The Devil's Advocate
Child abuse and the Men in Black

A survivor's account of the failings of Government, the
Churches, Religious Orders and our Criminal Justice System, in
understanding and responding to victims of sexual abuse in the
UK.

Graham Wilmer MBE

First Edition Published 2014 by Devil's Advocate Library

www.devilsadvocatelibrary.co.uk

ISBN 978-0-9928651-0-8

RRP £12.00

Typeset and design by Rory Wilmer

Cover Image: St.Vitus Cathedral Prague RAW2014

Photo credit: Rear cover – HM The Queen & BCA Ltd.

Printed and Bound in Great Britain

By Andrew Kilburn Print Services Ltd., Leeds.

For my family

'The sexual abuse and exploitation of children is one of the most vicious crimes conceivable, a violation of mankind's most basic duty to protect the innocent.' *James T. Walsh – US Politician*

'Graham Wilmer is a Liar and acting maliciously' *Extract from Police interview with Hubert Cecil Madley -19 April 2000 at Woking Police Station.*

'I have been asked by the police, if I recall a boy named Graham WILMER coming to see me and making an allegation of sexual abuse against a teacher called Hugh MADLEY. I do not recall any allegation of this kind being made. I am sure that if it had been, I would remember.' *Statement made to Surrey Police by Fr Edward O'Shea – 27th March 2000.*

'It rather looks as if this is an issue which is not going to go away, and it may well be that Wilmer is more trouble on his own than when acting though a solicitor.' *Extract from a letter to SDB from their solicitors – 24th October 2000.*

'Graham is a disturbed individual. His instability means he is not capable of sustained logical thinking.' *Extract from internal report written by Salesians, following the mediation on 12th Feb 2001.*

'I admit to being very puzzled by the fact that both Eddie O' Shea and George Williams both claim to have no memory of the events. The death of the boy in the rugby match is a well-known fact of school record, and the chalice in the community that commemorates him. I have to admit that I was rather convinced by the book that they were conveniently forgetting the past for whatever motive.' *Salesian Trustee – 19 August 2006.*

'Recommendation 70. Bishops and religious superiors should ensure that any cases which were known of in the past but not acted on satisfactorily ('historic cases') should be the subject of review as soon as possible, reported to the statutory authorities wherever appropriate, and that there is appropriate follow-up action including possibly regular continuing assessment.' *Extract from Nolan Report - 2001.*

'...In the exercise of your pastoral ministry, you have had to respond in recent years to many heart-rending cases of sexual abuse of minors. These are all the more tragic when the abuser is a cleric. The wounds caused by such acts run deep, and it is an urgent task to rebuild confidence and trust where these have been damaged. In your continuing efforts to deal effectively with this problem, it is important to establish the truth of what happened in the past, to take whatever steps are necessary to prevent it from occurring again, to ensure that the principles of justice are fully respected and, above all to bring healing to the victims and all those affected by these egregious crimes...' *Extract from Pope Benedict XVI's speech to the Bishops of Ireland, Rome, October 29th 2006.*

'The Vatican says it continues to receive around 600 claims of alleged abuse by priests every year, many dating back to the 1960s, 1970s and 1980s.' *Vatican press statement - March 2014.*

Acknowledgements

There are many people who helped me recover from the abuse I suffered in my childhood, especially my family - Barbara, Rory, Eve and Zachary, without who I would not be here. Neither would The Lantern Project, which I set up with their help and fellow survivor David Williams in 2003. Since then, the Lantern Project, with the support and dedication of our amazing volunteers, peer mentors and trustees, has helped many hundreds of other survivors, and is now a contracted NHS specialist service provider for victims and survivors of sexual abuse. So, to everyone who has helped me, in whatever way, I offer you my grateful and sincere thanks. I would especially like to thank Detective Constable John Hobbs, of Surrey Police, not only for his dogged pursuit of the truth, but also for continuing to help and support me, long after the trial of my abuser was over. I would also like to acknowledge the many other Salesian survivors who made contact with me after my first book was published and offered their support and solidarity in my quest for justice, some of whose testimonies also appear in this book. I would also like to thank Nicky and her family for their unwavering support during and after the trial, and my friend Noel Swift for his support, and for allowing me to include his story. I would also like to pay tribute to The Lantern Project's volunteers and trustees, especially David, Peter, Keith, Jill, Pippa, Barbara, Rory, Eve, Zach, Siobhán, Gary, Liz, Judy, Carl,

Christine, Alan, Pat, Sue, Ray, Candida and Angela, all of who have helped make the project what it is today, along with the solicitors who have guided me, Stephen Wilde, Peter Garsden and Edward Craven. I also want to thank Alex and Alice Parsons, who donated the assets of their charity, the Wirral Fellowship, to the Lantern Project to help us continue our work at a time when we were struggling financially. I also want to acknowledge my colleagues in the Stop Church Child Abuse Working Party: Anne Lawrence, Phil Johnson, Jo Kind, Lucy Duckworth (all of MACSAS), Sue Cox of Survivors Voice Europe, Richard Scorer of Pannone LLP Solicitors, Peter Saunders of NAPAC and the campaign's Chairman, David Greenwood of Switalskis LLP Solicitors, and everyone else who is helping and supporting the SCCA campaign. I am also grateful to the following press and media: BBC, The Hendon Times, The Surrey Herald, The Guardian, The Australian, The Independent, The Liverpool Echo, The Age (Australia), The Mercury (Australia), and The Catholic Herald.

I would also like to say thank you to my old school friend Ed Murphy for his thoughtful editing and patient proofreading of the manuscript. Finally, I would like to say a special thank you to Eric Baggaley, for his courage, wisdom and friendship, during a very difficult time. Without his skill as a mediator, and his courage in coming forward in the first place, this book could not have been written.

Forward

I have written this book to help expose the catastrophic shortcomings of the United Kingdom's government, the Churches, religious institutions and our criminal justice system, as they attempt to deal with the scale and consequences of sexual abuse in our country. The book is far from the full picture, but it should serve to remind those who hold power in our nation that, as a society, we are not dealing well with the enormity of the problem, which remains hidden in plain sight, despite the courage of the many victims who come forward, even though that usually means they face hostility, resentment and denial, rather than the compassion, understanding and acknowledgement they need and deserve. The cost of sexual abuse in our society, in whatever way one measures it, is on a scale that makes it both a national disgrace and a national health epidemic, neither being something that should be tolerated by any government, but tolerated it is.

What follows is not just about me, although it tells my story. It is about the ongoing failure of society as a whole to respond to and support victims of sexual abuse. It is also about the many conflicting and deep routed myths and negative perceptions about sexual abuse: what it really is and the devastating consequences of its long-term impact. Some of you may find the repetition of facts a little tedious, but I ask you to bear with it and read on, as it will help those of you who have not suffered the blight of sexual abuse understand the seemingly never-ending nightmare that survivors struggle with on a daily basis. For us, the story never ends, but with the right kind of support you can reach a level of recovery that is sustainable, and from that point onwards you become the master of your history, rather than its slave. For those victims who still struggle in silence, despite what I say about the lack of effective support services, you have nothing to fear from speaking out, other than fear itself. So, if you want help to tell your story, but don't know where to start or what to expect, contact me and I will help you.

Graham Wilmer MBE
grahamwilmer51@gmail.com
www.grahamwilmer.org.uk
www.devilsadvocatelibrary.co.uk

Prologue

I was born in Bedford, England on 20th October 1951. Three years later, my parents moved to Pyrford in Surrey, and at the age of six, I started school at Pyrford Primary, where, for the next five years I was happy and did well. In September 1963, aged eleven, I passed the entrance exam to an independent Catholic grammar school for boys, run by the Salesians of Don Bosco, a religious order that had a number of schools in England and one in Scotland. On the morning of September 6th, 1963, I was one of 36 boys standing proudly in our new purple blazers and caps at the gates of the Salesian College in Chertsey, Surrey. It was the first day of term in my new school. I was nearly 12 years old, eager, keen and excited at the prospect of meeting new friends and learning new things. A bell began to ring and we filed into the school, across the playground and through a large wooden door that led to our classroom.

Our housemaster - a dowdy old priest who smelt of BO and tobacco, showed us to our desks. The shoulders of his faded black cassock had a heavy dusting of dandruff on them that made him look a little like a cake decoration. He introduced himself and began to call out our names; each boy answering 'yes father' when it was our turn. We were ordered to sit down and be silent, but not all of us were. The punishment was swift and violent. With the stealth of a lion, the old priest moved quickly from the front of the class to the back, were I was sitting, and struck me across the face with his open hand. I had not even seen him coming, such was my excitement at discovering the books, pencils, erasers, rulers and bits of crisp in my desk, left by the previous occupant.

The blow left me stunned for a few seconds until I realised what had happened. I looked at the priest, who stared back at me with a fierce expression that filled me with dread.

'When I say silent boy - I mean silent. Do you understand me?'

'Yes father.'

'Yes father - what?'

'Yes father - sorry father.'

'Sorry eh? You will be boy - you will be.'

The rest of the class was so quiet you could have heard a pin drop as the old priest shuffled back to the desk at the front of the class and sat down. The boy sitting next to me looked at me with sympathy and smiled. Martin was to become one of my closest friends, but neither of us could have foreseen the tragic events that lay ahead of us.

By the end of the first term, I had settled into the routine of the school and learnt how to avoid the worst of the punishments that the priests handed out with relish and regularity to any child who failed to follow the strict rules of the Salesian teaching method, which were basic - do what we tell you or you get beaten. By now, I had also formed good friendships with three of the boys in my class, Martin, Michael and Paul. We sat next to each other in class, spent the break times together and travelled part of the way home together on the train from Chertsey to Weybridge where Paul lived, and where the rest of us changed trains - Martin going on to New Malden, while Michael and I went south to Byfleet. These were such happy times, filled with talk, laughter, teasing, jokes and, of course, girls - lots of them - from the Catholic girls school and a large independent school, both in Chertsey.

The four of us competed hard against each other in class, always trying to get the highest marks in end of terms exams. Martin and I also fought each other in Archery. I was hopeless at football and cricket, but I could shoot straight with a bow, as could he. Between us, we saw off just about everyone else in endless competitions, most of which I won by a narrow margin, but not all. Martin would often snatch victory from me with his last arrow, which would miraculously finds its way to the very centre of the target, much to the delight of the onlookers - many of whom had wagered pocket money or snacks from the tuck shop on the outcome!

As the months came and went, the friendships between us grew stronger as we got to know and understand each other better. We also shared another bond - our faith. As Catholics, we were already under a degree of influence from our parents, but none of us realised the power of the subtle brainwashing that was going on in parallel to the wider education we were receiving from the priests and teachers who ruled us, shaping the direction of our thinking to suit their own dogmatic beliefs. Most of what we did - we were told repeatedly - was sinful. Thinking about girls was sinful, lying was sinful, disobeying instructions was sinful, not completing homework was sinful, and so it went on. The punishment for these lesser sins was usually in the form of prayers, plus, of course, the corporal punishment that always accompanied the penance. Then there were the more serious sins such as missing mass on Sundays, taking holy communion, without first having gone to confession, and, worst of all, masturbating. These were among a long list of 'mortal' sins - which, we were told, would mean we would burn for eternity in the fires of hell if we died without having first been granted absolution by a Catholic priest. Naturally, we found such threats very real at the time, and much of our natural development into adolescence was fundamentally twisted by these rules - rules made by celibate men who neither cared for nor understood the damage they were doing to our young minds. In the absence of anything else, however, you accept what is in front of you, and we carried on in blind faith, worthless sinners, seemingly unable to find the purity of thought demanded of us - unaware that it was natural, normal and a vital part of the human condition for males to think about the opposite sex for most of the time!

Towards the end of the second year, Martin invited me to spend time at his home in New Malden. His parents were great fun and I seemed to blend into his family quite well from the first time I met them. His father was a surgeon at Kingston Hospital. He had a great sense of humour and there was always much laughter ringing around the house. His mother was a lovely woman, full of warmth and generosity. She was also a fabulous cook, and mealtimes were always a thing of wonder. But food was not the only thing of wonder in that house. Martin had three sisters and a brother. They were all older than him, but they all shared the same sense of fun and mischief that radiated round the house. The younger of the three girls, Nicky, was just 11 months older than Martin. I did not meet her the first time I went to stay there, but I heard a lot about her and saw photos of her. She was very pretty and it was obvious that she was very dearly loved. When I did finally meet her, some weeks later, I was completely mesmerised. Her smile, her laugh, her walk, her warmth; she was the most wonderful thing I had ever known. The first time you fall in love is so different to any other experience you will ever have. The waves of stomach churning butterflies, the bursts of rapid pulse rate, the hot flushes, the sleeplessness, the inability to eat - and it goes on and on for weeks. You think it will never stop - and then, if you are very, very lucky, you discover to your total amazement that the person you can't get out of your mind feels the same way about you. It was at the beginning of the summer holiday, 1966. I had met Nicky on several occasions now, but I had not yet plucked up the courage to tell her how I felt about her. I had told Martin, however. What I did not know was that he had told her! On this visit to their house, I had only been there a while when Martin asked me to come into the dining room with him, and without saying anything more, he led me into the room. Nicky was standing at the far end of the long, oak table. She was smiling. Martin turned and left the room, closing the door on the way out. Nicky walked across the room to where I stood, pulled me slowly towards her and kissed me gently on the lips. It was like being hit by a train. Could this really be happening? I put my arms around her and kissed her gently on her neck. I was falling in love for the very first time, and I was in heaven. But there lurked an evil force, moving slowly in my direction. None of us could have known it was there, but nor could we have done anything to stop it. When it finally arrived, it would destroy my friendships, my future and me. But for now, there was still a little time left to love and laugh and be happy.

In September 1966, a new teacher joined the school. Hubert Cecil Madley. Within weeks, he had separated me from my school friends, spending time with me in the playground. Then he started taking me home after school, and very quickly worked his way into my family, on the grounds that I needed extra maths tuition, which, he told my parents, he would be 'very happy to provide'. Then it began, and for the next two years he sexually abused me, as often as he could and wherever he could, ensuring my silence through a variety of threats and warnings about the dire consequences that would follow, if I dared tell anyone.

Then, on a cold Saturday morning in February 1968, the 5th Form rugby team assembled for a game against a visiting school team. Martin had been selected to play in the team but I had not and was at home, unaware of what happened during the game. It was not until Monday morning that I heard the rumours spreading in the College about an accident involving Martin. We were not told any details, but I learnt later in the day that he had gone down during a scrum and been fallen on heavily. He did not get up immediately when the scrum dispersed, but when he did, he was dragging his right leg as he walked. Although dazed and limping, Martin attempted to re-join the game, but was ordered off the field by the coach, Fr Tyler. The seriousness of his injury was not appreciated until he collapsed into unconsciousness, but even then, it was thought he had only suffered concussion. Eventually, an ambulance was called, but it was some twenty minutes, before he was taken to St Peter's hospital in Chertsey, where Doctors quickly discovered he had suffered a major internal head injury. Martin was then rushed to Atkinson Morley Hospital, where, frantic efforts were made to try and save him. On the Monday morning, we were told the terrible news that they had lost the battle and he had died the previous day, his parents by his bedside. For next two days, I was in complete shock, unable even to cry. A terrible atmosphere hung around the playground and the normal ribbing and name calling that we were all used to had fallen silent. None of us knew quite what to say to each other. On the evening of third day, Martin's father telephoned our house and asked to speak to me. His voice was gentle and calm and I told him how sorry I was. He thanked me and asked me if I would be willing serve as an altar boy at Martin's requiem mass. He said there would only be two altar boys - Martin's older brother, Paul and me. The priest taking the mass would be none other than Bishop Wheeler, a close family friend of the Allen's. I had met him on several occasions at their home and he certainly knew who I was.

I told Dr Allen that it would be an honour and I would try not to let him down. He thanked me and said it was what the whole family wanted. I put the receiver back onto its cradle and began to cry. As I thought about what was to come, I realised that I was now faced with a real dilemma. Ever since the abuse began, I believed that I had fallen from grace. I was in a state of mortal sin and could therefore not take Holy Communion unless I had first been to confession and confessed my awful sins. But how could I possibly go to confession and tell the priest, who also knew me well, that I had committed all these terrible homosexual acts? He would ask questions - it would all come out. The world around me would collapse. All hope would be lost and I would be an outcast.

On the other hand, how could I refuse to take communion from the Bishop at the requiem mass? You see, in the Roman Catholic mass, after the priest has consecrated the host he communicates himself, then the altar boys, and then the members of the congregation. When the Bishop offered me the consecrated host, all eyes would be upon me. How was I going to avoid taking communion? I couldn't avoid it. I would be unthinkable. Martin's family would be heartbroken to see me refuse communion at such an important event in their family life. What was I to do?

With the funeral now only two days away, I finally made up my mind that I would go to confession and face whatever the consequences were to be. It was, after all, 'my fault' that I had committed these terrible sins, so I deserved the punishment that was due. The following day, at break time, I made my way across the playground to the main school building and knocked on the priests' staff room door. The priest who opened it was my housemaster, Fr Madden.

'Can I see you a moment please, Father?' I said.

'Yes, boy, come in.' There was no one else in the room so I came straight out with it.

'I need to confess my sins, Father. Will you hear my confession now please?' The priest was clearly annoyed and began to scowl at me.

'Can it not wait until later?'

'No, Father. It must be now.'

'Very well, follow me.' He led me down the corridor and opened a large, oak panelled door into the priests' private chapel. There was no confessional box in the chapel so he pulled up a kneeling stool and a chair. He gestured to me to kneel on the stool. As I did, he walked over to a large wooden chest of drawers and took out a long, purple stole, which he kissed and placed around his neck like a scarf. He walked back, sat down on the chair next to me and made the sign of the cross.

It was now or never. I made the sign of the cross and began.

'Bless me, Father, for I have sinned. It is several months since my last confession. Father, I have had impure thoughts and done impure things.'

'What sort of things?' he asked.

I murmured in a low voice, unable to say it out loud. The words just did not want to come out of my mouth.

'Speak up, boy! What sort of things?'

'Homosexual acts, Father.' There was a brief pause and he repeated my words.

'Homosexual acts? What kind of acts, boy?'

I started to go through the litany of evil, dirty, disgusting, unspeakable things that I had done with Madley. Fr Madden interrupted me:

'Who did you do all this with, boy?'

This was the moment. The end had arrived. I said Madley's name out loud and waited.

'Do you mean Mr Madley, your science teacher?'

'Yes Father - Hugh Madley.' There was a further pause.

'Have you told me everything about this?'

'No, Father, there is more.' Explaining the acts of buggery was more difficult than I had thought, as I was not really quite sure which part of it was my sin. There was a longer pause when I had finished. Fr Madden began to tell me that these were very serious matters indeed, as if I didn't already know that. He went on, but in a more caring tone that he had used earlier. He said he wanted me to think about the wider issues that would result from what I had done with Madley. I didn't understand what he meant and I said so.

'The point is, boy, I will obviously need to take this further for your own protection, but I can't unless you repeat what you have said to me outside of confession. Will you do that?' Before I could answer, Fr Madden said:

'Look, make your act of contrition and I will give you absolution. You can then tell me again, once the confession is finished.' I was so relieved to hear those precious words - 'I will give you absolution' - I began saying my contrition prayer. Fr Madden spoke the words of the prayers of absolution and told me to say three Our Fathers and three Hail Marys for my penance. It was done. I was saved.

It was not done at all. It had only just begun. Far from being saved, I was about to be betrayed by my confessor. With my head still spinning with the relief at having been granted absolution, I repeated the story again. Fr Madden asked no further questions and then placed his right hand on my head and told me to go now and not to worry about it anymore. He said he would need to speak to the Headmaster, Fr O'Shea, and that I would probably have to see him as well. I didn't care. The heaviest weight in the entire world had just been lifted from my shoulders. I was free, or so I thought.

A few days later, the Salesian Provincial, Fr George Williams, arrived at the school to speak to me about my disclosure. I assumed that he had come to offer me help and tell me what would happen next, but instead of helping me, he asked me a series of prurient questions about my sexual knowledge and thoughts. He then swore me to silence; reinforcing the threats that Madley had placed me under. A few weeks later, Madley was moved to a new teaching post at the Salesian College in Battersea. I was left to fend for myself, without any support from the school, or from anyone else for that matter. Fr Williams had warned me that 'under no circumstances' should I tell my parents what had happened.

So I remained silent, and not surprisingly, when I sat my GCCE 'O' level exams a few months later, I failed them all; despite having been one of the top five students in my year. But worse was to come, as, rather than providing me with counselling and support, and allowing me to re-sit my exams, the following term, Fr O'Shea refused to allow me back into the school, thus ensuring my secondary education ended in disaster. I had been cut adrift; cast out by the very people whose only task was to provide me with the academic tools I would need to reach my potential. They would pay a heavy price for their betrayal, but it would take many years before I could hold them to account.

The abuse I had suffered created deep-seated, psychological problems in my mind, which would continue to plague me for years to come. The damage manifested itself in different ways. I developed a range of harmful behaviours, known as 'Coping Mechanisms', including alcohol abuse and self-harm, to block out the past. I also developed an addiction to casual sex, as it was the only way I could feel loved, as meaningful relationships proved very difficult to form in the years that followed. Over time, my character changed, as I tried to pretend that it had never happened. I buried the memories deep in my mind, and for the next 30 years I stumbled on through life, but the legacy of guilt, confusion and anger was never far from the surface.

Then, in 1995, the hidden memories began to re-emerge. A trickle at first, then more and more, each time becoming sharper in focus and more detailed. They pervaded my mind during every moment of every day, and haunted my dreams at night. Eventually, at the beginning of 1997, I broke down, unable to cope with the force of these awful images, which totally overwhelmed me and took me to the brink of self-destruction. I was lucky, though, I had someone who stood by me. She looked after me while I tried to find the support and counselling that I needed, and, eventually, I began to recover.

During my treatment, I was advised by my counsellor to tell the police about what had happened to me, so, in November 1999, I contacted Surrey Police, and made a formal complaint. The police launched an investigation, and in April 2000, Madley was arrested, but he denied that anything had gone on between us. Fr Madden had died two years before, but Fr O'Shea was still alive, and, like Madley, he also denied knowing anything about any such 'incident' involving me. But Fr O'Shea did more than just deny any knowledge of the 'incident', he went as far as to say that, despite his age, because his memory was 'still so good', if anything had occurred, he 'would have remembered it'. Consequently, based on the denials of a 'good man of the cloth' and a grubby, brown-suited science teacher, the CPS decided not to prosecute, due to 'lack of evidence', even though the police had not even interviewed Fr Williams by the time they made that decision.

Despite this, I was not prepared to give up, so, in October 2000, I informed the Salesians that I intended to start civil proceedings against them. They responded by offering to mediate with me, although they continued to deny having any knowledge of what I was claiming had happened, but saying that it would be 'far less painful and much quicker to mediate', rather than go through the courts. I agreed, and the Salesians appointed an independent mediation firm, although it turned out later that one of their lawyers was also a director of the firm of mediators!

The mediation took place in February 2001, at which the Salesians continued to deny having ever had any knowledge of what I was claiming, although, as you will see, they knew far more about Madley than they were letting on, as other serious allegations had been made against him just a few months before the mediation, but they kept that from me. However, they accepted that 'something must have happened', and offered me £20,000 'to alleviate the obvious distress' I was in, and to pay from some 'counselling', but on the understanding that I would not pursue them or Madley or Surrey Education Authority, through any court. Nor would I say anything about the matter ever again, either orally or in writing.

I signed their 'hush agreement' and I took the money, but I did not stay quiet. Instead, I began my own investigation, using some of the money to fund it. The breakthrough came In April 2004, when I tracked Madley down and told him that I intended to bring a private criminal prosecution against him. This time, instead of denying everything, he wrote me a series of letters asking me to forgive him, and he had numerous telephone conversations with my friend David Williams, in which he confessed everything he had done to me. He also disclosed the full nature of the conspiracy the Provincial, Fr George Williams, had cooked up with him in 1968 to keep the lid on everything. Surrey police decided that these letters, together with the phone calls, which David had taped, contained enough information to enable them to launch a new investigation, so, Madley was arrested again on October 17th 2004, at his home in North London, and taken to Colindale police station, where he was interviewed under caution, admitting everything he had done to me in very graphic detail. Madley was subsequently charged with buggery and indecent assault, under the Sexual Offences Act 1963, and sent for trial in December 2005. The story of what happened to me, and the struggles I endured during the first part of my quest for justice is told in my book 'Conspiracy of Faith – Fighting for Justice after Child Abuse', which was published by Lutterworth Press on 22nd February 2007. The book you are now reading tells the story of how Madley escaped justice for a second time, and what happened next. It also exposes the extent of clerical child abuse in our country today, and what I, and others, are trying to do about that.

While writing this book, more disclosures of church child abuse have emerged, and the ramifications of those disclosures continue to unfold, so this is not the complete story. Rather, it is a contribution towards the recording of a pivotal period in recent history, when victims of child abuse stood together to challenge those who abused us. In doing so, they have set in motion a process that will be seen as the point in time when the truth overcame the silence imposed on vulnerable individuals by people who held power over them, and used that power to harm them. Together we are making a difference, changing forever the balance of unequal and unjust dynamics faced by victims when they have tried to challenge the many corrupted religious and other institutions that have harmed us. Our collective truth telling has been both painful and rewarding, and it has also been at great cost to us all, but its merit is without question, and it will not be diluted or diminished by the excuses of those we have challenged. We have told the truth; they have not, and there is now nowhere for them to hide, following the announcement on Tuesday 8th July 2014 by the Home Secretary, Theresa May, that she is setting up two investigations into historical child sexual abuse in the UK. The first, led by Peter Wanless, Chief Executive of the NSPCC, will look into the allegations of a cover-up within Whitehall, while the second is a much wider investigation into child sex abuse throughout the UK. This second inquiry, was to be led by former senior judge, Baroness Elizabeth Butler-Sloss, but, within days of her appointment, the Baroness was forced to step down because of complaints about her suitability, due her links with the establishment, and the fact that her late brother, Sir Michael Havers, was attorney general in the 1980s, when the establishment cover-ups began.

At the same time, the Church of England and the Methodist Church have just set up a new National Safeguarding Panel, which also includes Peter Wanless of the NSPCC, together with two senior police officers, myself and two of my colleagues from MACSAS, Phil Johnson and Jo Kind, together with Bishop Paul Butler and a number of other experts with experience in safeguarding and child protection. So, the sea change many others and I have been calling for has begun, and is up to us to make it happen. Some have said to me 'be careful what you wish for', but I don't fear the challenge, as there are others who have said 'game on – lets do it'

Chapter 1
Letter from a stranger

The gravel crunched under the postman's boots. I was watching him through the front room window, but he didn't see me. He seemed burdened by more than the weight of his red shoulder bag, as he approached the front door. I could see he was muttering to himself - probably about the mountains of waste paper he had to stuff through people's letterboxes, along with the letters, of course, some of which might be important, but not to him. It was all wastepaper, as far as he was concerned, which was why he didn't give a toss if he put my post through next door's front door, and theirs through mine, which he had done three times already this week, and it was only Thursday. Today, he got it right. A pile of junk mail plopped onto the stone floor. There was a pause, then the letter boxed rattled again and two white envelopes popped through, both landing address side up, one typed, one hand-written.

I knelt down, scooped up the pile and walked back into the kitchen, examining the hand-written envelope carefully. I did not recognise the writing, which was neat, but emphasised with underlines and swirly tails, to make it seem important. The postmark next to the stamp read 'Cheshire- 21st February 2007'. I knew a few people in Cheshire, having lived there in 1998, but none of them ever wrote to me by hand.Whoever the author was, they seemed to know me. I sliced open the envelope with the silver paper knife my friend Peter had given me to mark his daughter's christening, at which, as her Godfather, I had taken an oath to protect her from evil. The letter said simply:

'Graham - you don't know me, but I have recently finished reading your book, 'Conspiracy of Faith', which raises my own unanswered questions. Please will you contact me? I would like to meet you and tell you in person what I have to say.' It was signed, simply: 'Eric Baggaley - a former Salesian priest.' As messages go, it wasn't really that mysterious, given all I had been through over the previous five years, but I had a strong sense that somehow this message was different. Perhaps - just perhaps, this might be the key to unlocking the secret door in the so-far impenetrable wall of silence I had faced in my long struggle for justice, but to explain why, and for those who may not have read my first book, let me take you back a few years.

On a bright, spring morning in April 2000, a 61-year-old man nervously walked into a police station in Woking, Surrey, accompanied by a solicitor. He was there to answers questions about allegations of sexual abuse at a nearby school, the Salesian College in Chertsey. The allegations, dating back to 1968, had been made two months previously by a former pupil of the school - me. Once inside the police station, WPC Sarah Harris arrested Hubert Cecil Madley, my former chemistry teacher. Sarah Harris was a child protection officer with Surrey Police. She had interviewed me for many hours over the previous weeks, after my disclosure.

Madley, on the advice of his solicitor, denied all of the allegations of abuse put to him by Sarah Harris. He said that I was 'a liar and acting maliciously', but he did admit he 'vaguely' remembered me, as a child he had once taught at the school in Chertsey. However, when she began to question him in more detail about what happened on the holiday he had taken me on in South Wales, in the Summer of 1967, he said he was 'feeling unwell', at which point his solicitor insisted that the interview be stopped. Sarah had no option but to suspend the interview until another time, when she hoped he would be 'feeling better'! A date to continue the interview was set for two weeks hence. Madley hurried out of the police station, released on police bail until then.

After the meeting, Sarah Harris phoned me to tell me how the interview had gone. She concluded by saying that, in her experience, Madley was 'as guilty as hell!' She said he had gone as white as a sheet when she asked about the holiday in Wales, as it was here that Madley had raped me, something she knew about in great detail from the hours of detailed interview with me, and, of course, so did he. But, today, hard as he tried to, he could not remember anything about any such holiday with me. 'After all,' as his solicitor complained, 'that was nearly 34 years ago!'

In the weeks before Madley's arrest, Sarah Harris

had also interviewed my old Headmaster, Fr O'Shea. He too seemed to have suffered a mysterious loss of memory: 'I have been asked by the police, if I recall a boy named Graham WILMER coming to see me and making an allegation of sexual abuse against a teacher called Hugh MADLEY. I do not recall any allegation of this kind being made. I am sure that if it had been, I would remember.' Equally convenient for the Salesians was the fact that, when she interviewed the headmaster at Salesian College Battersea, Madley's personnel file was virtually empty! Not a single piece of paper to explain why he had suddenly been transferred from Chertsey to Battersea, shortly after I had disclosed to the Salesians that Madley had been sexually abusing me for nearly two years! No contract of employment, no letter of reference; nothing!

The reality was very different, as not only had I told My House Master, Fr Brian Madden, what Madley was doing to me, he had then told the Rector, Fr Gaffney and the Headmaster, Fr Eddie O'Shea. O'Shea then contacted the Salesian Provincial, Fr George Williams, who came down to Chertsey and interviewed me about what had happened. Some weeks later, he also interviewed Madley, who confessed all, but I was not told that. Williams made Madley promise that he would never 'offend against another child.' Madley gave him his word, and, on the basis of that promise, Williams arranged for Madley to be transferred to the Salesian College Battersea, the then headmaster at Battersea,

Fr Blackburn, was given a full briefing on what had occurred, and told that he was to oversee Madley, and not to let him be alone with boys until further notice. I, on the other hand, was sworn to silence, by the Provincial, and subsequently thrown out of the school.

So, Here we had a school teacher and a headmaster both denying to the police that they knew anything about what had happened – despite the fact that the Sexual Offences Act of 1963 had been on the statute books for five years by the time I had disclosed to them, so, at the very least, they had a duty to inform my parents. But, as we shall see, the Salesian Order was no stranger to covering up child abuse in its schools, not just in the British Salesian Province, as it was known here, but in Salesian Provinces all over the world, of which there were and still are, many. Their approach in such matters, which followed that of the Catholic Church as a whole, was simple: even when confronted with credible evidence, 'deny, deny and deny'.

The full truth about what had really happened, and what some Salesians had known and done to cover it up, took a while to emerge, and it did not come willingly! Shortly after Madley returned for the continuation of his interview with Surrey Police, which proved to be just as unrevealing as the first part, due, no doubt to the coaching he will have had received from his solicitor in the two weeks since his arrest, Sarah Harris phoned me to say that the CPS had decided there was not enough evidence to prosecute.

So, Madley was released from police bail and sent on his way, a free man in the eyes of the law, but his journey towards exposure was only just beginning, as the fallout from the murders of Holly Wells and Jessica Chapman by Ian Huntley, in the village of Soham, Cambridgeshire on 4 August 2002, led to a change in the way the police recorded allegations of sexual abuse. Prior to the Bichard inquiry, which followed their murders, the police would only record convictions, but now that was no longer the case; allegations would also now be recorded.

To cut a very long story short, these changes allowed me to make a further allegation against Madley to Surrey police, which I did, to ensure that his name too would now be recorded on the police national computer (PNC), which, I hoped, would have at least prevented him from securing any further jobs working with children, as he was only 61 years old, and could, for all I knew, still be teaching. What transpired, however, was a suggestion from the police that I could also bring a private criminal prosecution against Madley, and two, long years later, he finally confessed everything to the police after being arrested for the second time!

The struggle to get Madley before the courts is told in my book 'Conspiracy of Faith', so I won't repeat it all here, other than to say that the wheels of justice, more often than not, do not run smoothly in cases of what is euphemistically called 'historical child abuse' like mine, which ended with Madley being let off again, but this time by the trial Judge, His Honour Judge Inman, who, after two days of legal argument at Guildford Crown Court, ruled thus:

'This is an application by the defence to exclude the evidence of the defendant's interviews, which he made under caution on 17th and 27th October last year (2004). The application is made under section 76(2)(b) and section 78 of PACE. The defendant was arrested and interviewed in connection with the same allegations as, those which form the basis of these proceedings in 2000 and a decision was made not to prosecute him. I understand the file for those matters had either been lost or disposed of, but in any event is no longer available. However, the investigating officer in this case, a Detective Constable Hobbs, I understand, had access to various relevant records from which he had learned that during the interviews, which took place in 2000, a solicitor and appropriate adult had been present. I have read the psychiatric report. A very long and detailed one, by Dr. Cree. This was served on the prosecution in July, I believe, and they have not sought to call their own expert. It is clear the defendant had been suffering from depression for a number of years and has been in the care of various doctors for his condition and has been prescribed medication, which he was in fact taking in October 2004. It is clear that the seriousness of his condition varies and can be controlled by medication. He was arrested at home on 17th October (2004) and taken to a nearby police station.

I have seen the custody record for that date. It is clear from that that the defendant had his legal rights explained and decided that he did not want a solicitor to be present at his interview. Before the interview the custody sergeant, Sergeant Barnes, filled in a form, 57M, which at Part A is an assessment of the medical risk relevant to the defendant and Part B assesses the need for an appropriate adult or other help. In Part A the defendant gave details of the fact that he suffered from depression and was taking medicine for it. Also that he had attempted suicide about four years earlier. In Part B at question 4 he was apparently asked if he needed special help and the box marked "no" has been ticked. I note from that form that attention is especially drawn to the action to be taken if any doubts about a person's mental condition arise and that the custody officer should explain the role of an appropriate adult to the detained person in those circumstances. Part D of that form has an entry "vulnerable, suicidal tendencies" and Sergeant Barnes in evidence said that he had no concerns about his mental well being and considered him fit in all respects to be interviewed. "I had no reason from my conversation with him to think he needed an appropriate adult" he said.

The defendant was interviewed, therefore, without a solicitor or appropriate adult. He was then bailed and returned to Woking police station on 27th October (2004). I have seen the custody record for that occasion, compiled by Sergeant Morris, who gave evidence. The defendant indicated again that he did not want the services of a solicitor. Sergeant Morris filled in a similar form, this time it was called a Form 38/37. Part A is in respect of an appropriate adult. Question 4 has the question: "Do you need special help?" and a "yes" box is ticked with an arrow pointing to the word "depression". Sergeant Morris had been told that the defendant had not had an appropriate adult present on 17th October, but he said he made his own assessment independently of that information.

The sergeant said that in answer to question 4 the defendant had replied: "I suffer from depression" and that is why he had ticked the "yes" box and put the arrow to the word "depression". He also said in evidence that he had put the questions verbatim as they appear on the form. He said he would expect to have explained the contents of the note on the form, but he could not recall if in fact he had done so in this case. He said (and I am quoting from the statement he made on 24th November, which he adopted): "During the documentation process and completing the medical care form, when asked, Mr. Madley stated that he was in good health but was suffering from depression.

However, when further questioned he stated that he was being treated by his doctor and that the depression was being controlled by medication. It was ascertained that he had been taking his medication as prescribed. I was completely satisfied that Mr Madley fully understood the process and when his rights were explained and administered he was adamant that he did not require a solicitor, stating: 'No, not at the moment.' I was also completely satisfied that Mr Madley was able to answer questions without the presence of an appropriate adult."

So, the interview proceeded without a solicitor and without an appropriate adult being present. Detective Hobbs told Sergeant Morris that he did not think the defendant needed an appropriate adult, based on his experience of the way that he dealt with the interview on 17th October. In re-examination Sergeant Morris had said: "I asked him if he needed one", that is to say an appropriate adult, "and he said: 'No'". The defendant gave evidence and said that on 17th October he had not indicated his need for special help and there had been no discussion involving the use of the words "appropriate adult". On 27th October he said that he was positive he answered question 4 in Part A by saying that he did ask for special help as he had had special help in the year 2000. He said Sergeant Morris had not explained the note on the form and also that Detective Constable Hobbs and said to him: "I understand you ask for an appropriate adult. Between the two of us I don't think you want one." "I trusted him", he said, "and I thought it was up to the police to provide an appropriate adult." He had taken the drug Largactil, I think it was, soon before the interview and he said that had the effect of calming him down.

I have to consider if there have been any breaches of the codes of conduct in respect of those two interviews. First I am asked to consider Code C 1 4, which sets out how an officer should treat a mentally disordered or vulnerable person for the purposes of the code and that has to be read in conjunction with a note at C 1 G. In his evidence Dr Cree had said that his diagnosis of the defendant showed him to be suffering from chronic depression, which he said came within the definition of mental disorder in section 1 subsection (2) of the Mental Health Act of 1983. The Crown seem to have accepted that he also comes under the description of mentally vulnerable, but I am not quite sure if that was the position at the end of the submissions. Note 1 G goes on to say: "When the custody officer has any doubt about the mental state or capacity of a detainee, that the detainee should be treated as being mentally vulnerable and an appropriate adult called." I appreciate that custody sergeants are not medical experts and they have a difficult job to do, often under great pressure.

Here we are dealing with two very experienced custody officers who both said that they carefully considered Mr Madley's mental condition and how he responded to their questions. I bear in mind the requirement of note 11 C to the effect that special care and caution should always be taken when questioning mentally vulnerable people and the appropriate adult should be involved if there is any doubt about a person's mental state. In this case the question of Mr Madley's mental condition had clearly been raised by his answers to the question he was asked by the custody sergeants.

No force medical examiners were called on either occasion to examine him.

It is my view that both custody officers erred in not providing an appropriate adult for the two interviews and, therefore, a breach of Code C 1 4, when read with the relevant notes, took place. The fact that a breach of a code occurs does not of course of itself render the subsequent interview inadmissible. So in this context I have to consider the provisions of section 70(6)(2)(b) of the Police and Criminal Evidence Act 1984. The burden is on the Crown to prove that the confessions in such interviews were not made in consequence of anything, which is likely to render them unreliable as a consequence of anything said or done. The correct approach to this problem is set out in Archibold at chapter 15, paragraph 384. That is to say, by consideration of what was said or done, considering the objective test: what was said and done renders it unreliable and whether the prosecution have proved it was not obtained in consequence of the thing said or done. In short, does the failure of the officers to provide an appropriate adult for the interviews render the confessions contained therein unreliable? I am also asked to consider whether the evidence of the interviews should be excluded under section 78 of the Police & Criminal Evidence Act. That is whether the admission of the evidence would have such an adverse effect on the fairness of the proceedings that the court ought not to admit it.

Of course every case has to be decided on its own

facts and in this case I have specifically been referred to the case of R.v. Aspinall [1999] Cr. App.R. 115. This is a case, which has some similarities to the present case. There, in Aspinall, the defendant was suffering from schizophrenia. He declined the services of a solicitor, as he said he wished to get home as soon as possible, but he was in fact actually seen by two force medical examiners who, in effect, confirmed the mental health diagnosis, but both concluded that he was fit to be interviewed. At the trial the recorder found that there had been a breach of section 78, but concluded the assessment of his being fit to be interviewed negatived the requirement for the safeguard of an appropriate adult.

The Court of Appeal held that the recorder had fallen into error. The question, which should have been determined, was not whether the defendant's condition obviated the need for an appropriate adult, but whether the admission of the evidence would have such an adverse effect upon the fairness of the trial that it should be excluded. In submissions before me the prosecution have submitted that the defendant in Aspinall was suffering from a much more severe mental illness than is the case here and to some extent I accept that, but I also note that he was examined by two FME's which of course was not the case in the present case. So here I conclude that at the very least the custody officers should have entertained a doubt as to Mr Madley's mental state or capacity on the basis of the information they had been given. They should have exercised the due care and caution necessary and when such an issue arises and the fact that they did not deprived the defendant of the safeguard he undoubtedly should have had, namely, the provision of an appropriate adult. So I shall not allow the evidence of the interviews of 17th and 27th October to be admitted because under section 76(2)(b) of the view that the confessions are unreliable as a consequence of there not being an appropriate adult present and under section 78 because the admission of the evidence would have such an adverse effect on the fairness of the proceedings that it should not be admitted for the same reason. That is my ruling.'

Chapter 2
'For what it's worth'

After the trial collapsed, even though Madley had walked free, I decided there was still a higher court I could appeal to; the Court of Public Opinion, only here the rules of evidence are not quite as precise as those in the Crown Court, and I could use that difference to bring down the Salesians' wall of silence and denial. The fact that Madley had walked free from the court did not mean that he was an innocent man. The court had not tried him, so he had not been convicted, but neither had he been acquitted. So, I would set up my own court, in the form of a another book, only this book, unlike my first book, 'Survivor', published in 2004, which his Honour Judge Reid had dismissed at a pre-trial hearing on August 4th as 'a lightly fictionalised account', My new book would be a forensic and detailed account of what had happened to me; who had hurt me and exactly what they had done.

It wasn't just Madley and the Salesians I wanted to expose, I wanted to challenge the ineffectiveness of the criminal justice system in its dealings with child abuse, and the case I wanted to make was this: On 15 December 2005, when Judge Inman refused to allow Madley's interviews with the police to go forward as evidence for trial, on the basis that he should have been allowed to have a responsible adult with him during the interviews, all that remained as evidence was my witness statement; Judge Reid having ruled previously on 4 August, at the pre-trial hearing, that the telephone conversations between Madley and David Williams were inadmissible due to the 'underhand' methods it was claimed David and I had used to 'entrap' Madley into admitting what he had done to me.

The fact that Madley had wanted to tell David everything willingly seemed to have evaded the judge, but then judges are a law unto themselves, and victims of child abuse don't, as a rule, get much sympathy from our system of justice, unless, of course, they have been killed by their abuser, but then, of course, it's too late. The judge paid no attention to the explanation I gave in court, in answer to the charge that I was only interested in compensation, when I said that I was trying to ensure that Madley could not go on to abuse other children. In fact, he dismissed my whole account, saying that he was 'unimpressed' by what I had said, as if I were the guilty party, not the victim. However, with Madley's confession having been ruled out as evidence that could be adduced, we were back at square one, where I had been in April 2000; the only evidence left in the case being my word alone, which, according to Judge Reid, who had referred to it glibly as being 'for what it's worth,' was not good enough to be tested before a jury.

So, having carried the pain and scars of everything I had been through for all these years, and for all the effort and heartache I had endured trying to bring Madley before a court, I had suffered the further indignity of having the door of justice slammed in my face by a two judges, even though the man who stole my childhood had finally confessed everything, albeit in his own cowardly version of the truth.

Madley may have escaped justice this time, but I have always believed that he will have abused other children, as do the police and just about everyone else who knows my story. In time, some of these victims will come forward, and hopefully, another judge may view their stories with more compassion, and punish this pathetic excuse for man for the misery he has caused us all. If there is any doubt in your minds as to what happened, here is what Madley told the police in the first of his two interviews with them. His account gives a chilling insight into the mind of a pedophile, particularly the way he transfers blame for what he did to me, saying that it was I who had initiated the sexual acts, not the other way round. His cruellest lie is when he says that, on the very day I had found the courage to tell the priests what had been going on, so that I could take communion at Martin's requiem mass, he claims I came to him for sex one final time. So, 'for what it's worth', this is what Madley told the police in the first of two police interviews:

Extract from police interview with Hubert Cecil Madley - October 17th 2004.

'Hugh - what can you tell me? Take as long as you want and in as much detail as you like, explaining to me your relationship with Graham, and what happened between the two of you.'

'To the best of my knowledge, I started teaching Chemistry (at Salesian College, Chertsey) in September 1966. Graham was asked by the Headmaster to show me round the school. He was about 15 years old. I found him a very pleasant person and very easy to get on with. We formed a friendship. I drove a motorbike at that time and I gave him a lift home occasionally. I remember once I went down to Wales. He was with a school party doing a trip to a place called St Brevills Castle, where they stayed the night. I gave several of them a lift on my motorbike as they were walking along the road, just to save them the extra five miles. I gave Graham a lift back (to London). Nothing had happened between us at that stage. After Christmas (1966), Graham's parents asked me to tutor him with extra lessons for Math, Physics and Chemistry. I started going to his home. In January (1967), I bought a signal generator kit, and built and tested it over a few months. I took it to his home and demonstrated it to him. On that occasion, I am a bit reluctant to say this, but I will say it, Graham said to me "My knobs gone all wonky." I looked and saw he had an erection. I asked him did he want me to feel it for him, and he said, "Let's go upstairs." In the letters I've had with him, he says that he didn't do this, but I do remember this now.'

'What I'm asking you to remember is your

memory, so if this is the way you remember it, then this is the way you remember it. Try not to let your memory be clouded by other stuff you may have heard since.'

'I don't want to turn it against him because I know he couldn't give his consent but.....

'You carry on. So, he said that his knob's gone wonky, and you saw that he had an erection. Then what happened?'

'We went upstairs, got undressed. I lay on his bed and he lay on top of me and we both ejaculated. As far as I know, it only happened that one evening. I don't think anything else happened that night. I think after that, when I went over to his house to give him private lessons, I did put my arm around him and I did masturbate him, and then he did the same to me.'

'So, as far as your memory is concerned Hugh, don't get me wrong, I appreciate your frankness - as far as your memory is concerned, was the incident where you had the radio - was that the first time you had physical, sexual contact with Graham?'

'I'm absolutely positive about this because I know he said, he uttered to me that I had touched him in the car, but...'

'Don't worry about what Graham has told you since. What we need to know is your memory.'

'I know I didn't have a car at the time. I was on a motorbike.'

'OK, that's all right. So, where did this take place?'

'That was in his house.'

'At Graham's House?'

'Yes.'

'What Address - is that the one in Pyrford?'

'West Byfleet.'

'So, we'll use that incident that you've just told me to start. At this point, you haven't been at the school for a full year yet, had you?'

'No.'

'You started in the previous September. You got on with Graham and what you're saying is at parent's evening, his parents asked if you would give him extra tuition, and you were happy to do that, and the payment would be a meal or whatever? So, it was around about March of '67 that you made this radio? Was it a radio?'

'No. It was a signal generator.'

'Was he expecting you to come around with it?'

'Yes. I think I'd given him a lift over from the school.'

'You'd gone to his home address, after school presumably. Was anyone else at home?'

'No. Apparently, as far as I remember, his parents were away at the time.'

'So, you've gone in there, where you have set up your transmitter in the house?'

'In the lounge.'

'How come, then, that this came about - Graham said that his knob was wonky, then?'

'Bonky.'

'Bonky? I've never heard of that one. I mean, had

you been talking about anything sexual?'

'Not at all, no. It was completely out of the blue.'

'So, you're there; he's here. How old is Graham then - '67?'

'15, coming on 16.'

(He was actually 14 years and 4 months old at the time.) 'You say to him, would you like me to touch it? Is this something you've discussed before with Graham?'

'No, never.'

'Had there been anything even remotely sexual between the two of you?'

'I'd never interfered with him at all up until then.'

'When he told you that his knob was bonky, and you looked and saw that he had an erection, what effect did that have on you?'

'I got an erection as well, obviously.'

'How old were you at the time Hugh?'

'About 23 - 24.'

'So, the fact that he told you and you saw that, it had a physical reaction for you, and you got an erection yourself.'

'Yeah.'

'First sequence of events. Were you aroused when you asked Graham if he'd like you to touch his penis?'

'I think I was aroused when I saw he had an erection.'

'Take me through what happened next.'

'What went through my mind?'

'Everything physically. Who's suggestion was it

that you went upstairs?'

'Graham's. He did actually say, "Someone might see us - let's go upstairs."'

'You went upstairs. Where did you go?'

'To the bedroom - Graham's bedroom.'

'Whereabouts in the house was Graham's bedroom?'

'As far as I know it was immediately above the lounge. That's too far back for me to really remember.'

'You've got into the bedroom. Then what's happened?'

'We both got undressed.'

'Completely?'

'Yes, but not initially. As far as I remember, we didn't initially get completely undressed. Graham lay on top of me and then we did eventually get undressed.'

'So, when you lay on the bed, were you naked?'

'Eventually, yes.'

'Was it like a slow strip, or how did it work out?'

'I can't remember that far back.'

'But you can remember lying on the bed. You're naked, sexually aroused?'

'Yes.'

'And Graham is doing what?'

'He was lying on top of me, rubbing backwards and forwards.'

'What, rubbing penises?'

'No, well, um, physically he was on top of me....'

'Facing each other?'

'Yes.'

'You're lying on your back, he's facing down, so, what, rubbing your bodies together?'

'Yes.'

'Rubbing penises presumably?'

'Yeah.'

'Then what happened?'

'We both had an ejaculation.'

'What, you had an ejaculation brought on by him rubbing you penis with his penis?'

'And vice versa.'

'Then what happened?'

'Basically, that was it.'

'Was anything said after that?'

'I honestly can't remember.'

'How did you feel after that?'

'I know how I felt when he said, "Let's go upstairs."'

'Tell me?'

'What do I do? Do I walk out? I think that this distance was going on through my mind. Do I walk out - embarrass him, and he probably would never want to see me again, or do I go upstairs? To my shame, I went upstairs.'

'Were you in a relationship with anyone else at the time?'

'No.'

'Were you aware that you might have feelings for another male at that time?'

'Yes. I thought I was under control. I didn't expect

it to happen. I hadn't planned it to happen.'

'I'm not saying that you did. What I'm saying is when were you aware that your interest was towards - I'll say Graham to start with - or was it towards men in general?'

'Men in general, I would say.'

'When did you realise that you were having those thoughts and feelings? Are we talking about something that's years and years ago, or is it something that you've lived with for...'

'It's impossible to remember back then. My memory was very much affected by what happened to me in the '90's.'

'As a young man, growing up in the sixties, was that a problem for you?'

'I did...there were a couple of girls I was fond of, but I was always a very, very shy person. I think I was too afraid to approach them and say, "Let's go out."'

'And before this thing with Graham, had you had any sexual experiences before that?'

'Not that I know of.'

'I'm talking about either with girls or boys.'

'I've never had intercourse with a girl, no.'

'What about any sexual play with a male?'

'I'm not aware of it.'

'So, what we're talking about really is this sexual encounter you've described with Graham is, could be, the first sexual encounter that you've had.'

'As far as I can recall, yes.'

'You had a thought - do I walk out, or do I go upstairs?'

'I should have walked out.'

'Obviously, of course you should. But this is, as far as you can remember, the first time that anything sexual took place between you and Graham?'

'Absolutely, yes.'

'Now, when you saw Graham after this incident, was anything said about it?'

'I can't remember.'

'The only thing I will say about that Hugh is that we're talking about something that's quite monumental in your life. It's quite a big thing to take place, and you've remembered it. Obviously, it's in your memory. You've remembered it in a lot of detail.'

'Most of the talk between us was as friends, and honestly, I did look on Graham as a friend. I would have loved to have had a brother. I would have loved Graham to have been my brother. My intentions had been to do the best for him. Knowing that now is one of the things that's upset me so much, which is why I wanted to help him. I feel so ashamed.'

'We've talked about the first sexual encounter between you and Graham. How many times did you have a sexual encounter with him?'

'If you mean masturbating him, I presume about six or seven occasions, which happened ...where was it now....that would have been when I came over to give him lessons.'

'To the best of my knowledge, nothing happened outside school until we went down to Wales in, I think, the summer of '67.'

'We'll chat about that in a second. That's obviously towards the later end of the relationship with Graham. So, would it follow a pattern?'

'How do you mean?'

'You go and do the tuition, and then go on to masturbation. How would it go? Did it follow a pattern?'

'I'm not aware of any particular pattern.'

'Who would generally start the sexual activity then?'

'After the first time, I would have done.'

'How would that manifest itself? How would you do that?'

'I'd put my arm around him, and then perhaps masturbate him.'

'And would this be in his bedroom in his house?'

'He had a study bedroom, yes.'

'What about him doing stuff to you?'

'Yeah, he'd do the same.'

'Masturbate?'

'Yeah.'

'What, to ejaculation?'

'Oh no, we were dressed then.'

'OK, but masturbate him until he ejaculated?'

'No, we were fully dressed.'

'So, when you masturbated Graham, did it go that far?'

'Not on those times, no.'

'What, he didn't ejaculate?'

'I wouldn't know. He was dressed at the time.'

'So, was it over his clothing, or what would you do? Put your hands inside his clothing?'

'No.'

'Over his clothing?'

'Yeah.'

'What would he do to you?'

'The same.'

'Would you take any of your clothing off and get your penis out?'

'No, because we were in the family house then.'

'Did that ever happen, apart from the first occasion?'

'Not to my knowledge, no.'

'So, it was rubbing each other over your clothing? Yeah.'

'So, when he rubbed you over your clothing, did he make you ejaculate?'

'No.'

'Did he ejaculate?'

'I have no idea.'

'Was anything said after these things? Any expressions of pleasure, of joy or anything like that, or regret or anything at all?'

'I don't think regret was ever mentioned.'

'So, would it be the case that, once it had actually got to the physical sexual side of things, as you've described in the first instance, would it be a regular thing then for you to sort of mutually masturbate each other after homework?'

'It's difficult to say.   '

'But was it a number of times?'

'It was a number of times, yes.'

'Did sexual activity ever take any different forms?'

'You're talking about the rape now?'

'I'm talking about any sexual activity you had with Graham. Did it take any other forms apart from masturbating?'

'As far as I can recall, it was only either masturbation or laying on top of each other.'

'What about oral sex?'

'Oh, no. I couldn't stand it. I can't stand the idea of that.'

'OK then. I'll ask you the question. Did you ever suck his penis?'

'No fear.'

'And did he ever suck yours?'

'No.'

'You say these things took place mainly in Graham's house?'

'Yeah.'

'Anywhere else where they took place? We're not speaking about Wales for a minute, we're just speaking about any sexual activity between you and Graham taking place anywhere else?'

'He said that he stayed one night at the flat I

had, which is true, but no sexual activity took place that night. I absolutely know that.'

'Did any sexual activity take place between you and Graham in your digs?'

'No.'

'Are you sure about that?'

'Positive.'

'Did Graham ever visit...'

'At that time, nothing has happened between us.'

'Did Graham ever visit your digs?'

'Just that one time.'

'What was that in relation to?'

'I think we'd been out to the pictures and I have a feeling there was something wrong with my motorcycle. He'd missed the last train home. He phoned his mother for her to come and collect him, and she wouldn't. So, basically, he had to stay with me for the night, plus I didn't have enough money to get him a taxi home.'

'Did anything happen that night?'

'No, that's the night I'm talking about before....'

'I'm asking you now, really testing your memory now, and asking you again, just for your frankness really. Did anything sexual take place between you and Graham in any of your digs?'

'In the second digs, yes.'

'This was right next to the school?'

'They sold the other flat and moved me to a flat right next to the school. In fact that was the night that Graham told me that the Salesians knew what was going on, and that would have been February or March of '68. It was after the summer of '67, to the best of my knowledge, there had been no sexual activity between us in the Autumn term, or up until that time when he said he wanted to speak to me, and came to the flat - that was the other flat.'

'And sexual activity took place on that occasion?'

'Yes'

'And what was that?'

'That was exactly the same as before - he laid on top of me...'

'Mutual masturbation - oh, what naked?'

'Yes.'

'So, you got naked and...so how many times - I know it sounds like a funny question. You've described one set of sexual activity where you're rubbing his penis over his trousers, and he's rubbing you, and then you've described the first time you had sexual contact with Graham was when you were both naked and he laid on top of you. So, how many times was it when you were both naked, and he laid on top of you?'

'I would say, obviously the first time. The only other time I can recall is when we went down to Wales.'

'We're going to talk about Wales in a little while. We've got this occasion at the flat. So, three times, as far as you can remember, where you were completely naked?'

'Well, it's twice, plus what happened in between - yeah.'

'So, Wales was in between?'

'Yeah.'

'So, we're talking about Graham's home address, your second work address, and we're talking about this trip to Wales now. So, what happened on that trip to Wales?'

'By this time I had use of my father's car, as I'd passed the test, and sometime during the summer term, I started to use the car. Sometimes the car, sometimes the motorbike. My father had a derelict cottage in Wales, which I would go down to occasionally and see if it was alright, and hadn't been vandalised. I was planning to go down there almost at the start of the summer holidays of '67, I think it would have been. I asked Graham if he would like to come with me, and he did.'

'How old was Graham now?'

'He was just going from year 10 to year 11. I'm not sure when his birthday is, so he could have still been 15, he could have been 16. I don't know'. (He was 15.)

'What about his parents? What did they think about it?'

'They were happy with that.'

'So, you've gone off on this trip to Wales. When, approximately, do you think it was?'

'I think it was probably the first or second week of the summer holidays of '67.'

'So, that would be early August.'

'Might have been the end of July. I can't remember. We arrived fairly late as the car was giving trouble on the way. I took and old tent. It began to rain and the tent leaked, so we slept in the car, or in the back kitchen of the cottage. The following day, I took Graham to Ross on Wye to buy a new tent. That day we put up the tent, and we had sexual relations as before.'

'When you say as before...?'

'I was lying on the ground - Graham was on top of me.'

'Naked?'

'Yes.'

'Did it go beyond the laying on top of each other?'

'I was sort of, back in my memory, and I honestly can't remember this happening.'

Was there any sort of penetration?'

'No, this is what I mean.'

'What, you can't remember it, or...?'

'To the best of my knowledge, it didn't happen, but I have really sought in the back of my mind about this, and what I can remember, I have said. I don't know whether I attempted it and failed, or what, because that's what he said in the...'

'What Graham is saying, on that matter, is that you had sexual intercourse with him, in the fact that you managed to get your penis into his anus, and you had sexual intercourse that way, and then he tried it with you, and he couldn't do it. Does that ring any bells?'

'No. I remember from what he said on the stuff on the internet, that I penetrated him and then withdrew. I just can't remember this. If I did, well, I just can't believe it.'

'What I'm saying, Hugh, now, just be honest with me, and really think about this now. We're talking about a sexual relationship - let's take the mechanics of who's who out of it. It's a sexual relationship between two people. It's gone from mutual masturbation, and it's progressing, as it would do in any sexual relationship. I am just asking you to be as honest with me as you can. Did sexual intercourse take place between you and Graham on that holiday?'

'If I could remember it, I would tell you, but, honestly, I can't. I hope it didn't. I can't say it didn't.'

'What about when Graham tried to penetrate you anally?'

'I'm saying I don't remember this incident at all.'

'That's all I need to ask you about this trip to Wales.'

'I know afterwards, we did tour around Wales.'

'Was there more sexual activity afterwards?'

'Masturbation. I can't remember if we lay on each other after that.'

'This, when you're laying on each other? Were you touching him? Were you holding his penis, and him holding your penis, or..?'

'That would be a bit difficult because I had my arms around him.'

'That's what I'm thinking of. So, it was in a cuddling sort of way, but a rhythmic movement between the two, like sex?'

'I presume so.'

'When did your sexual relationship finish with Graham?'

'The night he told me, in the flat - well, actually, can I explain a little bit?'

'Please do.'

'It was several weeks after Martin died. He wanted to speak to me, and came round to the flat after school. He came round and we both got undressed again, and exactly the same thing as before happened. He lay on top of me, and then he said he had to go. This would be about 5ish, and he then asked me if I could meet him later on. At this stage, I didn't know what he was going to tell me.'

'You didn't know what had been said, or who'd been told, or anything. OK. Were you concerned when he said that he wanted to meet you later on? No worries?'

'No. I was completely all right. I went to his house between about 6 and 7 o'clock, and spoke to Graham's mum until Graham came home. We went for a drive, and after a few minutes, stopped to talk. He said to me, as far as I can remember, these are his exact words. "They know about us." And, as you can imagine, I was absolutely shattered.'

'How did you take that to mean, when he said they know about us.? What did you take it to mean? The school knew?'

'Yeah.'

'Did he go into any details as to who was told

or...?'

'He didn't - he didn't.'

'You carry on then.'

'I asked how did they know, and he said he didn't know, and it wasn't until recently I knew that he had told them. I thought they'd found out by some other means.'

'So, you weren't sure. He told you that he didn't know how they knew about it, and you didn't...'

'But he told me that they wanted me to resign.'

'Graham told you that?'

'Yes. So, they sent him with a message, effectively, but I didn't realise that until recently.'

'Graham told you that the school wanted you to resign over you're sexual relationship with Graham?'

'I was absolutely shattered. I said to Graham at the time that I would deny it. I remember saying that now, and I know that's actually caused him some problems since, which I didn't realise until recently.'

'What we need to concentrate on is that time, Hugh.'

'I dropped Graham back and went for a drive for a while. There was an un-gated level crossing near Chertsey, and I was going to go over under the train.'

'Because of what Graham had told you?'

'Because of the shame.'

'Well, thankfully, you didn't do that. What did actually happen after that, Hugh?'

'I just thought of my family. They wouldn't have wanted me to do that. So, I knew it was no good denying it, so, I went to see the Headmaster, who was Fr O'Shea, but he wasn't around at the time, so, the rector was Fr Gaffney. I went to see him that same evening.'

'What, after Graham had told you?'

'Yes.'

'So, it's Fr Gaffney you went and spoke to?'

'Yes, and I told him basically what I've told you, except it was much shorter.'

'But, he was left in no doubt that you had told him you'd been having a sexual relationship?'

'He was expecting me to come round. He obviously knew what had been going on.'

'But, what you told him, Hugh - I know you said it wasn't in as much detail - was he aware that you'd been having a sexual relationship with Graham, as a result of your conversation with Fr Gaffney. Is that what you told him?'

He knew. Yes, but he knew before, from Graham.'

'Did you tell him?'

'Yes I did.'

'So, he was aware that you'd been having a sexual relationship with Graham?'

'Yes.'

'And what was his advice - what did he do about it?'

'I can't remember exactly what he said, but I offered him my resignation there and then, and he said that he would see the headmaster in the morning. I presume he'd been away. I didn't know what was going to happen, whether the police would be called in at the time. I think, the following day, I saw Graham at the bottom of the stairs leading to the Chemistry lab, and I started to tell him that I had been to see Fr Gaffney, and it's alright, they believe me. Then I had to break off, because I think someone was coming down the stairs.'

'So, what you were telling Graham is that...?'

'When I said, he must have thought that I denied it. I didn't get the chance...'

'To tell him that you'd told the truth?'

'If I can go back to the day before? Fr Gaffney told me to avoid being alone with Graham, as far as possible, except in a professional capacity.'

'So, this Fr Gaffney, he was what, the Deputy Head?'

'No, he was the Rector.'

'But he was aware of it?'

'And he told the Headmaster the following day.'

'And his advice, when you told him, was don't be alone with Graham.'

'Yes. He didn't say I had to go from the school immediately.'

'So, then what happened, Hugh?'

'Well, I suppose the next three or four weeks, I was just...'

'You were still working there?'

'Yes.'

'Still teaching?'

'I worked until the end of that year, and not long

after that.'

'So, was anything else said to you by any of the other staff?'

'No. Fr O'Shea didn't come to me. I was expecting to be called into him, but I wasn't. Not long after this, Fr Gaffney died, as it happened. I can't think of a gap, but it would give some idea of the time if you can find out when this happened. At his funeral, the Provincial Rector - he's the boss of the Salesians in England and Scotland and Wales. He was at the funeral, and I went to see him to apologise for what I'd done, and the difficulty I had caused the Salesians. He knew all about it.'

'What was his name?'

'Fr George Williams.'

'Is he still about?'

'Yes, to the best of my knowledge.'

'So, Fr George Williams is like the sort of Head Honcho, and you told him at Fr Gaffney's funeral?'

'But, he already knew.'

So, somebody had told Williams, then? Were you surprised that this Fr George Williams knew what had gone on, or not?'

Yes and no. I didn't know how far things had spread.'

'Still, nothing happened to you - you were still teaching?'

'I'm still teaching, but, obviously, I'd given my resignation at that time.'

'You had resigned, so you were working your

month's notice out, what ever it was?'

'The year's notice, isn't it, until July? I can't remember exactly when it happened, when I resigned.'

'So, it was at the end of the teaching year that you were going to go?'

'Yeah.'

'So, that would be the beginning of the summer holiday?'

'Yes. Anyway, basically, I told him what I'd told Fr Gaffney, and what I've told you. We talked about a few things, I can't remember, and he asked me what I was doing next year. I said that I hadn't got anything sorted out. I'd applied for a few jobs, and I'd either been too late, or they were filled with more qualified people, or whatever. So, he said to me "There's going to be a post for a Chemistry teacher in Battersea."'

'What, a Salesian school in Battersea?'

'Yeah. After I got up off the floor, as you can imagine, he made it clear that, if I applied for the job, there wouldn't be a problem getting it.'

'That must have been a surprise for you?'

'I couldn't believe it!'

'Him being aware of what happened between you and Graham, then, offering you a job at another school?'

'It maybe they wanted to keep their eye on me there, rather than me going to another school.'

'Did you, at any time after it had come out, have any other sexual encounters with Graham?'

'No. Absolutely not.'

'OK. I am going to ask you one question, and it's a matter for you whether you answer it or not. Since the last sexual encounter with Graham, has anything taken place between you and any other pupil?'

'No. I learned a very hard lesson.'

END of interview.

Chapter 3
More questions than answers

On the 27th October 2004, Madley was re-interviewed by Surrey Police at Woking Police Station. The following is an extract from that second interview:

Person interviewed: Hubert Cecil MADLEY
Place of interview: Woking Police Station
Date of interview: Wednesday, 27th October 2004
Time Commenced: 12:27 Hours
Duration of interview: 37 minutes
Interviewing Officers: DC JH, DC AM.

Persons present introduce themselves. Tape procedure explained. Entitlement to free independent legal advice explained. Caution given, explained in full and understood.

'This is the second time I've spoken to you. We had an interview on Sunday 17th October at Colindale Police Station. I came to your home address and we went to Colindale Police Station. I arrested you on suspicion of Indecent Assault and Rape, which is all to do with what happened between you and a boy called Graham WILMER back in 1967/1968, at the school Salesian College, at your digs and at his home address. I was very grateful to you at the last interview because you spoke to me a lot and explained a lot of things that had been going on between you and Graham, and I mentioned last time that I might need to speak to you again.'

'Are you going to be speaking about the same things?'

'Some of it, in a little bit more detail. I wont be repeating things I've asked you about before. First of all, what I want you to do is cast your mind back to the trip to Wales that you had. When was that? Can you remember what year that was in?'

'That would be in 67'

'What school holiday did that take place in?'

'Summer holidays – end of July, first week of September.'

'When about during that 6 week period was the trip planned for?'

'Either the first week or second week.'

'Who went on the trip?'

'Myself and Graham.'

'Right, just the two of you. I've know we've spoken about this before. You went to your mum's place?'

'My Father's.'

'Your father's place up in Wales, and you explained to me before about a tent and all the rest of it. Now, the bit I need to ask you about is where you stayed in the grounds of this cottage. Was it an occupied cottage?'

'No. It was completely derelict.'

'This is owned by?'

'My father.'

(MADLEY explains the property in Wales has old cottage gardens, an orchard and a field, near a place called Harkhouse, with the nearest town being Monmouth)

'You explained before that you pitched a tent there, and it was a rainy night, and you said some sexual activity took place between you and Graham in the tent?'

'Yes.'

'What vehicle did you use to get there in - can you remember?'

'It was an old Ford Anglia – my father's.'

'Was there a point in that evening or night where you ended up inside the cottage?'

'That's something I cant remember – whether we slept in the car or in the cottage. The reason I'm not sure is we might have slept another night at the cottage.'

'It's an important point, Hugh. How many times did you spend the night in the cottage with Graham?'

'I'm honestly not sure, probably only once, because I remember there was a stone floor and it wasn't very comfortable. I think that was only because it was just so wet in the tent, because it was leaking.'

'What did you do to make yourself comfortable in the cottage, then?'

'I think I had an oil stove, which I did some cooking on. After all this time, I can't remember.'

'Can you remember lighting a fire in there at all?'

'No.'

'What about getting anything out of your car to put in there, to make things a bot more comfortable – the back seats of the car?'

'I can't actually remember doing that – taking the back seats out, but if he says I did, I did.'

'Can you remember taking the seats out of the car and putting them in the cottage?'

'I can't honestly remember.'

'What you need to remember, Hugh, is that it's your memory I'm after, not anything you may have found out since.'

'I didn't realise what had happened until about January this year.'

'So, this trip to Wales, then. You've already explained there was some sexual activity. I think we discussed that before. There was mutual masturbation in the tent. What sexual activity took place in the cottage?'

'The same.'

'Did the sexual activity progress from mutual masturbation? Was there a time when it went beyond that? It's you I'm asking Hugh?'

'He says it did, but I think it must have done.'

'Tell me why you say it must have done? What were you saying, you think you must have done?'

'He says that I raped him by inserting my penis in his rear.'

'I'm just asking you to be as honest as you can

now, Hugh. That is what Graham says took place in the cottage. That's what Graham tells me. I wasn't there – you and Graham were there.'

'I've been trying to visualise as much as I can. Since January, things have been coming back to me, a little bit at a time, sometimes in a rush, sometimes in nightmares. It's not something I wanted to do, I think.'

'No, we're not saying that you wanted to do it. We're talking about something that happened, for whatever reason.'

'I believe I did do it, but I can't visualise it.'

'I'm going to have to go into a little more detail, because it is a very important point, alright. So, from what I understand, from what you have told me there, you can't actually remember doing it, but you may have done?'

'Yes.'

'What would you call that sort of sexual connection between you and Graham? What would you call it? Would you call it sexual intercourse?'

'I suppose that's what you'd call it.'

'So, if we call it sexual intercourse, then, how many times did sexual intercourse take place between you and Graham?'

'If it happened; it must have been once only. I can't imagine I would have done it more than once. Can I say something? I was reading what he'd put on the internet. He says I just started to penetrate him, and then withdrew, and I didn't compete anything sexual. I can't explain it.'

'Did that happen, then?'

'It must have done.'

'So, what about Graham what Graham did to you, then?'

'I presume he did the same.'

'How have you got a problem remembering, then? You remember quite a lot of detail, don't you?'

'It takes a lot to go through it again.'

'But it happened, didn't it?'

'I think so.'

'As far as that's concerned, what you're telling me now is that's the only time that sexual intercourse, as in you pushing your penis into his anus took place, and if he tried to do it to you, that was the only time he did it to you?'

'Yeah.'

'But you're sexual relationship carried on after the holiday?'

'The only time I can remember afterwards was the night he told me about the Salesians knew about it. That wasn't until March/April 1968.'

'So that would be more mutual masturbation?'

'Yeah'

'So, sexual activity did take place after that?'

'Yeah, but I don't think...I can't remember – not in between that time and right the way through.'

'I know I've covered it in detail in a previous interview, and I'm not going to go through all that again, but sexual activity too place between you and Graham at Graham's home address that was mutual masturbation, basically rubbing each other, etc?'

'Yeah.'

'Sexual activity took place in one of the rooms at the school provided for you where you lived, just in one of those rooms?'

'That was in 68, although I'm not positive.'

'Again, that was mutual masturbation. So, all the time that you were having a sexual relationship with Graham, how many times was there any sexual activity between you and Graham? What do you think?'

'It had been causing a bit of an argument. We did lots of things, which were absolutely nothing to do with this. We got on well together, or at least I though we did.'

(General conversation, as MADLEY becomes upset and is asked if he wants a break, but he does not.)

'Why wouldn't you have wanted to have sexual intercourse with him, when you say: "I wouldn't have wanted to", why wouldn't you have wanted to?'

'I couldn't see doing it, to be honest, because it would cause pain, I suppose. I never wanted to hurt him at all.'

'It would appear to be a natural progression of the sexual activity between you and Graham?'

'I can understand that, but it wasn't something I wanted to do.'

'Was it ever discussed between you and Graham after the event?'

'Possibly.'

'How was Graham after the trip to Wales. I mean, I'm talking about like the next morning. How was Graham with you the next morning?'

'I don't think he was any different. I know afterwards we went on a tour around Wales, and we certainly slept in the car at least one night. I've been trying to remember events. We went to an area I love very much. I did actually write to Graham afterwards.'

'Did any more sexual activity take place in Wales?'

'If it did, it was only masturbation.'

'Let's move on a little bit now then. You explained before that you'd already been interviewed before by police about what had happened, and we covered the point at that time you couldn't honestly remember what had happened?'

'I just had no clue.'

'So, when I interviewed you at Colindale, and what I'm asking you now, these are memories that you've got of what happened, and you're telling me the truth now, not because somebody's told you, but because of your memory, so what you're telling me is stuff that you remember that you've done?"

'Yes.'

'OK, that's important. When it all sort of came to light again, back in 2000, when you were first interviewed, nothing became of that at the end of the day, so just in brief sequence or brief chronology, if you like, how did it all start up the? Was it following this article on the internet about the Salesians?'

'I don't think it was about the Salesians in particular. I had been sent most of the material from Graham, that section he put out in November 2000, and I'd thrown most of the stuff away.' [It later transpired that the MADLEY had been tipped off by the head teacher at Salesian College Battersea, that Graham had placed material on the Friends Reunited web site, detailing what MADLEY had done to him.]

'What prompted you to contact him this year?'

'I felt so bad.' (MADLEY becomes upset).

'How did you go about tracing him, Hugh? Just concentrate on the question; try not to get too emotional?'

'He wrote to me in April, and for the first time since, probably 2000, I had his address.'

'This is his address up in Wallasey?'

'Yes.'

'So, he wrote to you. What did you do following that?'

'I wrote back to him and asked him if he'd like to meet me and talk to me, and he was obviously very nervous about that. We exchanged, initially, very tentative letters, and then he agreed for Stephen WILLIAMS, who was a supporter, I suppose you would call him that, from The Lantern Project. He got him to phone me up, and I sent him my telephone number, and basically I poured everything out to him, what had happened.'

'What you told me in these two interviews, you told him, did you?'

'Yes, we spoke a number of times.'

'Hold on. I'm a little bit confused. How did that actually come about? Who rang who?'

'Stephen WILLIAMS rang me.'

'What, was that something that you'd arranged to do?'

'Graham was unwilling to come to speak tome directly. I was too nervous to put stuff on paper. Unfortunately, I didn't keep a copy of what I'd written to him, but I've got his letters.'

'So, you've got Graham's letters at home?'

'Yes. I think I suggested, because he'd mentioned this person before, I suggested Graham might like to ring me, or meet with me, perhaps when Stephen was in his presence.'

'So, apart from the letters between you and Graham, you haven't spoken to Graham?'

'No.'

'But you have spoken to this Steve WILLIAMS, who works for The Lantern Project?'

'Yeah.'

'You spoke to him and you've disclosed to him what you've told me in interview, the same stuff that you've told me?'

'Probably in more detail. We did speak for a very long time.'

'Lets just concentrate on the letters, now. How many letters do you think you've sent Graham this year?'

'7 or 8 – somewhere in that region.'

'What is the content of those letters, Hugh?'

'Basically, I'm apologising, and I said I wanted to try and help. I'm sorry for what I did to him. I don't want him to hurt anymore. I wanted to try and put things right,'

'So, that's why you started to send the letters, was it? To try and put things right, as you put it?'

'Yes.'

' If I was to show you some letters, perhaps you can confirm for me that they're the ones you sent Graham. Would that be alright?'

'Yes, that's fine.'

'I'm not sure whether there's 12 or 13 letters. Would that be about right?'

'As many as that? I've no idea.'

(MADLEY is shown a ring binder containing his letters. He becomes upset again. The officer explains that he is not going to go through the letters, or make judgements about the content. He just wants MADLEY to confirm that they are indeed the letters he wrote and sent to GRAHAM.)

'Are there any more letters you sent to him prior

to this?'

'No.'

'So, it started on him sending you a letter at the beginning of April (2004), informing you he was going to re-open the investigation, or do something along those lines, wasn't it?' How did you feel about that when you got the letter?'

'I didn't really think too much about it. All I wanted to do was get in contact with him. I just knew I ad to do something. I have a conscious.'

'I think everybody does, Hugh, really. Just compose yourself and calm yourself down.'

'I just wanted to do what I though was right. I had no idea that I'd caused him so much harm over the years.'

'What made you realise that? From reading that on the internet?'

'Yes. I didn't realise what he'd been through.'

(The officer asks MADLEY to compose himself.)

MADLEY is then asked about the content of the telephone conversations with Stephen Williams – who was, of course, David Williams. Graham had originally asked his lawyer, Stephen Wilde if he would speak to MADLEY, and he had agreed to, so Graham had asked MADLEY in one of the early letters if he would be willing to speak to 'Stephen.' Graham did not give a surname. However, after MADLEY had agreed to talk to 'Stephen',

David Williams suggested it would be much better if he spoke with MADLEY, as Stephen Wilde did not know as much about Graham as David did. Stephen Wilde agreed, but, rather than tell MADLEY that there had been a change, which might have scared him off, the planned phone call went ahead, and David just introduced himself as Stephen Williams. It had seemed like a sensible thing to do, but when the case came before the courts for pre-trial hearings, the presiding judge, judge Inman, said this about the phone calls: 'So far as the telephone conversations are concerned, were I the trial judge I would not for a moment admit them in evidence. I was extremely unimpressed both with Mr Wilmer and with Mr Williams. It seemed to me that Mr Wilmer, in particular, was dishonest and disingenuous in his account of how the telephone calls came to be made. I have no doubt that he was a deliberate party to seeking to get Mr Madley, the defendant, to incriminate himself by pretending that these phone calls were being made for an entirely different purpose.' What planet was he on?

The interview continued:

'But, everything that you've said during those conversations – did you make anything up, or did everything happen?'

'I don't think I made anything up.'

'You told me in the first interview, Hugh, that, following all this, you were expecting to be in serious trouble, back in 1968, with the school, and, to your surprise, nothing happened! They moved you to a school in Battersea (Salesian College Battersea), where you carried on teaching for a number of years?'

'31 years.'

'I'm going to ask you some questions about what happened since Graham, and I don't want you to be offended by the questions I'm going to ask. I've got to ask questions because of what you did to Graham. That's why I've got to ask the questions. You remained in teaching; is there anything else that you want to tell me about anything that happened between you and any pupils since Graham?'

'I've never touched another pupil since, and that is the truth.'

'Have you ever touched another young person, not necessarily a pupil – somebody you come into contact with, or somebody you've met, socially or whatever?'

'No.'

'So, is there a partner in your life at the moment? Is there somebody in your life?'

'No.'

'Has there ever been?'

'I was hoping to get married in 63, but it didn't work out.'

'Nobody since then?'

'No, I just wanted to be trusted.'

'Is there anything hat you feel we've discussed

that you want to go through again, or anything you want to clarify about what you've told me today?'

'The only thing that's worrying me is this business of whether I raped him or not. I think I spoke to Stephen about it?'

'What did you say to Stephen?'

'I've actually spoken to Stephen since we've spoken, and he said I did say it. To be honest, my memory isn't very good.'

'So, if there is a tape recording of that conversation and you're telling Stephen that you had, I don't know which way you would term it – sexual intercourse or buggery or whatever. If that's on tape (MADLEY states if he said it, he said it.), but is that an honest thing that you told him, or have you told him something you think he wanted to hear, this is what I'm saying?'

'I can't answer that. I thought to dispute anything that Graham said would make things worse.'

'What you're saying is that you accept that sexual intercourse took place between you and Graham in the cottage.'

'If Graham said it happened, then it happened.'

'What I'm saying is Graham might say he'd been on a trip to the moon. The main important thing is do you remember penetrating Graham with your penis in his anus on that trip to Wales?'

'It Comes in and out of my mind. I'm sorry.'

'My view is that it would appear a natural progression of, I don't know, the expression of physical tenderness that you had between each other, at the time.'

'I don't agree with that, because if that was the case, then I'd have wanted to do it again and again.'

'It might not have been a good experience, but it might not have been a good experience for either of you, in which case you wouldn't want to do that again.'

'I certainly wouldn't have wanted to hurt anyone.'

'By that act, you may have done that. It might have caused some pain, and it might have put you off him, or whatever. Graham tells us that is what happened in his statement. In those days, in 1967, when this took place, a male couldn't rape a male in law. It's all changed now. In those days it was a buggery. It was (a buggery) in law, but it wasn't a rape. When I discussed this with you back in Colindale (Police Station), I explained to you what a rape was. There's a huge difference now, and the law changed - now a male can be raped. In 1967, a male couldn't be raped, but could be the victim of buggery. It's the same thing, but before the law changed recently, the only sex that could be raped was a female. A male couldn't be raped. That technicality of law has changed, so if there was a confusion, then that was my fault, and I apologise for that, but the actual offence at the time was buggery, which is basically sexual intercourse to an anus with a male, so that is what we are discussing, and I think we've covered that now. Is there anything else that you feel we want to go over? Have you seen Graham recently?'

'No. I just hope he's not suffering right now, and getting better. I did speak to Stephen after we'd spoken, and he did say Graham was making good progress.'

'That's good, then. That was something positive, wasn't it?'

'You were saying back then that things were coming in and out of your mind. What is the extent of that? What is going into your mind, then?'

'I remember more things we did, where went to 2 cricket matches.'

'What about the actual penetration at the back?'

'I can't visualise it. I can accept it happened. I believe Graham if he said it happened. I'm just lost (for) what to say.'

With nothing further to add or clarify, the interview concluded at 13:04 hours.

For the record, Hugh Madley joined the teaching staff at Salesian College, Battersea, in September 1968, where he remained teaching young boys for the next 31 years. He was supposed to be monitored during his time there, but within a matter of months, he was taking boys from that school on camping trips, visiting their houses and taking them back to his house. He continued to do this even after he had retired from teaching, but no one seemed to notice until a concerned parent phoned Wandsworth Education Department in September 2000 and made an allegation about his activities. However, no one investigated the allegation, even though the police had become aware of it. But, in 2005, after Madley was charged with the offences against me, one of those boys contacted me after reading my first book, 'Survivor': 'Date: Wed, 02 Feb 2005 - Subject: Hugh Madley - Hello Graham, I think there are possibly a few others like yourself, and I would like to try and find them if possible. I feel very frustrated about this situation as Madley is a born and bred liar, and always has been. He is refusing to tell me the truth and is trying to stop me from attending Guilford Crown on the 3rd March, as he is worried about what I might find out!! As I said to you before I suspect that he has abused my brother. If he has, then I do not want him to escape punishment. I have read the book and to be honest the majority is almost identical to the way he was around me. Whenever we stayed with him he would try to get in the same bed, but we used to kick him out. I know you are telling the truth, and after reading your book (Survivor), it struck me that there HAS to be others. Madley has admitted to my Wife that he has had feelings for me since I was younger, and still has; and also that if I had been that way inclined he would have slept with me. In other words, because I was strong enough to stop him he didn't. He has also confessed to masturbating over photos of me that he had taken whilst I was attending Salesian College Battersea. In the picture I had just crossed the line at the Inter Salesian sports events. He is a very stupid man as I was only 13 years old when he started hanging around me. He confessed this to MY WIFE though!!!! Why does he still have that picture??? I thought that was illegal??? He only confessed all this as my Wife told him she would not tell me, (yeah right). She put the phone on loudspeaker and even my mother in law heard it. I feel absolutely sick to think that all this time I thought he was a friend, and all he wanted to do was abuse me. This validates my suspicion of my brothers ILLNESS further. I have also found out that he burnt most of the video's that he had taken of the many other pupils, but I think they are actually under the floor in his room (he has a small section of floor boards that can be lifted out in a square approx. 2 foot by 2 foot under his bed) and that he is lying again, as I know that he hides stuff under there. If they are not there then they may be in the shed, or at his Uncle's house, who lives only 10 mins away. In his bathroom there is a panel by the bath taps that can be lifted and also hides stuff in there. He sits shampoos and other items on top so that you would never suspect it. Good luck with everything. Take care, Best wishes.

Chapter 4
A war of words

When I sat finally down one afternoon in January 2006 to write my new book, Conspiracy of Faith, I set myself two golden rules to govern my writing; being totally honest was one of them, even if that meant exposing my darkest secrets, while the other was to write a book that was a good read, not just a diary of hurt. Apart from that, I would let the story emerge, as it wanted to. The path it took did not entirely surprise me, but it soon developed a life of its own; one of the joys of writing when unimpaired by guilt and free from fear. Memories and emotions, some sad and some happy, seeped from the deeper regions of my mind, memories I had once tried hard to bury, as deep as I could, only to discover that, there they were, lying just below the surface after all. Once I had found the courage to look at them again, only this time square in the face, they looked different now, not just as a consequence of hindsight, but more because I was a child when I buried them, and I was now looking at them as an adult.

They were still very uncomfortable, but they were no longer so frightening, but that was in the daylight! When the darkness came, and I went to sleep, they would re-emerge like demons, screaming, jabbing and clawing at me, without mercy. Those nights were long and terrifying, but they provided the impetus to keep writing, keep digging, until I had searched out every corner of every recess of my memory, leaving no quarter for the horror of what he did to me to lurk and fester, feeding on the anxieties and vulnerability of the child, alone, confused and frozen within me. I was in charge now. I was the adult, and those who had once tried to destroy me, and then to deny me, would now face me once more, this time not in secret, enforced by threats of damnation, pain and obscurity, but under the glare and sharp focus of the truth; oh how I was relishing the comfort and safety of the truth, which, at long last, was setting me free.

It took about four months to complete my story, after which came the search for a publisher, which was not as difficult as I had thought it would be, unlike my earlier book Survivor, which took two years of rejections before I finally found Methodist Publishing, who published it, but only on the condition that I changed all the names and places, and removed all references to Catholic priests, hence Judge Reid's comments about the book being a 'lightly fictionalised account'.

But, having found a publisher for my new book, which did not hide anything, getting the book into print was not as straightforward as I had hoped! Adrian Brink, the managing director of Lutterworth Press, had secured an initial interest in my new book from the Mail on Sunday, subject to the usual caveats: 'depending of space in the paper at the time of publication...etc.,' But that was enough for him to go ahead and commission the work and start the pre-publication marketing, which took the form of a write up about the book on Lutterworth's web site, under the heading 'the first book to uncover sexual abuse in Salesian schools in Britain.' It wasn't long before the first letter from the Salesians' lawyers landed on his desk, threatening to take immediate action if he went ahead with publication, based, presumably, on their mistaken belief that Madley had maintained his silence, and so anything I had to say in the book would be a breach of the 'hush' agreement I had signed with them in 2000. It was obvious that the Salesians and their lawyers had not kept up with developments, as they seemed blissfully unaware of the fact that in 2005, there had been two pre-trial hearings, which, although the case had not gone to a full trial, the hearings had still been in open court, and there had been reports of the case in the local press, so, although the agreement was technically still enforceable, we calculated that, once they found out about the trial, the very idea that the Salesians would want to have the whole story dragged out again in the civil courts was highly unlikely. Adrian agreed with me that we would press ahead and see how serious they were, so he wrote back to them and said neither he nor I were under any legal obligation to stay silent. It transpired that they were not aware that Madley had been arrested for a second time, and that he had confessed all, including how much the Salesians had always known about what had happened to me, because he had told them himself before being moved to the Salesian College Battersea! I continued to explain that Madley had been charged with various specimen counts of buggery and indecency against a child, i.e., me, and had subsequently appeared twice at Guilford Crown Court, once on 4th August 2005, and again on 15th December 2005, and that everything I had written in my book had therefore already been aired in open court, including, of course, the fact that Madley had told the police that he himself had admitted to the Salesians back in February 1968, that he had been sexually abusing me, and that they had then moved him to Battersea to cover it up.

Their paranoia is evident in this internal memo, which shows an almost desperate attempt to protect their 'reputation' at all costs. Their view was that I was a tiresome troublemaker, and they must do all in their power to distance themselves from me and from any criticism. Had they not read Lord Nolan's report, especially the sections on how to support victims? Clearly they had not, or should I say they had, but they were choosing to ignore it, as indeed was the Catholic Church itself.

"Record of a meeting on April 24th 2006 about the publication of the book 'Conspiracy of Faith', by Graham Wilmer."

Background

In 1999 Graham Wilmer alleged that between 1966 and 1968 he had been sexually abused whilst a pupil at the Salesian College Chertsey, by Mr Hugh Madley, a lay teacher employed by the school. The abuse had not taken place on the school premises. Mr Wilmer stated that he reported the matter to Fr O'Shea, the head teacher, that Fr Harris the rector also knew of the matter, and that he was interviewed by Fr O'Shea and a Salesian from another school. Fr O'Shea now in his late 80's has no recollection of the allegations.

Having reported the matter in school Graham Wilmer was not abused again. Mr Madley left the school three months later at the end of the school year taking up a teaching post at the Salesian College at Battersea. At the end of that same year Graham Wilmer took his GCE exams but did very badly and was not allowed back to the school the following year - this would have been normal practice for a person gaining poor results.

In 1999 none of the Salesians still alive who might have known about the case had any recollection of it, and Mr Madley denied the allegations. Though there was no evidence to support Graham Wilmer's allegations he was clearly in a distressed state and with the advice and guidance of (lawyers) in 2001 he was made a payment of £10,000 by the Salesians 'towards any expenditure in connection with the diagnosis and treatment for PTSD' (Post Traumatic Stress Disorder) as part of a mediation agreement. In return, Wilmer agreed not to subsequently name the Salesians or their schools in any oral, written or electronic publication. Mr Wilmer was also given £10,000 to cover his legal costs associated with the mediation process.

In 2004 Graham Wilmer claimed that Hugh Madley had now admitted the abuse and that Hugh Madley had named to him the Salesians who had dealt with the matter in 1968 and arranged for his transfer to Battersea. Wilmer now took the view that when the 2001 mediation process took place the Salesians of Don Bosco were being deliberately misleading in saying that no Salesians could now remember the 1968 allegations, and so he seems to have decided that the 2001 agreement is no longer binding on him as in his view he was deceived by the Salesians when it was drawn up. In fact no Salesian questioned about the allegations in 2001 could remember them.

Currently Graham Wilmer has a website in which he gives his account of his alleged abuse by Hugh Madley and of the actions taken by the Salesians of Don Bosco and other parties. The Lutterworth Press are planning to publish his story in book form in June 2006 under the title 'Conspiracy of Faith' and there is a full page advertisement for the book on the press's website which names the Salesian School at Chertsey, Hugh Madley as the abuser, and the Salesians of Don Bosco as seeking to cover up the abuse and conspiring against him.

1. We are advised that though a judge would seek to uphold a legal contract such as the 2001 mediation agreement in which Graham Wilmer agreed not to name the Salesians or their schools, a judge might also consider that it was in the public interest that Graham Wilmer's book should be published. In his opinion there was probably a 60% chance that a judge would opt in favour of upholding the contract but that this was not a strong enough chance for lawyers to advise the Salesians to take legal action to seek to halt publication of the book. Such action and its failure could create significant adverse publicity and support Graham Wilmer's case that the Salesians of Don Bosco were trying to silence him. It was also the case that there was no agreement between the Salesians and the Lutterworth Press that would limit the actions of the Press.

2. In the light of this advice, it was agreed not to recommend to the Salesian Trustees that they take any legal action to try to stop publication, but that it was necessary to draw up a Salesian response to the book to be issued as a press or public statement if required.

3. The question of whether to approach Lutterworth Press so that a Salesian chapter or contribution to the

book could be inserted was raised, on the grounds that such a joint venture would show that the Salesians were not antagonistic to Graham Wilmer but had a different perspective and points to make. On reflection it was agreed not to take this line as this could be considered as association with, and implied approval of, this kind of book and Graham Wilmer's campaign against Hugh Madley and others.

4. It was agreed that though no action should be taken against Lutterworth Press, nevertheless they should be informed that Graham Wilmer had entered into a confidential agreement with the Salesians of Don Bosco preventing him from identifying the Order or its schools by name. It was agreed that this letter should be a factual statement of the situation and not imply that legal action would be taken against Lutterworth Press – to avoid any accusation that the Salesians were trying to block publication.

5. Graham Wilmer's website was considered and it was noted that an earlier website active in 2000 had been withdrawn, probably because action was taken against a UK host for the site by the NASUWT teachers union. If the current website was not using a host in this country then such action was not now possible.

Agreed Action

1. SDB, consulting on draft versions, would draw up the press/public statement in response to the book. This could perhaps include a section with answers to likely questions. The statement would only be issued in response to need and would probably have to be revised in the light of the book's actual content

2. Lawyers would write to the Lutterworth Press.

3. Lawyers would check to see if Graham Wilmer was using a UK host for his Lantern Project website.

SDB

18.04.2006

The Salesians worked on several drafts of their press statement, each draft being passed to their lawyers for scrutiny. Here are some of those drafts, from which one can see that they had no interest in me, their efforts being entirely to protect themselves and limit any damage to their precious reputation:

Short Press Statement DRAFT 1

'Conspiracy of Faith' by Graham Wilmer: Statement by the Salesians of Don Bosco. The Salesians of Don Bosco became aware in '1999 of Graham Wilmer's allegations of childhood abuse by a lay teacher in one of their schools in the 1960s. They offered support and assistance in the light of his clear distress and reached an agreement with Mr Wilmer, though the allegations could not be substantiated. The Salesians followed current guidelines and legal advice at all times. The alleged abuser was a layman and not a priest or member of the Order. Neither the Salesians nor the Catholic Church were in any way responsible for the alleged abuse.

Short Press Statement DRAFT 2

'Conspiracy of Faith' by Graham Wilmer: Statement by the Salesians of Don Bosco.

The Salesians of Don Bosco became aware in 1999 of Graham Wilmer's allegations of childhood abuse by a lay teacher in one of their schools in the 1960s. They offered support and assistance in the light of his clear distress and reached an agreement with Mr Wilmer, though the allegations could not be substantiated. The Salesians followed current guidelines and legal advice at all times. The alleged abuser was a layman and not a priest or member of the Order. Neither the Salesians nor the Catholic Church were in any way responsible for the alleged abuse.

The way the matter was handled in '1968, according to

Mr Wilmer's account, would now be seriously deficient. The Salesians apologise for and regret this fact but it is not always possible to judge past practice on current thinking.

Short Press Statement DRAFT 3

'Conspiracy of Faith' by Graham Wilmer: Statement by the Salesians of Don Bosco.

The Salesians of Don Bosco became aware in 1999 of Graham Wilmer's allegations of childhood abuse by a lay teacher in one of their schools in the 1960s. They offered support and assistance in the light of his clear distress and reached an agreement with Mr Wilmer, though the allegations could not be substantiated. The Salesians followed current guidelines and legal advice at all times. The alleged abuser was a layman and not a priest or member of the Order. Neither the Salesians nor the Catholic Church were in any way responsible for the alleged abuse.

The way the matter was handled in 1968, according to Mr Wilmer's account, would now be seriously deficient. The Salesians apologise for and regret this fact but it is not always possible to judge past practice on current thinking. The Salesians of Don Bosco have been accused of conspiring against Mr Wilmer and trying to silence him, neither of these accusations is true.

Short Press Statement DRAFT 4

'Conspiracy of Faith' by Graham Wilmer: Statement by the Salesians of Don Bosco.

The Salesians of Don Bosco became aware in 1999 of Graham Wilmer's allegations of childhood abuse by a lay teacher in one of their schools in the 1960s. They offered support and assistance in the light of his clear distress and reached an agreement with Mr Wilmer, though the allegations could not be substantiated. The Salesians followed current guidelines and legal advice at all times. The alleged abuser was a layman and not a priest or member of the Order. Neither the Salesians nor the Catholic Church were in any way responsible for the alleged abuse.

The way the matter was handled in 1968, according to Mr Wilmer's account, would now be seriously deficient. The Salesians apologise for and regret this fact but it is not always possible to judge past practice on current thinking. The Salesians of Don Bosco have been accused of conspiring against Mr Wilmer and trying to silence him, neither of these accusations is true.

There is now no recollection of the 1968 allegations by those still alive who may have dealt with the matter.

May 2006

DRAFT 8

'Conspiracy of Faith' by Graham Wilmer Statement by the Salesians of Don Bosco.

'Conspiracy of Faith' by Graham Wilmer, to be published by the Lutterworth Press in June 2006, presents his account of indecent assault at the hands of a teacher whilst he was a pupil at the Salesian College, Chertsey between 1966 and 1968, and the effect this has had on his life.

Though not yet available, from advance publicity it is clear that the book is critical of a range of organisations including the Salesians of Don Bosco, the Roman Catholic Religious Order responsible for the school at that time. If the book illustrates the devastating effect that childhood assault can have on the health and mental wellbeing of a person, righteous anger might also result in a story that could in parts be potentially misleading.

In the light of this possibility and seeking to ensure that no one's good name is unjustifiably called into question, the Salesians of Don Bosco wish to state the following: 1. The alleged offender in 1968 was a layman and not a priest or member of the Order. Neither the Salesians nor the Catholic Church were in any way responsible for the actions of the alleged offender in Mr Wilmer's case.

2. Mr Wilmer's account of assault came to the attention of the Salesians of Don Bosco in 1999. The alleged offender denied the accusations.

3. Mr Wilmer states that he first told his story in 1968 to a priest in confession at the school and the priest told him that he should report the matter to the school authorities. This was the appropriate advice.

4. According to Mr Wilmer's account after he reported the matter the assaults ceased but neither the police nor his parents were informed, nor did he receive any personal support. The teacher left the school a few months later, taking up a post at another Salesian School. In terms of current thinking and practice this 1960s response would now be regarded as inadequate and the Salesians of Don Bosco regret this fact, though it is not always appropriate to judge past practice against current thinking.

5. Mr Wilmer left the school because poor GCE results, which meant that he was not able to return to the Sixth Form. He attributes his poor results to his turmoil over the assaults he had suffered. This may well be the case but the lack of a Sixth Form place, whilst unfortunate, would have been in line with normal school policy at the time reflecting the absence of GCE re-sit provision, and should not be seen as action taken against him because he had made a complaint against a teacher.

6. Mr Wilmer takes the view that the few Salesians still alive whom he says knew of his allegations in 1968 cannot now claim to lack knowledge of them. The fact is that those still alive who may have dealt with the matter are now very elderly and do not have a clear recollection of what happened in 1968. Any suggestion that they and the Salesians are guilty of some sort of conspiracy against Mr Wilmer is totally false.

7. When the Salesians of Don Bosco became aware of Mr Wilmer's allegations in 1999, though they could not be substantiated, the Salesians in the light of his clear distress offered support and assistance following current guidelines and legal advice at all times. This support and assistance was accepted by Mr Wilmer.

May 2006

Chapter 5

"Truth? What is truth?" Pilate asked.

The arguments and exchanges of letters went on between Adrian, myself and the Salesians for several months, but, despite their lawyers recommending them to that they take out an injunction against me, The Salesians accepted Adrian's offer to let them see the manuscript, on condition that they did not take out an injunction against its publication, but, instead, they contribute a chapter to the book, giving their reasons for treating me the way they had done back in 1968. They accepted the offer to see the manuscript, but having read it, declined to make any contribution to the book, which they submitted to a line-by-line scrutiny by their trustees and their lawyers, who then produced eight different drafts, as they attempted to mitigate any responsibility for what had happened. This is the final version, sent to and Adrian Brink, my publisher, and to myself:

SDB final version of response to Conspiracy Of Faith.

The book is well written in a narrative style that holds the reader's attention. It is a powerful, moving and convincing statement of the devastating and lasting effect that childhood sexual assault can have on the life, health and mental wellbeing of a person. Graham

Wilmer's righteous anger against his abuser and his passionate desire for justice is entirely justified. His denunciation of the Salesians of Don Bosco, the criminal justice system, the Catholic Church in general and a range of other bodies is understandable, and at times justified, but his righteous anger leads him into some intemperate comments and accusations that are either wrong, misleading, or cannot be substantiated. The Salesians of Don Bosco have a number of particular concerns and ask that the author and publisher revise the text in the light of the points that follow.

1. The Book is written on the basis that the Salesians of Don Bosco were being false and duplicitous in their dealings with Graham Wilmer from 1999 onwards.

Graham Wilmer takes the view that when his accusations against Hugh Madley were brought to the attention of the Salesians in 1999, the Salesians knew that those accusations were true and so were being false and duplicitous when they said that they had no knowledge or evidence to substantiate them. This leads to claims in the book that there was a conspiracy to silence Graham Wilmer through the mediation process, and efforts to protect Hugh Madley.

In reality the Salesian Child Protection Team (SCPT) and the Salesian authorities dealing with the matter in the period from 1999 onwards did not have any knowledge or evidence to support the accusations until Hugh Madley admitted his guilt in 2004 and so legally they had to deal with the matter as unsubstantiated allegations. The two elderly Salesians still alive who had dealt with the matter in 1968 (Fr O'Shea and Fr G Williams) stated that they did not remember the matter.

Even in the unlikely event that they did remember, but stated that they did not, that still means that the SCPT and the Salesian authorities dealing with the matter from 1968 did not have any knowledge or evidence to support the accusations and were not being false or duplicitous, nor were they conspiring against Graham Wilmer.

On the basis of the way he was treated in 1968, and various assumptions in recent years, Graham Wilmer has come to the view in the book that the Salesians cannot be trusted. It will not be easy for him to set aside his conviction of a post-1999 Salesian conspiracy against him, and perhaps that even this very response to the book and the meeting of July 28th are part of such a conspiracy, but in the end it is only the truth that can bring closure and reconciliation and a post-1999 conspiracy is not the truth.

In the light of this we would ask that the following, much of which is libelous, be rewritten:

(a) The account of the mediation meeting and in particular references on page 80 that "1 knew then that I was in the presence of conspirators who had no intention of admitting their guilt....they were committed to continuing to deny any knowledge..." and "smug smiles of the two priests."

(b)The third paragraph on page 84 about priests being "corrupt, abusive, lying, evil..."

(c) The second paragraph on page 92 implying that the Salesians had played a trick on Graham Wilmer (to silence him).

(d) Much of the content of page 93; in particular the second paragraph and the reference to "mealy mouthed vault farce" (sic) in the third paragraph.

(e) Much of the content of pages 100 and 101. If this is an accurate account of the conversation between Graham Wilmer and David Williams, then some comment needs to be added (as is often done elsewhere in the book) to the effect that the deep rooted anger of Graham and David was making them jump to wrong conclusions about a Salesian conspiracy. Terms such as "attempt to pervert justice", "total pack of lies", "wicked secret', "the bastards", "treachery' are based on a false premise and even if said at the time need to be qualified as examples of the point Graham Wilmer makes elsewhere on page

49 where he says "1 had come to view almost everyone and everything in life with suspicion and doubt."

(f) The references on page 103 in the second paragraph to a "cover up" and putting the Salesians "in front of a judge and jury", in so far as they appear to relate to an alleged post-1999 conspiracy.

(g) Much of the first paragraph of page 105 about Salesians covering up and protecting Madley, and "those bastard priests", near the bottom of this page.

(h) The middle paragraph of page 115, which includes the comment that "Madley's confession had blown their conspiracy wide-open." And statements on this page such as "my battle was with the Salesians", Fr O'Shea being "cowardly 'and "found ouf", and "these despicable men.,,

2. The book is coloured by the general conviction that the Salesians were 'bastards' and 'conspirators'

Graham Wilmer's account of his school years at the Salesian College Chertsey, his view of the head teacher and Salesian teachers of that time and of the way he was treated after his confession to Fr Madden seem to be coloured by his conviction that the Salesians are and were "bastards" and "conspirators".

This comes out in a number of ways as indicated below:

(a) The absence of any positive comment about the Salesians who taught him at Chertsey, the description of "a dowdy old priest " on pages 5 & 6 and references on pages 6 & 7 to Salesians handing out punishments with "relish", "daily brainwashing", and an educational method based on "do what we tell you or you get beaten". Graham Wilmer may wish to present this picture of the school at that time and the Salesians within it, but one of the Salesian Trustees was himself a pupil at the Salesian College Chertsey from 1957 to 1964 and does not have such recollections. Corporal punishment was used, but in general no more than was normal in boys' schools at that time.

(b) Graham Wilmer states on page 20 that he was "betrayed by my confessor". This is simply not the case. The key here is that Fr Madden asked him to repeat his story immediately after the conclusion of the confession. All current guidelines from statutory agencies stress that if an adult receives a disclosure from a child, to the effect that they have been abused, then that adult has a serious obligation to inform the appropriate authority and must do so. Fr Madden would not have been able to report the abuse Graham Wilmer was receiving if he had only heard it in the context of confession, as there is a solemn church requirement that forbids a priest from revealing the content of anyone's confession. By getting Graham

Wilmer to repeat the matter after confession Fr Madden was rightly putting himself in a position where he could report the matter. This was an entirely appropriate and proper thing for Fr Madden to do and completely in line with current guidelines. Graham Wilmer may wish to describe this as "betrayal' but any knowledgeable reader would know that it was not. On page 73 Graham Wilmer states that Fr Madden "used my confession against me" and on page 77 Peter Green is reported to have said in the context of the mediation that the headmaster had been "fold the details of Graham's confession". Neither of these statements is correct. Fr Madden rightly reported what Graham Wilmer repeated after the confession and the head teacher was not told the "details of Graham's confession" but what he had told Fr Madden after confession. This is not splitting hairs but a vital distinction.

(c) The presumption is made at the top of page 23 that Fr O'Shea had arranged for the "specialist priest" to interview Graham Wilmer. In fact in those days the local rector Fr Francis Gaffney – Fr Harris named on page 21 as rector had finished in the summer of 1967) was very much in overall charge, and it is most likely that the rector (to whom Hugh Madley had in fact admitted his guilt) would have arranged for the "specialist" priest to come. This final paragraph tries to present Fr O'Shea in the worst possible light, as do other passages in the book. A particular case is the first paragraph of page 25 where in decidedly uncomplimentary terms the text predicts a betrayal 30 years in the future. Fr O'Shea's inability to remember the matter 30 years later would be judged by a person who has not "come to view almost everyone and everything with suspicion and doubt" (Graham Wilmer's self-description on page 49) as the forgetfulness of old age.

(d) In the middle of page 52 there is a statement that police constable Sarah Harris's enquiries had "shaken the school to its foundations" and a passing, but by implication damning, reference to "disturbing circumstantial evidence" uncovered that the school-" had gone out of its way to cover up what they knew to be true...". These are unsubstantiated comments.

(e) On pages 65 and 66 reference is made to comments Graham Wilmer received by email from two unnamed people one alleging a "regime of abuse perpetrated by a small minority" at the school, the other alleging abuse by Fr Madden. These comments are potentially very damaging to the good name of those involved, and to the Salesians generally. Since they appear to be wholly unsubstantiated, or made by unattributed sources, they should not be included, or made less specific.

3. The mediation meeting and process is presented as a 'Court of Conspirators' (The title of Chapter 12)

The account of the mediation process and meeting in chapters 11 and 12 is a matter of considerable concern in its presentation of the whole process as a conspiracy, its gratuitously insulting and unjustified comments about the two Salesians present at the mediation, their solicitor and the mediator, and in the inclusion of much material which is not in the public domain and is confidential. In particular:

(a) We would draw to your attention the agreement made between the Salesians, Mr Wilmer, the mediator and the Centre for Dispute Resolution in which all those parties agreed to "keep confidential and not use for any collateral or ulterior purpose'"

* the fact that the mediation had taken place,
* all information (whether given orally, in writing or otherwise) arising out of, or in connection with, the mediation including the fact of any settlement and its terms.

It therefore follows that there should be no reference in the book to correspondence or conversations in connection with setting up the mediation, any documents produced for or statements made in the course of the mediation, or any subsequent negotiations which led to the settlement of Mr Wilmer's complaint.

Finally, on this point, we would remind you that even

if Mr Wilmer and we were willing to waive his and our rights of' confidentiality under the mediation agreement (which, for the avoidance of doubt, we are not prepared to do) the publication of such information would not be lawful without the prior approval of the other parties to the agreement.

Most of chapters 11 and 12 will therefore have to be omitted from the final text of the book. Nonetheless, for your information, we set out below a number of misconceptions and inaccuracies in the text as currently drafted. We do so in the interests of accuracy and completeness, and not so as to relax or release the entitlement of ourselves and others to a solemn commitment to confidentiality.

(b) It is suggested that the proposal of mediation was a trap (page 71). This is not correct. On 7th December 2000, Mr Wilmer had written to the Salesians' solicitors: "In the meantime I have prepared the necessary documents.. ...to file a claim in the High Court for damages (aggravated and exemplary) agains the Salesian School"

The courts now expect disputing parties to use mediation (or a similar process) before starting legal proceedings. Against that background, therefore, the author's assertion that the Salesians were "just trying to put more pressure on me in the hope that I would go away" does not make sense. The very purpose of mediation is to resolve the dispute on terms acceptable to both parties (as indeed happened in this case). It is entered into entirely voluntarily by all parties. There can be no settlement unless all parties agree to the terms, again entirely voluntarily. Accordingly, a proposal of mediation cannot be used, or reasonably be perceived to be used, as a litigation tactic designed to put a party under pressure.

(c) In pages 72-73, the Salesians' case summary of the mediation is criticised for pointing out that the burden of proof was on the author. It is said that "Their position is one of total denial, yet they wanted to mediate! It was a joke".

In the first place, the content of the case summary is entirely confidential, for the reasons explained at 3(a) above. Secondly, it is highly misleading to characterise the position as set out in the case summary as one of "total denial'. We were perfectly entitled to remind Mr Wilmer, and correct in doing so, that if he proceeded with his claim, he would as a matter of law have to prove his claim. This is elementary. Far from maintaining a position of "total denial', the case summary expressly acknowledged that following Mr Wilmer's complaint investigations had been carried out by the school (see, for example, paragraph 5.3).

(d) In the context of the mediation, the Salesians are also criticised for refusing "to accept any knowledge of what I was claiming" (p.72). This is unfair and incorrect. The mediation proceeded on the assumption that Mr Wilmer was telling the truth. This point was expressly made by our solicitor in his opening statement on behalf of the Salesians (our solicitors have his notes prepared for the mediation). As a matter of logic, let alone law, there would have been no reason for us to propose or enter into a mediation, nor for that matter to settle on the terms that we did, had we not proceeded on the basis that Mr Wilmer was telling the truth.

It should be noted that this is a separate point from the evidential position, namely that at the time of the mediation there was no evidence to corroborate what Mr Wilmer was saying, and that had he proceeded with a claim, he would have had the burden of proof.

(e) The Salesians are criticised (page 73) for pointing out in the case summary that it was for the claimant to show that he was entitled to compensation. This is described as "an insult". This is incorrect. In order to succeed in a claim for damages (which was what was threatened by Mr Wilmer), it is necessary for the claimant not only to prove that the events took place but that, as a matter of law, they caused him the loss for which he claims compensation. Again, this is an uncontroversial statement of the law which appears to have been misunderstood by the author.

(f) It is said that the Salesians' case was "crap", i.e. weak or worthless and/or advanced in bad faith. This is not correct. Indeed, the author himself concedes that his case was so weak that a barrister specialist in the relevant field put his prospects of success at only 30%. A defense with a 70% prospect of succeeding cannot on any view be described as "crap".

(g) The account of the mediation process also repeats the false and highly defamatory allegation that Fr Madden and the Salesians generally had used the author's confession against him and had therefore betrayed the confidentiality of the confessional. We would refer you in this regard to paragraph 2(b) above.

(h) It is said (p. 80) that the mediator was incompetent and/or unsuitable because she was "nervous" and "clearly had no idea about the real impact of sexual abuse on children". This is clearly unsubstantiated. So far as the Salesians and their legal representatives are aware, X is not of an unusually nervous disposition. Mr Wilmer had considered and approved her CV before agreeing to her appointment as a mediator. In any event, there is no requirement for a mediator to be expert in the subject matter of a dispute; the expertise lies in the conduct of mediations.

(i) The account of events after the mediation (p, 81-82) is incorrect. The correct chronology is attached. The Salesians did not ask the author "to withdraw the complaint he had made to the police", nor did their solicitor "lie through his teeth".

j) On page 105 it is asserted that the Salesians had been hypocritical in assuring the author at the mediation that they would never cover up child abuse "yet that is exactly what they were still doing, because they had continued to protect Madley, believing he would never spill the beans". For the reasons set out in section 1 above, this allegation is based on a mistaken assumption. There was no conspiracy to protect Madley in 1999 and subsequently. So far as the position in 1968 is concerned, while it is now widely recognised that pedophiles cannot be trusted, in the 1960s most people were rather more naive. On Mr Madley's own account (accepted by the author) both the Rector, Fr Gaffney, and Fr George Williams formally asked Mr Madley to promise that he would never abuse again. Although they should not have been, they were probably both reassured by this - a Catholic young man solemnly promising a Catholic priest not to offend again.

It is in the Salesians' view quite likely that Fr George Williams would have offered Mr Madley the teaching post at Battersea because, having resigned his post at Chertsey, he was an unemployed young teacher who deserved the opportunity of a fresh start. This seems a more plausible explanation than that Fr Williams sought to cover up one scandal by knowingly creating a risk of further scandals at Battersea. In other words, the more credible explanation is that Fr George Williams (albeit naively) genuinely believed that Mr Madley would not offend again.

4. The book cover and Lutterworth Press website and publicity for the book.

Concern was expressed at the July 28th meeting about the content of the advance publicity for the book and seeing the proof text this concern extends to the back cover text. In particular:

(a) The comment on the back which reads 'This is the first published account of the failure of the Salesian Order to deal with child abuse in one of its schools" implies that other books are in the pipeline which is not the case, and that the abuse was not dealt with, i.e. that it was allowed to happen or to continue, which is not the case. We would wish for the ambiguities to be removed or the sentence to be removed.

(b) The first paragraph includes the sentence "He exposes the Salesians in the UK for their role in covering up the abuse and protecting the teacher....". Graham Wilmer may feel that such a summary of the situation is merited but we ask that consideration be given to alternative wording such as: "He exposes the Salesians in the UK for their failure to report the abuse or to recognise the trauma that he had suffered..."

(c) The second paragraph's opening words "Despite the recommendations of the Nolan Enquiry, and the reference to the Bichard Enquiry imply that there was a failure to take account of these Enquiries and their subsequent reports (2001 and 2004) in Graham Wilmer's case, but most of the action of the book predates these Enquiries.

5. Conclusions

The Salesians of Don Bosco believe that Graham Wilmer's book could make a significant contribution to a fuller understanding of the traumatic and lasting effects of childhood sexual-abuse. They do not wish to hide from the truth of their response to the abuse Graham Wilmer suffered at the hands of a lay teacher in one of their schools in the 1960s, but are concerned that their actions and statements since 1999 have been wrongly judged to be a conspiracy of falsehood and deception. Tragically on Graham Wilmer's own admission (page 49) one of the long-term effects of the trauma he has suffered is to make him "view almost everyone and everything in life with suspicion and doubt".

If it is to be a true story, the text needs to acknowledge that his tendency to "view almost everyone and everything in life with suspicion and doubt" was even more active than he has as yet acknowledged or realised, leading him into a conspiracy theory against the Salesians that in its details since 1999 cannot in fact be justified and has led to some distortion in his judgment of people and events in the past. It is hoped that consideration will be given to the revision of the text of the book in the light of this response of the Salesians of Don Bosco.

Dated: 18 September 2006

Eventually, to get the book into print, I agreed to make some of the changes they wanted me to make, but not all, as I was determined not to let them have any further control over me. There were other reasons why I was not willing to make many of the changes they had pressed me to. For example, I had been approached a couple of months before by another former member of the Salesians, who had told me of his serious concerns about the Salesian Order he had once been member of, and abuse that he had witnessed himself. He gave me a credible account of an incident of abuse involving a young boy and Fr Brian Madden. I knew that there would be other victims, and I was convinced that my book would help them break free from their silence. As Margaret Thatcher had said to President Regan, during a telephone discussion over the Falklands: "This is no time to go wobbly".

Chapter 6
Under Pressure

And so it was, on the 2nd February 2007, just a year after I had begun writing it, the book was finally published, an event that was to lead to a series of new disclosures that surprised even me, starting with that letter from a stranger, which I mentioned in Chapter 1, and which had arrived 18 days after my book was published. I read the letter several times before I picked up the phone and called the number written at the top. A quiet-spoken male answered in a controlled tone, but when I said who I was, the tone changed to one of great excitement. Eric spoke of his long association with the Salesians, and the close relationship he had with them, but he said that he was deeply troubled by my book, and he would really like to talk to me in person, so I invited him to come to New Brighton. Four days later, a knock at the front door announced his arrival. I had not known quite what to expect, but the sight of this neatly dressed man in his 60s, with a long, grey overcoat, silver beard, white hair and broad smile, put me instantly at ease. I invited him in and took him through to the kitchen, where David had made us coffee. He was a not surprised to see David, as he had read about him in my book, and had expected him to be standing alongside me, as he had done for the past seven years, as I had battled my way through my breakdown, and the subsequent fight back against the men in black. He sipped his coffee for a while, then, slowly started to tell me what he had to say.

At first, I found it hard to believe that this former Salesian priest, who had worked with and lived alongside almost all of the Salesian priests I had talked about in my book, was here telling me that he believed many of them had abused children, but here he was! He continued to talk for several hours, until his entire life was laid out in the same, neat order as his appearance portrayed. Eric was a very methodical man. He appeared calm and collected as he laid out his life, until he came to talk about Fr George Williams – the same Fr George Williams who had sworn me to silence back in February 1968. His eyes narrowed and his tone dropped, as he reached into his brief case and pulled out a sheaf of hand-written notes, which he handed to me in silence. I read through the pages:

"Graham: Some straws in the wind. I cannot give the names of my sources since I do not have their permission to use their spoken and/or written comments. However, although these quotes cannot be verbatim, I can guarantee that these are accurate, as they have been spoken and/or written directly to me. I know all of these sources as my fellow Salesians and/or my pupils when I taught at Salesians schools. At present, Graham, you must NOT quote my name, since I am still very closely involved with the Salesians and with all of these friends.

"Fr Hoey offered me chocolates…when he put his hand on my knee and began to stroke the inside of my (short) trousers. I left his room…I was very wary and very suspicious of him and another Salesian Brother."

"Fr Bamber and Fr Wareing were bad men and bad priests on the Staff at (Salesian College) Chertsey. They abused; I was unhappy there."

"George 'Gus' Williams bought us presents. He was the Sacristan. He put his hands up my trousers. Another boy took off all his clothes for him."

"My brother was very unhappy at (Salesian College) Shrigley. He did not like what happened to him there. He was abused. He has long refused to go near the place. Fr George Williams was the Rector."

"There are lots of stories about Fr George Williams. When he was RectorHe gave me sex instructions. He told me to take my trousers down."

"I believe that George Williams was fanatical and obsessive, and fundamentally unsuited to the job he was in – to any job he was in – to any job, in fact, in charge of boys. I did not prosper under his regime, and I worry about any organisation in which he was subsequently and successfully promoted."

"When I made a General Confession to Fr Terence O'Brien, he asked me to tell him all the 'dirty jokes' I knew."

"Fr Terence O'Brien was under police investigation for allegations made against him from boys who had been in 'The Guild of Dominic Savio'. It was about his sex instructions. The Salesians 'hid' him."

"Fr Pilbeam was under police investigation for child abuse at Botley Park Mental hospital – Chertsey. The Salesians transferred him their Australian Province."

"The promotion of Fr George Williams through their years of training by the Salesians of Don Bosco (Philosophy, Teaching Brother, Theology, Ordination), raises the whole question of how much they actually found out and knew about him. Did they know the truth? If they did know about his liking for his little charges, and still defended, promoted and protected him? How guilty does that make them then, and now?"

The last page was signed: 'Eric Baggaley' and dated 25/02/2007. Eric watched me intently, as I read through the document. My face would have told him all he needed to know. I was in shock. Here in front of me were credible allegations of much more than just the one-off conspiracy of silence that I had believed was behind what had happened to me back in 1968. Here was what appeared to be evidence of institutional child abuse, spanning decades, involving Salesian priests several of the Salesian schools in the so-called British Province, from the bottom of the Order right to the very top. I needed some fresh air, so David suggested that we all walk down to the river, which was only ten minutes away, and stroll along the prom. Fifteen minutes later, we had reached the Magazine pub, and once inside, Eric began to explain to David and I why it was that he had felt so compelled to meet me. It was a long, complicated tale of personal philosophy, Catholic indoctrination, religious ideology and disillusionment with the Salesian Order, in which he had grown up, and which had shaped his very existence, until now. My book, he said, had made it impossible for him to 'remain silent any longer'. He wanted the abusers, the corrupters of children, to be exposed for what they were, and punished, especially Fr George Williams, who he quite clearly held in utter contempt, which suggested to me that there was more to their relationship that he was making out, but he would not be drawn on that when I questioned him.

We walked back to my house, and I explained what I would like to do next. Eric listened carefully, making notes as I talked and nodding in apparent agreement. Before he left, however, to catch his train home, Eric asked me to promise 'that, for now, I would not say anything about what was in the document he had given me, or mention that he had come to see me. He said that he needed to talk to the current Salesian Provincial, Fr Michael Winstanley, before I did anything.

I agreed, as I could see that there was nothing to be gained from acting without his support, not yet, anyway. And so, the stranger who knocked on my door only a few hours before, was now leaving, but now as an ally and possibly even a friend?

A couple of weeks before Eric had come to talk to me, a North London newspaper, the Hendon Times, published an article, under a front-page, banner headline: Teacher: 'I abused boy'. This is an extract from the article: 'A retired teacher from Mill Hill has admitted he sexually abused one of his young pupils 40 years ago - despite never being convicted of any offence. In an interview with the Barnet Times, Hugh Madley, 63, of Hale Lane, confessed he indecently assaulted the boy at Salesian College, a Catholic boys' grammar school he taught at in Chertsey, Surrey. His victim, Graham Wilmer, now aged 55, says Mr Madley sexually abused him over a two-year period between 1966 and 1968, when he was aged between 14 and 16 - and was twice taken to Mr Madley's Mill Hill home to be abused. Mr Madley was questioned by police in 2000 and 2004 about the claims and was due to be tried in 2005, but the case collapsed over a legal technicality. But on Tuesday - after learning Mr Wilmer has written a book detailing his experiences and naming him as his abuser - Mr Madley confessed that he had sexually abused Mr Wilmer, but said he did not remember doing so.' © *6:41am Friday 9th February 2007 - Copyright 2001-2013 Newsquest Media Group.*

In the days that followed, as he said he would do,

Eric wrote to, and then met with the Salesian Provincial, Fr Michael Winstanley. A few days before their meeting, Eric sent me a copy of the notes he had written, as an aide-mémoire to give to Fr Michael at the meeting. Here is an extract from those notes:

'I have learned (to date) of at least 4 or 5 former Salesian pupils who have read Graham Wilmer's Conspiracy of Faith, an expose of his sexual abuse by Hugh Madley at Chertsey. They are now also logging on to his website and following up various Press reports. They are concerned, as you and I are, that named Salesians at Chertsey, Battersea and Provincial Office are being portrayed in a very bad light. They are talking about a "cover-up" by the Salesians when Fr George Williams was provincial.

From correspondence and conversations I have had, more and more "anecdotal" evidence is emerging linked also with various names (he names 8 Salesian priests and one Salesian brother). One name is especially arousing numerous stories: "hands up trousers", "stripped naked", "sex instruction, beginning with 'take your trousers down'" etc., and these refer to the time before he was a Salesian, and when he was a Salesian priest.

How long can it be now before these two strands, Graham Wilmer's abuse and these other allegations converge? Graham's book Conspiracy of Faith, and his website, plus the continuing Press attention, seem to show that this connection (the abuser, Madley, and the

Salesians who defended/protected him) could well be among the stories soon to emerge. Michael, my respect for you, for your intelligence and your integrity, are very great. I am sorry that this issue is coming to a head on your watch – but it is! Personally, I did not suffer abuse from Fr George Williams. For me, it is clear that the only choice facing us all now is to be for, or against, TRUTH – JUSTICE – LEGALITY – MORALITY.

This crisis is not all doom and gloom: it is a challenge and an opportunity...to change direction towards Graham, with Graham, to forget the adversarial and very expensive games played by lawyers "moving the goal posts constantly", seeking tiny legal loopholes to block the truth and justice, to prevent them being found, to prevent them being exercised. This is a challenge and an opportunity to meet and to listen to Graham Wilmer; to begin to show empathy; to talk through what he sees, feels, needs and wants to happen; to talk through with him what you, Michael, see, feel, need and want to happen. We need to work together for a closure and a healing which is a "win-win" solution escaping from the lawyers' "win-lose" confrontations, and from the morass of "lose-lose" we are now all at present bogged down in. Eric -27.02.07.'

The meeting took place on the 8th of March 2007, at the Salesian headquarters in Bolton. The following day, Eric phoned me with a brief account of what had been said, and then sent me a more detailed account of their meeting:

Friday 9 March 2007. 'Graham, a good idea for you to have, in more permanent form, my impressions of yesterday's meeting with Michael. I am VERY happy to be able to say that it went as positively and as well as I imagined and hoped it would. Thanks to Martin, Nicky, you and many "angels", Michael and I spoke in great calm and concentration, respect and empathy. I asked him first to say a prayer; he improvised absolutely perfectly, asking for light, courage, understanding, and forgiveness; to do what is right. I then said that I regarded this meeting, what I was about to say and what we were about to discuss, as "the most important of my life". I also asked that we listen to each other from our "depths"; the depths of our shared Salesian spirit, our shared Priesthood and shared integrity and humanity. He agreed, and listened, in wrapt silence, as I very slowly and deliberately read the whole of my "paper" exactly as you know it.

He made the following points: He personally told Fr Mervyn Williams that he HAD to give an apology at the mediation meeting. It was and is sincere, from Michael. What was done in 1968 was not right on all the counts mentioned. Furthermore, he has no problem with an apology now being in writing and in the public domain. He intends to meet you face to face. He prefers to communicate in this way, has done so before, in contentious cases, and found in good for all concerned. He would come to Wirral willingly.

He has no problem with a Salesian donation

to the Lantern Project, but he has not been happy with what could appear as the total responsibility of what you have endured being placed on the Salesian Congregation, so that all the failures of Police, Lawyers, CPS, Surrey Education, NASUWT, etc. could be dumped on the Salesians. He has a concern about "Conspiracy" being one of Faith, and covering the whole period 1968-2001. He sees that there WAS a conspiracy - of SILENCE - due to the wrong doings of George Williams. All we have said should have happened for you and for Madley were not done. When Fr George Williams handed over office to Fr. Eddie Fox (a much respected and loved Salesian), he was told nothing about the matter, and George Williams bombed off to Italy for many, many years. Michael was visibly shaken and amazed about the stories circulating about Fr George Williams and other Salesian priests. Michael said these gave 'a new slant on everything George Williams did/did not do'.

Michael has a concern about "confidentiality", in the sense that his lawyers are of the opinion that you have broken this in the past. Michael hopes that nothing done now, in terms of mediation, apology, donation and the rest - could ever be turned round and used as a weapon against the Salesians. Michael wants reconciliation, healing, closure and the like to be precisely that. He told me that he is tied up for a few days now (I gather there was a Provincial Council Meeting in the offing!), but that he would be in contact with you, Graham, very soon after that. I think I have been fair to his thoughts, without verbatim quotes on any of them. I am confident that you can have a very good meeting with him, and that you both will be the better for it! If I can be of any help to him or to you, Graham, you know that it would be a privilege for me. I have tried, and shall always try not to hold any secrets for one person against another. Very bad and dangerous for any Counsellor! So, I now feel that you and Michael can meet and discuss at a truly adult, mature and deep level of empathy. I Hope so. All the best to you, for the moment, Graham. I thank you, Nicky and all the angels on the team, for your love, honesty and support and I shall do my utmost to repay you all in kind. Courage – Shalom! The answer to the question "QUO VADIS?" must be "Towards Truth, Justice, Healing and Peace", of course.'

Eric came back to see me a few days after they had met, and told me that if I wanted to re-open a dialogue with the Provincial, the door was open. He suggested that I should phone him, right now, and from a pocket notebook, he read out the number, which I dialled. A quiet voice answered, and I introduced myself. It was a very different conversation to the many I had had over several years previously with the lawyers who represented the Salesians. Gone was the hostility, the defensive tone, the outright denials of prior knowledge and cover-up. Now what I was hearing was contrition, sorrow, the need for reconciliation, or so that is what it sounded like, and by the end of the conversation, I had accepted his offer to meet with him at a place of my choosing to talk face-to-face, one reason being, perhaps, the growing alarm within the Salesian Order as reviews about my book began to appear in the national and regional press, the second story appearing in the Surrey Herald, which was printed just down the road from the school in Chertsey where I had been abused! The paper had also been speaking with a former Salesian Brother, who had first contacted me in August 2006, just prior to my book being published. He sent me an email, saying he had read something about my forthcoming book, and he wanted to let me know that he had serious doubts about them, so much so, he had left the Salesian Order in disillusionment back in the 70's, as a result!

I replied, and over the next few weeks, he told me his story, which gave yet more evidence of the scale of child abuse being perpetrated by Salesian priests, and in particular, one priest - Fr Madden. The very same priest I had originally disclosed my abuse to back in February 1968, after confession. This is part of the discussions between Martin Gormally and a reporter at the Surrey Herald:

'It's surprising how a telephone conversation can trigger off memories! And I also realise how easier I find it to express myself in writing rather than on the phone. I offer a few more elements of memory in the hope that they may give you a more balanced view of what happened 40 years ago. Memory is very fickle, and I'm not sure how much one ought to rely on it. There must be some elements of truth, if we sift through it carefully.

I didn't, in fact describe the incident, which brought the driving school parent to complain to the Rector of Salesian College about Fr. Madden. I think it might be useful for you. It happened on the football field, during a match when his son received a ball in the groin, just where it hurts. Fr. Madden came to the rescue with massage, which went apparently beyond relieving pain. The boy was profoundly disturbed, and reported the incident to his parents'.

'THE horrors of child abuse and the toll it exacts on its victims have been laid bare in an explosive new book called Conspiracy of Faith. In it, author Graham Wilmer, claims he was sexually abused for two years by a teacher at Salesian College in Chertsey during the 1960s. STEVE BAX reports:

'IT was the dead of night in a remote part of South Wales and 15-year-old Graham Wilmer stood with a shotgun in his trembling hands. Hugh Madley, the man he hated with a passion, had just taken a shot at a group of rabbits and left the weapon in the boy's hands while he inspected the area where the creatures had been. Madley, then a teacher at Salesian College in Highfield Road, Chertsey (where Salesian School is now based) had persuaded Graham's parents to allow the teenager to accompany him on a camping holiday. Graham's heart was filled with dread at the thought that "something awful was about to happen" but he could not bring himself to use the gun against the man he would one day accuse in court of molesting him.' After rain put paid to their plans to sleep in a tent, the pair went into a derelict cottage and lit a fire. It was here that Graham alleges, Madley raped him.' Extract from Surrey Herald - February 2007.

Chapter 7
A Provincial's Confession

We met on the 26th March 2007, at Eric's house in Cheshire. David and I had arrived early, so there was time to ask Eric to give us an idea of the likely scenarios we might expect. He was polite, but seemed as much in the dark as we were. After about 30 minutes, the doorbell rang, and there stood not one, but two men in black. The taller of the two I recognised; Fr Mervyn Williams, the priest who had represented the Salesians at the meeting with their lawyers, in London before my book Conspiracy of Faith was published. The shorter of the two, by some measure, was Fr Michel Winstanley, a mere five feet six inches in his stocking feet, totally dwarfed by myself, David, and Fr Williams, all of us being over six feet tall! Michael's diminutive stature was not, however, matched with the bombastic temperament often associated with small men in positions of power. Far from it, he was genteel and charming, quite the opposite of the former Provincial, George Williams, who had asked me all those prurient questions, when he had quizzed me back in 1968.

Eric escorted us into the front room of his small, but tidy cottage, then made his apologies and left us to talk. Michael was the first to speak, asking me to explain to him what exactly, if I could remember, was it that George Williams had said to me when he interviewed me at Chertsey, back in 1968? When I had finished going through the litany of prurient questions he had put to me, most of which were exploring my sexual development; when had I started to masturbate? What did I think about when I masturbated? Had I ever touched another boy's penis, and so on and so on? Bearing in mind that I was only 15 years old at the time, and that I had just disclosed to him that my chemistry teaching had been sexually abusing me for the past two years, and that there was no one else in the room with us to hear what was being said, you might well ask yourself, what's wrong with this picture? Certainly, by the look on Fr Winstanley's face, he had already asked himself that question, and now he was about to deliver to me his answer.

'Graham', he said, 'I have a confession to make to you.' He paused, briefly, then said: 'Eighteen months ago, another Salesian pupil told me that he had been sexually abused by Fr George Williams. I have spoken to George Williams, who has denied the allegation, but I do not believe him. I am still deciding how best to deal with that situation, but what is it that I can do to make amends to you?' I told Fr Winstanley that there were two things he could do that would make a difference, not just to me, but to the way my family and other victims would view the Salesian Order. The first was to convert the verbal apology he had given me through Mervyn, at the meeting with their lawyers, into a written apology, signed by him. The second was to make a significant donation to my charity, The Lantern Project, which was now supporting a number of Salesian victims, in addition to the hundreds of other victims we supported nationally, through our Survivors Forum. After another brief pause, Fr Michael, as he preferred to be called, agreed to both my request. The first, he said, he would do as soon as he got back, but the second would require a little longer, as he would need to seek permission from his Provincial Council. I said that was not a problem, and we ended the meeting, gave our thanks to our host, and went home. Three days later, another letter dropped through my letterbox.

29 March 2007

Dear Graham

I write subsequent to our meeting last Monday. It was, I believe, a landmark event, a genuine meeting of minds. I am grateful to you and to David for making it possible for us to move forward in such a positive and constructive manner. You assured me that you had already accepted the apology, which you received via Mervyn at your July meeting in London. But I wanted to make it to you personally, and would now like to put it in writing.

As Salesians of Don Bosco, we exist in order to serve young people with genuine acceptance, compassion and care, and to do all we can to promote their well-being.

There are many Salesians across the world and in our own British province who do this with great generosity and commitment. I am profoundly saddened to realise that this has not been your experience. The manner in which you were treated in 1968, after revealing the child abuse you had suffered through the actions of Mr Hugh Madley, was seriously deficient. There is no way in which we would wish to condone or defend the way in which this matter was handled at the time. As the current provincial of the British province I offer you a heartfelt and unreserved apology, and I ask your forgiveness.

I firmly believe that we can continue together our journey towards reconciliation, healing and closure. That will be my prayer over the season of Easter. May God's peace accompany you, always.

Yours sincerely

Michael T Winstanley SDB
Provincial.

Two weeks later, I received another letter from Fr Michael, in which he declared that he was going to make a donation to my charity of £10,000, per year for the next four years, in recognition of the work I was doing to help other survivors of child abuse. This time, however, I would not be bound by any legal restraints, as I had been when they gave me £20,000 back in February

2001. This time, there were no strings attached, and Michael even stated that I could say whatever I wanted about his apology and his donation to my charity, but, as time would tell, this turned out to be more of a personal act, rather than one which reflected the wishes of all of the other members of his Provincial Council, or indeed the wider, Salesian Order.

So far, so good, but on the 23rd August 2007, Eric phoned me to say that he had just finished writing an open letter, addressed to me and to Fr Michael, in which he had expressed his frustration at the Salesians for the lack of action in tackling the allegations being made against Fr George Williams. I asked him what he wanted me to do with it? He replied: 'Whatever you think is right.' A few moments later, the letter appeared on my computer, attached to an email from Eric. Its contents were, to say the least, disturbing!

Dear Fr. Winstanley,

In March 2007, having first read his book Conspiracy of Faith (Lutterworth Press, 2007), I corresponded with and then met Graham Wilmer. The account of his experiences of sexual abuse while attending the Salesian College, Chertsey, Surrey (1968) and the struggles he has been through, especially since contacting the Salesians in 1999, moved me greatly. I offered my help both to him and to you, Fr Winstanley, hopeful that it would be possible to achieve a measure of understanding, truth, justice and possibly healing, which have not been possible in the past.

Our intention in this work has been to attempt to repair some of the damage and right some of the injustices which began when the teenage Graham Wilmer, having suffered repeated sexual abuse by a lay teacher on the staff of Salesian School Chertsey, told his Salesian confessor, who persuaded him to allow these accusations to be revealed to other Salesians, including the Rector of the Community, the Headmaster of the school and the Provincial Superior, amongst others.

I believe that the subsequent silencing of the teenage victim, followed by the provision of a new teaching post at Salesian College Battersea for the abuser, Hugh Madley, giving the latter further access to young, vulnerable boys, greatly compounded the injustices already suffered by Graham Wilmer. These morally reprehensible and legally blameworthy courses of action were arranged and supervised by the then Provincial Superior, Fr. George Williams SDB. To their credit, the present Salesian Council members, under your leadership, Fr. Winstanley, have recently issued a letter of unconditional apology to Graham Wilmer and have also voted to support the Lantern Project (the Charity founded by Graham to help adult survivors of childhood sexual abuse) with an annual "ex gratia" donation of £10,000 for the next four years.

There remains, however, one grave issue as yet unresolved. The reprehensible and clearly indefensible conduct of Fr. George Williams, following on from the detailed interviews which he conducted with both Graham Wilmer and Hugh Madley, as revealed in Conspiracy of Faith, have prompted further disturbing disclosures of a sexual abuse. Former Salesian pupils have revealed certain facts to me. I know and respect the fact that these men depend on me to preserve the confidentiality of their disclosures. I shall never betray their confidence. I confirm that the anecdotal evidence of these men demonstrates that, as young boys, they were the innocent victims of predatory sexual behaviour by Salesian priests, who subjected children and young people to emotional, psychological, religious and sexual abuse and trauma.

I am not at liberty to reveal any names, dates, places or details of these allegations, but I make this statement and deposition in the conviction that I am duty-bound to speak out in support of Graham Wilmer who has come forward to accuse Fr. George Williams of silencing him about sexual abuse at one Salesian school, while protecting and prolonging the teaching career of a known and self-confessed pedophile at another Salesian school. I also speak out in support of those other victims, who, while as yet choosing to remain silent, or not to pursue matters in public, affirm that some Salesian priests have proved themselves to be sexually predatory adults, prepared to abuse innocent, vulnerable boys.

As one of my correspondents writes: " I do believe that he was fanatical and obsessive and fundamentally unsuited to the job he was in – to any job, in fact, in charge of boys. I did not prosper under his regime and I worry about any organisations in which he worked."

I believe that only a perverse and misguided sense of "tribal loyalty" could now persuade any Salesian or any true friend of the Salesians to approve of any form of "cover-up", mute denial of the truth or silent inactivity as either viable or sensible options regarding paedophilia and paedophiles. Whether such cases or allegations are present or historic, any such course of action would prove to be ultimately futile, dangerous and damaging for the Congregation and its British Province.

The recommendations and requirements of the Nolan Report and other, more recent Child Protection documents, provide the Catholic Church and the Salesian Congregation with positive challenges and opportunities for good. The cloak of silence which Fr. George Williams imposed, not only on Graham Wilmer but on Salesian priests in posts of responsibility, must now be unequivocally condemned by the Salesians of the British Province. I have been informed that Eddie Fox has recently confirmed that Fr. George Williams told him nothing about the Hugh Madley/Graham Wilmer case when the then Fr. Edward Fox SDB took over the post of Provincial Superior in 1970. Consequently, Fr. George Williams made sure (he hoped) that the Province would never know the truth of what he had done or not done in its name.

Conspiracy of Faith has now blown apart that

conspiracy of silence orchestrated and perpetuated by Fr. George Williams. Consequently you, Fr. Winstanley and your present Council cannot, I believe, morally or legally continue to keep silent about Fr. George Williams. Silence now means that you acquiesce in, approve of and cooperate with his guilt. The fact that other sex abuse victims are remaining silent for the time being does not excuse the Salesians from acting decisively on the disclosures which have been made by Graham Wilmer and by the one other victim, who has spoken to the Child Protection Officer for the Salesian British Province, even though this individual did not press for any further action at the time. Graham Wilmer clearly is pressing for further action and is determined to pursue justice – for himself (the victim) for Hugh Madley (the sexual abuser) and for Fr. George Williams (the abuser's protector).

It seems to me, therefore, that the Salesians of the British Province have a clear and stark choice to make: either they themselves voluntarily do what is right and just now to clear their name of any complicity with Fr. George Williams, or be forced to do so through a slow, ignominious series of accusations, revelations, admissions and condemnations at a later date.

The Catholic Church in USA and Britain has accepted that transparency and honesty about the pedophiles in their midst represent their only routes back to credibility and dignity. Fr Winstanley, I put to you as strongly as I possibly can that only complete transparency and courageous honesty in the search for truth and justice are worthy of the name Salesians of Don Bosco. Only such complete integrity is compatible with the Salesians' proud mission statement of commitment to the total good and well-being of young people.

Eric Baggaley - 23.07.2007

Chapter 8
The can of worms opens

Although Eric had given me his verbal permission to use the letter as I saw fit, I sent him an email to asked him to confirm his permission in writing, which he responded to immediately, adding that I could even use it in the press, if I wanted to. I knew once the Salesians had sight of it, however, they would very quickly try and get Eric to withdraw it. So, before they could act, I sent a copy to my friend, the journalist and author, Francis Beckett, who had expressed an interested in writing about me for the Guardian. The content of the memo was all he needed to give his story a news angle, rather than writing just a book review.

The Salesians did indeed react to the 'open letter' in the way I had thought they would, sending Eric a very clearly worded letter from the Provincial, on 12th August 2007, lambasting him on his actions, as the following extract shows: 'I was aware that your 'open letter' would be shared with Graham, so that he would know that you had acted – since it was obviously a cause of some perplexity and irritation to him that you seemed to be sitting on the fence. I am surprised, however, at your decision to let him use it as he wishes. If other people read it who are not aware of the reason for its being written, and written in the language and style you adopted, they would get the wrong impression.

I did not think that the letter was to be published on the open market. I also feel that it is not right that the confidential information, shared with you by other victims, should be used for Graham's agenda. Its feels to me (I use the verb deliberately) that you have allowed yourself to be pressurised and manipulated, and have lost the impartiality of the intermediary which I took to be the role you had adopted. Whilst Salesian bashing may be in vogue, the people who get hurt are not the ones concerned.'

Eric wrote to myself and to Michael Winstanley the following day, withdrawing both his permission for the letter to be used, and apologising unreservedly. I fired one back to him, suggesting that he had obviously been got at by the Salesians, and shame on him for caving in so easily! He reacted with indignation, saying that he had not bowed to any one's pressure. But I knew how the Salesians worked, even though I had not seen the Provincials letter at this stage, so I ignored his 'withdrawal' and carried on using it, as indeed did the Salesians in a letter their Child Protection Coordinator sent to the NSPCC South London Safer Communities Project, also dated 12th August 2007:

'Dear Sir, Re: Salesians of Don Bosco UK - Allegations against Fr Williams. The Provincial of the Salesians has asked me to contact you in you in your role as Independent Chair of the London South Coast Regional Religious Commission. I enclose a copy of an article from the Guardian (03/08/07) together with a copy of Francis Beckett's Blog (05/08/07) and a copy of an Open Letter and Memo sent to the Provincial (23/07/07). I realise that we have a Commission Meeting on 10th September, but I felt this matter could not wait till then. I wish to come to discuss this case with you in more detail.'

Ten days earlier, on Friday 3 August 2007, the Guardian had published the article Francis had written under the heading 'Breaking the silence'. This is a small extract: 'When Graham Wilmer was sexually abused by a teacher at his strict Catholic school, he was ordered to keep quiet about it. But 30 years later he decided to bring his tormentor to justice. As Francis Beckett reports, it proved a harrowing task. Today the present head of the Salesians in Britain, Father Michael Winstanley, admits the abuse. "We have apologised for what happened." But it has taken all Wilmer's obsessive anger to bring the institution to this point. I asked Winstanley if Madley was the only child abuser employed in Salesian schools. There was a long pause before he replied: "He is the only abuser who has confessed."'

Not long after the Guardian article appeared, other victims began to contact me, saying they too had been abused in Salesian schools. I was also contacted by a teacher, who had worked alongside Madley, at the Salesian College in Battersea. He told me he knew the mother of a Salesian pupil with learning difficulties, who claimed Madley had abused her son while he was on a school camping trip. The camping trip scenario was very familiar to me. The boy's mother said her son was badly affected by what had happened, but she didn't want to make a complaint, in case it caused him even more difficulties, but yet she wanted to support me. I told her that what she had already said was enough, and that she should not worry about anything, as evidence from other pupils was emerging almost by the day, the nature of which painted a picture of wide-spread abuse of children that was not only known about, but was tolerated by those at the top the Salesian Order, as the following testimonies demonstrate.

'Dear Graham, my brother and I were at Salesian College Chertsey until June of 1968. Recently, via the Salesian College website, he found your website and passed it on to me. I read your account with sadness, but little surprise, as Father Brian (Jock) Madden had also been my housemaster, and had attempted to molest me and two other boys in the showers in the spring of 1968. If you remember the showers there, they were closed cubicles, which one entered, shed one's clothes, and showered in private, then re-clothed prior to leaving. Jock's penalty to us for having done poorly for the house in cross-country was to run ten miles after school, or take a cold shower. Given that the showers were enclosed, we opted for the cold shower. Once in the shower, he knocked on the door, and demanded I open it so he could watch me turn around and around under the cold water, naked, freezing and humiliated. Once he said I could turn off the shower, he came forward with a towel to give me a rubdown. I closed the door on him, dressed and fled. I fear the other two boys weren't so lucky.'

'Dear Graham, Father Darwell went with us on a trip to Turin. I was given a double room at the place we were to stay. I think it was a Salesian college or retreat. I was alone in this single room, which had an en-suite. The first morning there was a knock at my door and it was Father Darwell. He claimed that he wanted a shower, and for some reason he couldn't use his own, as he was sharing with another priest (I don't know why). He started to undress at the foot of my bed (not in the en-suite bathroom). He was, as usual, aroused - he always seemed to be. I pretended to be tired, but he called me from the shower and asked me to wash his back, and then other parts of him. It was soon after this that he started to wash me, and attempted to bugger me, but he was unable to do so. It was at this point I realised I could not go on.'

'Graham - I was sexually assaulted at Salesian College Chertsey. I have lived in shame and guilt, made many suicide attempts and hurt myself in the years since. They stole my life and ensured it would never get on track, no matter how hard I try I fail at what I start - like a programme been put into me. The events in question happened in the late 80's Graham - really pleased you've exposed this. You're a brave man.'

'Dear Mr Wilmer, whilst at Salesian College Blaisdon, I became the object of the attention of a particular priest. I was a very naive lad and had lived a fairly cloistered existence; most definitely not up on worldly matters. It was only on reflection in recent years, and having come across a paedophile (without at the time knowing what he was until his being discovered and subsequent imprisonment) that I realised just what this priest was. Your experience, and mine, to a lesser degree, are not isolated ones.'

'Hi Graham, I have come across your story recently, and am very distressed for you. I was at Chertsey from 1964-71, so I knew all the main characters in your story. I know from personal experience, which fortunately stopped short of abuse, that Madden was a dangerous individual, who should never have been working with children. With 40 years of perspective, I recognise both the "grooming" and cunning on his part, and the feeling of not being able to tell anyone on my side, which makes the whole scenario possible. There also has to be a feeling that the hierarchy was aware of the dangers but did nothing to separate him from potential prey. Can't say much more, but just wanted to express sympathy and solidarity in case it helps - Regards'.

'Dear Graham, my abuser was Fr Terence O'Brien, during the time period 1969/1970/71 when I was 12/13/14 years old. He also abused my brother, who continues to live a socially withdrawn & dysfunctional life. He had made several attempts to get to know my parents, and visited our house (uninvited) on many occasions. This was almost certainly a classic case of grooming.'

These extracts tell the same story. The sexual abuse of children at Salesians schools in England was endemic. How many others would come forward, and how many other victims could there be? The evidence from experts now tells us that recidivism by priests who have been convicted is a factor in all cases. One-off offences are almost unheard of, whereas multiple offences are the norm, with some offenders committing dozens of sexual assaults over many years. It is not unreasonable, therefore, to estimate the overall number of victims of sexual abuse by priests in Salesian schools in England to be many hundreds.

Chapter 9

CTRUK - The Commission for Truth and Reconciliation

The months rolled on, and the number of victims contacting the Lantern Project continued to rise, not just victims of abuse at Salesian schools, but from all over the country. They all told the same story, albeit in different forms, but essentially, they were all the same, and they were all suffering in the same way, years after the abuse had stopped. One of the most saddening aspects of the stories recounted to me was the loneliness and isolation that all victims said they suffered from, something I knew only too well from my own experiences. It began to dawn on me that the scale of abuse was so huge, we needed a national commission to expose what was, in effect, a national health epidemic in our country, albeit one which no government seemed to be willing to admit to. I knew that this was not something I could achieve on my own, but It may be possible to get others to lend me their support, which I could then use to float the concept in front of Ministers, but first I would need to gather support for the idea from people who had influence, and to do that, I would need to put together a concept document, which I posted on a website: www.ctruk.org.uk, which my son Rory set up for me:

'The Commission for Truth and Reconciliation UK Statement of purpose:

Since the foundation of The Lantern Project in 2003, we have worked with hundreds of victims of sexual abuse, the majority of who were abused during their childhood. The psychological and emotional damage caused by the abuse they suffered has affected them throughout their lives, but, until they made contact with us, they have had little if any help in dealing with the aftermath of the trauma forced upon them.

In recent months, much attention has been focused on the extent of child abuse perpetrated by Roman Catholic priests in Eire, and more recently, in Germany and the Netherlands, investigations have begun into the extent of child abuse by Catholic priests within those countries.

Since June 1994, when pedophile priest Father Brendan Smith was sentenced to four years in prison for the abuse of children in Northern Ireland, there have been three major reports into the abuse of children at the hands of Ireland's Catholic clergy:

October 2005 the Ferns report detailed extensive child abuse and the cover-up of pedophile activity in the southeast of Ireland.

November 2005 Judge Yvonne Murphy was appointed to head a commission of investigation into clerical child abuse in the Dublin diocese.

May 2009 the Ryan report detailing abuse at

orphanages and industrial schools run by Catholic religious orders across the state was published.

In this country, in 2000, the Catholic Church commissioned Lord Nolan to investigate child abuse by Catholic priests here, which resulted in various recommendations, subsequently adopted by the Church, the aim of which was, essentially, to stop future abuse taking place by improved safeguarding policies and procedures, but not to address and repair the damage of abuse already committed. The Anglican Church is also engaged in similar efforts to investigate abuse by Anglican priests.

What has not happened in this country, but which is much needed, is a wider inquiry into the extent of childhood sexual abuse in the country as a whole, not just within religious organisations, and the establishment of better support for victims to help them deal with the long-term impact and consequences of the abuse they suffered.

The purpose of this initiative is to persuade the British government to establish a commission to do just that. If you would like to take part in this initiative, either as a victim, or in any other capacity, please complete the declaration of interest, and we will get back to you.

The CTRUK concept had three aims:

1. To provide a non-judgmental forum through which victims of sexual abuse can submit testimony, in person

or by other means, to enable their voices to be heard and the harm they suffered acknowledged and responded to.

2. To evaluate the damage caused to victims of sexual abuse over their lifetime, and to quantify its true cost to individuals and to our society.

3. To develop and effect the delivery of a comprehensive therapeutic intervention and support programme that will enable victims to reach a nationally recognised and measurable standard for recovery.'

In March 2010, having set up the web site, I began to contact people of influence who I thought would respond to the idea. First on my list was, of course, the head of the Salesians in the UK, Fr Michael Winstanley, a man I had come to trust over the years; in spite all of the wrongs the Salesians had done to me. He responded to the idea by saying that he thought I should talk to the Catholic Church itself, and that I should write to the Archbishop of Westminster, Vincent Nichols. I did, but the Archbishop was lookwarm to the idea, although he asked me to take it up with the Chairman of the National Catholic Safeguarding Commission (NCSC), Bill Kilgallon, 'who I am sure will give this matter careful consideration.'

I also wrote to the Pope: 'Your Grace – I write to you as a survivor of sexual abuse in my childhood, at the hands of members of your church. My story has been told before, but my struggle for justice goes on, as does the struggle for the hundreds of other survivors, who sought my help after my story was published. Despite the recommendations of the Nolan Review and the Cumberlege Commission, we are still meeting hostility, obfuscation and denial from your bishops and safeguarding officers, as we seek the reconciliation and healing we need to enable us to move on. What we lack is the support of an independent commission, with the credibility and experience to act as a forum for all victims of child abuse in the UK; a place where victims can disclose the harm done to them without fear, shame or prejudice, have their experiences recognised and accepted, and seek and obtain the therapeutic support they need to recover. I have laid out the rational for such a commission on a web site: www.ctruk.org.uk. You have the power to enable such a commission to be created. All that is needed is a single sentence of support from you, no more, no less. I ask you, therefore, to help me help those who still suffer in silence and in darkness, so they may be guided through their turmoil and be, once more, free to achieve their potential, as they were once, briefly, in childhood, before your priests laid waste to their futures.'

The Pope did not reply, and Archbishop Nichols made no further comment. However, Bill Kilgallon, Chairman of the NCSC, along with his colleague, Adrian Child, the Chief Executive of the Catholic Safeguarding Advisory Service (CSAS), invited myself, and a number of other survivor groups, to attend a meeting in London to 'explore how we might work together.' There were meant to be three of these meetings, but, it soon became clear, after the first meeting, that the Catholic Church was trying to use us to improve their media image over their lack of support for victims of church abuse. I urged Vincent Nichols to work with us to clear up some of the mistrust that was emerging:

28th March 2011
'Dear Archbishop Nichols

A year ago, you kindly suggested that I make contact with Bill Kilgallon, the then Chairman of NCSC, to discuss my proposals to establish a national commission for truth and reconciliation for all victims of childhood sexual abuse in the UK.

David Williams (Co-founder of The Lantern Project) and I subsequently met with Bill on a number of occasions, to discuss our proposals and seek his support, which he gave, albeit on the understanding that he had very little influence, and would therefore be unlikely to be able to help us move our proposals forward.

However, in July of last year, we were invited by Adrian Child and Bill Kilgallon to attend a meeting, with a number of other survivor groups, to explore how the Catholic Church, through NCSC and CSAS, could reach out to victims, and develop a more appropriate response to their needs. The meeting did not achieve very much, save to highlight the extent of the differences in the way we all felt about what should be done to improve the way the Church was acting towards victims.

To help move the process forward, I wrote the attached paper 'Working Together To Support Victims Of Childhood Sexual Abuse', which was circulated at the subsequent meeting of the NCSC and CSAS in February of this year. The paper was responded to by Sr Jane Bertelsen, on behalf of NCSC, who said "It is impossible to read (the document) without a deep sense of regret, sadness and shame. This is work we want to learn from and support in every way we can and it confirms our determination to change things."

This is encouraging, but the pace of change is proving to be painfully slow, with actual progress being rather hard to illustrate. Could I ask you, therefore, to read my paper, and add your support to it, in a way that would allow me to explain to others, including the press and government ministers, that I have your personal blessing, and that of the Church itself, to move our proposition forward, by bringing it into the wider public arena. Such support from you would allow me to knock on the doors of those who do actually have the influence that Bill Kilgallon said he did not have, which is what is required to enable us to widen the support we give to the many victims we support, and to the many others who are still locked in silence and fear, not knowing who to turn to or how, in order that they may find a way to come to terms with their ordeals, and, in doing so, recover from the trauma they have suffered. With all best wishes - Graham Wilmer - Founder The Lantern Project.'

This is an extract from the paper I sent to Archbishop Nichols:

Working together to support victims of Childhood Sexual Abuse. A proposal for discussion with NCSC/CSAS and Partners.

WARNING: THIS DOCUMENT CONTAINS EXPLICIT DISCLOSURE DETAILS OF SEXUAL ABUSE.

For victims, overcoming the many challenges of childhood sexual abuse requires more than their individual courage. With the right kind of support, it is possible, but that support is very hard to find, so the majority of victims continue to suffer in silence for most of their lives, at a cost to themselves and to society at large that is simply unacceptable.

Working with the Churches to overcome the many obstacles that stand in our way, we could make a real difference to the lives of victims, and to our society, but this will require collective courage, of a kind that that is usually only found in times of disaster. Child abuse is just that, a disaster. So let us act together with courage to put things right.

Proposition: The purpose of this document is to propose working with the Churches together to determine a complete understanding of the impact and legacy of childhood sexual abuse, with the sole aim of developing and implementing a practical, holistic and sustainable recovery process through which truth, reconciliation and healing can be achieved for victims, their families, the Churches and society at large.

Since the foundation of the Lantern Project in 2000, I have worked with more than 2000 victims of childhood sexual abuse. The hundreds of similar support groups that exist in the UK and elsewhere have also supported many thousands of other victims. In England and Wales, the Survivors Trust (TST) represents the majority of these support groups at national level, enabling us to get on with the work of supporting victims in our local areas, while TST engage legislators and other influencers on our behalf.

The nature of our work (I only speak for the LP here) has varied widely, depending on the type of support we have been asked to provide. In some cases our support has involved assessing the needs of victims, referred to us by GPs and local psychology services, based on disclosures those victims were able to make to us, but unable to make, for whatever reason, to their GP or counsellor.

In other cases, we have only become involved when police have asked us to accompany victims to court for the duration of trials, where their abusers have been prosecuted. This has inevitably led us to provide ongoing support, long after the trails have been concluded and the police have gone away.

In other cases, we have been asked by the prison service and the National Offender Management Service (NOMS) to spend time in prisons, talking to prisoners who have harmed themselves because no one would listen to, or could deal with, their disclosures of abuse, suffered in childhood, which, in the majority of the cases we worked with, also had a direct causal link to their subsequent offending behaviour.

We have also attended psychiatric hospitals and A&E departments, to support victims who have attempted suicide, no longer able to cope with the symptoms of depressive illness and post-traumatic stress disorder, which they were suffering from, as the result of mental breakdown, often due to the re-emergence of their childhood abuse memories.

We have also acted as mediators for victims who have wanted to confront the organisations, where they had been abused as children, work which has involved us with the Churches, care homes, social services and the criminal and civil justice systems, all of which has been technically challenging and extremely difficult.

EXAMPLE: 1 as an example of the difficulties we have faced, I have the permission of Noel Swift to discuss his case with you. Noel was sexually abused over a prolonged period by his local parish priest, at Christ The King Catholic Church in Bedford, England in the 1960s.

This is his testimony: Statement by Noel Swift

about the sexual offences committed against me by Fr John Parr in Bedford, England, which took place in the Roman Catholic Church of Christ The King, Harrowden Rd, Bedford, and in Fr Parr's house and in other places in the locality, between 1965 and 1968.

This testimony is a true account of the sexual offences committed against me by Fr John Parr, while he was parish priest at the Roman Catholic Church of Christ The King, in Bedford, England.

The abuse began shortly after I went with my mother to talk with Fr Parr about what was going on with my father. My dad was a great provider but a weekend drunk. My mother was at her wits end with what he was doing. I was 10 years old at that time (1965). Why I was picked to go with her to this day, I don't know?

The abuse started soon after that. At first it was very soft and caring. He would tell me that he knew all about my father's problems with drinking. He would tell me that he really cared for me and that he wanted the best for me. We would walk down to the moors and look for blackberries and birds' nests, as I had told him that my brother and me collected birds' eggs.

The first time anything real happened was in a field near the moors. We were sitting down in the long grass looking at a skylark hovering in the sky he told me to come closer and watch the bird start to land; that it would land away from the nest and run up to it so as to lead predators away.

He pulled me onto his lap and slid his hand up

my trouser leg and started to rub me on my upper leg and then went all the way up to my penis. He undid my belt and top button on my trousers and pulled them down and then my underpants were pulled down.

He rubbed my penis and my bum for a long time, and then I got what felt like an electrical shock. He said to me "Your daddy does not love you like this does he?" I said "No Father." He then said, "Your daddy does not make you feel like this either, does he?" I replied "No Father." He told me to get dressed and then he wanted me to listen carefully to what he was going to tell me.

He said that I was very special and that he wanted to take care of me, but I must promise not to tell anyone about what we did or where we went, for if I did I would "go to Limbo for a thousand years." I made the promise; we left the moors and I walked home.

After the first time the abuse became a regular occurrence. I would meet him after school or after Mass, as I was an Altar boy and I also sang in the Choir.

The places changed, but the abuse always went the same: up on his knee, then his hand would move gentle up my leg to my penis, and he would start to rub it, while telling me that I was his "special boy." Then he would ask me to do the same to him. At first I could not do it, but then he would take out his penis and put it in my hand and tell me to pull it back and forward. When we were done, he would always end with "Your daddy does not love you like this, does he?", and then the warning not to say anything to anyone.

I was taken on numerous occasions to his bedroom, where he would lay me on the bed, take of my clothes and perform oral sex on me, putting my penis is his mouth, and when he was done, asking me to do the same to him. I could not put his penis in my mouth. I think it was the smell of it that just wouldn't let me do it.

I was also taken to the church sacristy, where he would dress me in vestments, and call me his "little boy priest". Then, he would lift up the cassock, pull down my trousers and underpants and put my penis into his mouth. One of the times we were in the sacristy, and he was performing oral sex on me, his housekeeper came in. She stood there just watching, then, without saying a word, she just turned around and left the room, as if nothing was going on.

There was a time when we were on the moors, and after he had done all the things that I have written above to me, as I was walking home, an older boy appeared and said to me "I have seen what you did with Father - now you are going to do it with me." He was riding a bike, so I took the pump and began to hit him with it until his face and nose were bleeding. I threw the pump down and ran home. One of the things that truly bothers me about this episode is that I could say 'NO' to the older boy, but yet I would let Fr Parr do whatever he wanted to me.

Another thing that happened, frequently, was the punishment I would get for coming home late from school, because I had been with Fr Parr. I could not tell my mother or father that I had been with Fr Parr; because of the promise he made me keep. So I would get a beating with a belt from my father, and then be sent up to my bedroom. Other times, I was hit for having dirt on my trousers, because of the grass stains; so it was go with Fr Parr, get assaulted by him sexually, and then go home and get hit and kicked for getting home late, and having dirt on my clothes or socks.

The things that Fr Parr did to me, not only traumatised me and ruined my education, but also resulted in me have to leave home at a very early age, and the only place I could really go was to join the Military, which is what I did. I stayed away from Bedford as much as I could; became a soldier and became very good at what ever I needed to do to be safe and survive. Life meant nothing to me.

Since then, as you already know, I have suffered very considerably through the rest of my life, from the long-term impact of the abuse I suffered as a child. And I am continuing to suffer because of the way the diocese has treated me since 2004, when I came back to the UK to ask you for help. Noel Swift – 14th September 2010'

To understand Noel's last paragraph, you also need to read the following letter to Bishop Peter Doyle, Bishop of Northampton, written by Noel as part of the disclosure process I helped him with.

2/09/2010
'Dear Bishop Peter

Further to my last letter, I have begun the process of producing a detailed account of the abuse I suffered at the hands of Fr Parr; the impact it had on me over the course of my life, and the subsequent difficulties I have experienced in my quest to seek justice and recovery from all I have endured.

In writing my testimony, it has become clear that to try and put the whole story into a single letter to you would require much of the detail to be condensed to a point that it would fail to get across to you the full nature of what was happened, and why you need to reassess your approach to dealing with me, not just for my sake, but to enable you and the Diocese to have a more comprehensive understanding of child abuse, and, as a result, be able to develop more appropriate procedures when dealing with victims. Graham Wilmer, who, as you know, has been helping me for some time now, is also currently working to develop just such procedures, as it is recognised that the way individual bishops are currently deal with child abuse is a long way short of what is required, and my case is one of several that from the basis of Graham's work, more about which you will hear from Graham directly.

So then, having decided that I will write my full testimony in a number of separate parts, so that the complete detail can be included, the purpose of writing to you today is to deal with what happened when I came over in October 2004, the history of which you say you are not familiar with, according to your letter, in which you said: 'The diocesan file contains some differing and confusing accounts of what happened surrounding your visit to the UK in October 2004 but it appears that there were some misunderstandings regarding where certain meetings were to take place with the result that those meetings did not take place at all.

This is what actually happened: I came to the UK with my niece, Andrea, to attend a meeting at the bishop's house. When we arrived, we were asked to wait in the hall while they talked. A young priest then showed us into the office, where Virginia Bird, Mons McDermott and Sean Healy, the Acting Bishop, were waiting for us. I knew Sean from childhood, of course, as we had served as altar boys together. As soon as we entered the room, Sean Healy came over to me and I handed him a 3-page letter from my therapist telling him why I needed to come back to UK. He read the letter slowly; looked at me, read some more then folded it up and put it in his jacket. He made no comment about the letter. I suspected then that the visit was going to be a waste of time.

We sat down and Sean Healy asked me to tell him what Fr Parr had done to me. I told him in detail what had happened, and asked him if he was shocked about this? He replied: "Well Noel, it depends on how you define the word 'shocked." He then went on to tell me that there had been the other allegations against Fr Parr.

In particular, he disclosed to me that Fr Parr had had a long-standing sexual relationship with his housekeeper. This, of course, is at odds with the statement in your letter: "there was no record of any other complaints having been made against Father Parr. "

I asked Sean Healy what had happened to Fr Parr's vow of celibacy? He did not answer me. My niece then asked "what are all of you present in this room doing for victims like my uncle and others like him?" They gave virtually no answer, so she said: "You are not doing anything", and she started to cry.

At this point, I said that this meeting was over, and we then arranged to meet again with Sean Healy at some of the places Fr Parr had abused me, including the priest's house (Christ The King Church), which was what Sean Healy had suggested we do when he had phoned me prior to me coming over to the UK. We then exchanged phone numbers – Healy took my niece's mobile phone number and mine and I took his office number.

On the day of the meeting (two days later), my niece and I went to the agreed place and time of the meeting - Bedford bus station. We arrived there twenty minutes early, and we waited around for two hours, and made a total of nine phone calls – to his office, to the bishop's house, to Virginia Bird's office and to Christ The King church. We got no response from any of these places.

We then left the bus station and went to Christ The King Church, in case that is where Sean Healy might have gone. When we got there, I knocked on the door of the priest's house, and Fr Brendan Gorman came to the door. He was the current Parish Priest. I introduced my niece and myself, and he asked me if I was related to Bridget Swift – who had just passed away? I said yes, she was my mother. He said she was well respected in the parish. I then told him why I was there. He asked me in and I told him what had been done to me by Fr Parr. He appeared genuinely caring. I told him we were there to meet Healy. He said he would call Healy to see where he was. He did, but no one knew where he was. He then said he would call Mrs Dunne – a friend, who Healy would always go to see whenever he came to Bedford - to see if he was there.

She said she knew nothing about him coming to Bedford that day. Fr Brendon asked me how old I was when Fr Parr had abused me. He then said that would all fit into a time line. I asked him what did he mean? He said that at that time the then bishop was being elevated, and he would not have wanted any stain on things at that time. He went through the scenario – I told him that he had abused me in the house – so he said where, and I described to him every room in the house from memory. He said we could go over to the house and I could make my peace. I asked him if he knew about a place in 'Aylesbury', which is where I had been told they had sent Parr for treatment? When I had previously asked Healy about this, he had always denied that there was any such place, let alone a place where Fr Parr had been sent for treatment. Fr Brendon replied: "Noel it's Aylesford not Aylesbury - and it does exist." (I have subsequently talked to the director of the Aylesford Centre, John Roberts, and he has confirmed exactly what they do there.) Fr Brendon then asked me to disclose more details about what Parr did to me, so I told him what had happened with my mother, which is this: During a meeting with Fr Parr, my mother had asked me to tell Fr Parr about my 'dream.' I said no, at first, but she forced me to tell him about the 'dream' I had told her I kept having. I said that I had dreamt that I was dressed in priest's clothes, but I was only a boy at the time. Fr Parr went ballistic at this point telling me I was "wicked" and all sorts of other angry things – how dare I say such a thing - only an ordained priest can wear holy vestments. My mother was looking amazed at this exchange. She, of course, did not know that Fr Parr had dressed me in priest's vestments when he abused me.

Not long after that meeting, Fr Parr was sent away. Fr Brendan told me that after I had confronted Parr about the dream, he had probably gone to the bishop and told him what had been going on – but the bishop was not going to have any scandal to mar his tenure, so Fr Parr was moved to Aylesford for treatment. The police, of course, were not told anything about this. I told him that Healy had said he was going to come and pray with me in Jubilee Park, where Parr had also abused me. Fr Brendon said we could go now – which we did, and he prayed with me at some of the places I was abused. Fr Brendan became concerned, and told me to be careful. He then blessed us both and we got in the car and left.

We tried to call Healy several times again, but he would not come to the phone. I eventually got through by pretending to be someone else, and I asked him why he had not come to the meeting. He said that he had gone there and he had waited for three hours! When I asked why he had not come to the priest's house, he gave a nervous laugh and said, "I don't know." He gave me the same answer to the question "why did you not phone the priest's house?" I then said "Sean – if you only knew how angry you are making me by laughing at me?" He said he was not laughing at me, so I asked him why he had not told me that Fr Parr had been sent to Aylesford and not Aylesbury as I had thought? I said to Healy you knew that when I was saying Aylesbury that it was Aylesford so why did you not say so? He said he did not know. I said I am done here and the next time I call you it will be through a lawyer.

I then called Virginia Bird, and told her and told her the same thing – she responded in a really snide way, telling me not to waste my time, as "no court would sue a dead man." I said I was going to sue the diocese – she said I would bankrupt the diocese and how dare I do that – she never once tried to be kind to me, so I hung up. Just before I left the UK, Sean Healy called me and said he had a cheque for me to cover my 'expenses', which he wanted to give me. I told him that I did not want to meet with him, so please would he post it to me at home in the USA. To this day, I have never received the cheque.

In Dec 2004, I got a call from Virginia Bird after I had left a message on her phone to say I had hired lawyer. She said to me that I was "the antichrist", and that my therapy (which you had organised the payment for) had turned me into this. She also condemns my therapist saying that he was turning me against the Church. I mentioned another of Parr's victims – MD, to which she said: "MD was a very troubled boy and that if he thought he could get money from the diocese by saying He was abused by Fr Parr, he would be the first to do that."

I spoke to MD in 2005, after tracing him, with the help of an old friend, MT. I told him what Bird had said and he laughed. I asked him if Parr had abused him and he said he didn't want to go into that now as it was in his passed. He was happily married and had a 26yr old daughter and a Grandchild He did not attempt to try and say no he had not abused him.

Virginia Bird then tried to warn me off talking to the Observer – she started shouting at me and said: "I better be very careful what I told the Newspapers because they would not want to print gossip." I said to Her "So you are saying all I have told the Diocese is just gossip" She replied with "No that is not what I mean, Just that the Newspaper will fact check your story" I said to her great that is what I want them to do. At this she said "If you think you are going to get millions, from us, like those yanks – you are wrong. She kept asking: "What more do you want from us?" I hung up because she would not leave it alone. I was told subsequently to desist from trying to contact Bishop McDonald.

MT who had helped me find MD subsequently told me that he did not want anything more to do with me again. Someone had got to him (it turns out he was responsible for church buildings in Bedford). Fr Brendan also told me subsequently in a phone call to "forget it – the past is the past". He said he couldn't talk to me anymore. Had you got to him as well?

I will end here, for now, as the whole process of writing this is difficult and distressing, however, I realise that it needs to be done, if you are going to have a better understanding of what I have been through at the hands of so many people in the diocese.

I ask you to reflect on this, and I will write to you again soon, with other aspects of the trauma I have been through. In the meantime, I hope you will ask those involved to confirm what I have said here, and think again about your statement: "Nor will I agree to any further formal procedure such as mediation or arbitration which you are demanding in order to gain financial compensation from the diocese."

There has to be some form of structure to the dialogue between us, so if mediation is not an acceptable way forward for you, please will you let me know how else you propose to settle this? Yours sincerely - Noel Swift'

EXAMPLE 2. My own abuse began at a Catholic school run by the Salesian of Don Bosco, the full story of which has been well documented over the past five years in books, magazines, newspapers and on national TV and radio, so I do not intend to go through it again here. However, after my first book was published, numerous other victims of abuse in other Salesian schools in England came forward and told me their stories. This led to a number of revelations and police investigations into numerous allegations of sexual abuse of children in Salesian schools in England, spanning decades and involving many Salesian priests, including a Provincial of the Salesian Order.

The difficulties faced by myself and these other victims when trying to engage the Salesian Order has clearly demonstrated (as in Noel Swift's case) that, despite the fact that these difficulties have all happened post Nolan (which was itself instrumental in the eventual creation of NCSC and now CSAS), there is still no agreed or practiced set of protocols or procedures, geared towards the needs of the victims, that are exercised when individual victims come forward. Instead, victims are met with a wall of obfuscation, denial and legal frustration, all of which is designed to protect the institutions at the cost of the victims, and the cost can be very significant in terms of the additional damage it does to the victims, damage that, to date, has not been recognised either in law, or by the institutions involved. This must change.

To illustrate this second example, I have been given permission by a fellow Salesian victim, to share the following letter:

'10th November 2010
Dear Salesians

I am writing to ask for your help in getting a response from the headmaster or the chair of governors of Salesian College Battersea, in response to my claim for the harm I suffered, as a result of being sexually and physically abused at the school by Fr Paul McAleer and Mr Tony Grundy, while I was a pupil there between 1967 and 1970.

After a meeting with your Safeguarding Coordinator in May, where I disclosed to her what had happened to me, I was asked to think about what I wanted to happen next and let her know, which I did in the form of a letter, dated 8th September. On 27th September, I received the following e-mail from her:

'Dear Sir

I'm contacting you again to follow up my previous Emails. The Salesians apologise for the delay in responding to your letter dated 8th September, which I forwarded on to them. Fr Tom Williams is now the Salesian who has responsibility for safeguarding matters. However, unfortunately, he is out of the country, and won't be back until after 6th October. I will ask him on his return to make contact with you. As you are aware the Salesians are a registered charity, which means that if they receive a claim for compensation they are required to seek legal advice as to how they should respond. In order not to cause further delay this process has been initiated and you may also receive a solicitor's response to your compensation claim. This is the due process which I'm sure Graham will explain further to you if needed. The Salesians have asked me to let you know that they wish you to have pastoral support at this time. Please do contact me if you wish to discuss this further.'

I subsequently received a letter from your lawyers, informing me that the Salesians of Don Bosco bore no responsibility for what happened to me, and that it was a matter for the board of governors. Although I disagree with that view, I subsequently wrote to Mr McCann, the headmaster, and that was the last I heard from anyone. You will understand that the wishes you expressed for me to have pastoral support has so far amounted to nothing. I feel totally abandoned now, particularly as your safeguarding coordinator has now also written to Graham Wilmer, who has supported me from the outset, and told him that he should withdraw his support for me, as she says he is not impartial!

This apparent wall of silence is very difficult for me to deal with, as it is generating feelings within me that are so similar to the awful silence I have had to live with for years, not wanting to tell anyone what happened for fear of being ridiculed and humiliated all over again, but that is exactly how I am feeling now, so will you please tell me what is going on, and ask Mr McCann to write to me as well and let me know what the position is.

Yours sincerely.'

These examples show very clearly that the recommendations put forward by Lord Nolan in 2000 have had very little, if any, real benefit for victims of childhood sexual abuse, committed by Catholic priests, or others working in Catholic run institutions.

NEXT STEPS: In the Spring of 2010, the Lantern Project put forward an initiative for consideration by government, the basic concepts of which were as follows:

1. To provide a non-judgmental forum through which victims of sexual abuse can submit testimony in person or by other means to enable their voices to be heard and the harm they suffered acknowledged and responded to.

2. To evaluate the damage caused to victims of sexual abuse over their lifetime, and to quantify its true cost to individuals and to our society.

3. To develop and effect the delivery of a comprehensive therapeutic intervention and support programme that will enable victims to reach a nationally recognised and measurable standard for recovery.

We sought the support of a number of influential people in government and among the religious. The Archbishop of Westminster, Vincent Nichols, indicated his support in principle, and asked me to contact the Chair of NCSC, Bill Kilgallon, to develop the concept further. I did this, but so far, nothing has come of our discussions, for a range of reasons, not least of which, has been the lack of any effective communications mechanism that we can engage with.

As said at the beginning of this paper, my purpose to propose working with the Churches together to determine a complete understanding of the impact and legacy of childhood sexual abuse, with the sole aim of developing and implementing a practical, holistic and sustainable recovery process through which truth, reconciliation and healing can be achieved for victims, their families, the Churches and society at large.

I am asking you, therefore, to incorporate these ideas into the developing work of the NCSC and the CSAS, supported by survivors groups, to achieve these objectives for the benefit of us all.

Graham Wilmer Founder – The Lantern Project.
27th January 2011.'

The Archbishop refused to meet us, saying that we should 'continue to work with his Commission,' but as the Guardian reported on October 2011, the talks broke down:

Shiv Malik - The Guardian, Friday 14 October 2011 17.41 BST

Abuse victims accuse Catholic Church of using talks as a smokescreen. Negotiations on a support package for victims are on the verge of breaking down after two survivors' groups pull out'

Negotiations on delivering a package of care for English and Welsh victims of sexual abuse by Roman Catholic priests are on the verge of collapse after survivor organisations accused the church of using the discussions as a smokescreen for inaction.

Two groups have pulled out of discussions led by the National Catholic Safeguarding Commission (NCSC) and the Catholic Safeguarding Advisory Service (CSAS), describing them as shambolic, toothless and unlikely to achieve anything by May 2012, when the pope's deadline for a progress report expires.

Graham Wilmer, who heads the Lantern Project and was himself abused by a Catholic priest as a teenager, said: "We were prepared to talk to [the institution] that had harmed us, even though it was uncomfortable, because the end of it should be worthwhile," he said. "[But] we can't trust them. What has effectively has happened is nothing."

Wilmer said the talks were meant to create "a comprehensive support package" for victims of sexual abuse by clergy but there was still no system in place for a victim to request support by telephone and that calls were answered by lawyers for the church's insurance company.

Archbishop Vincent Nichols, the head of the Roman Catholic church in England and Wales, declined to meet Wilmer or the forum before the two groups walked out.

Wilmer said another aggravating factor for his organisation was that the church had continued to oppose victims seeking compensation over the past year.

He said: "There certainly is the intention to deliver what looks like an attempt to produce a better response to victims of abuse, but when you test it, you just end up with a bunch of lawyers ... they [the Catholic church] are not prepared to deal with the victims of its abuse in any way other than to fight them through the courts."

Dr Margaret Kennedy, founder of Minister and Clergy Sexual Abuse Survivors (Macsas), has also pulled out of the talks, describing them as "a complete shambles". She said: "Macsas has always been very uncomfortable with this particular group, partly because it started off with no aims and objectives and no money on the table... to put [recommendations] into place."

She said church representatives "were continually refusing to even mention clergy abuse" in the meetings, preferring to widen out their remit to all survivors of abuse in society.

"We said: 'Isn't your first response to the victims of clergy abuse whom your priests have raped and tortured?' ... And they didn't want to talk about that. 'You're not the only victims of abuse' was the message we basically got," she said.

Kennedy said that one of the group's purported aims, to "reconcile" victims of abuse to the church, had angered her.

"They have this great idea that they are going to heal victims that they have actually harmed in the first place. They haven't a clue of how victims of clergy abuse feel," she said.

Pete Saunders, from the National Association for People Abused in Childhood, said his organisation and three others were sticking with the talks because there was still a "chink of light".

Saunders, who was sexually abused by two Catholic priests as a child and believes there are "thousands and thousands" of UK victims like him, said confidential proposals on survivor treatment were now going to be put before the Catholic bishops' conference in mid-November and this represented a make-or-break point.

He said: "We are aware that the Catholic church have got a lot to answer for in terms of the way that they protect abusing priests and nuns. They have an appalling record on that and the colleagues around the table, including the Catholic Safeguarding Advisory Service, have all agreed that."

But Saunders said the church's senior clergy were "now going to have it laid on the line". In November, they would be told to "stop making life difficult for survivors and challenging very legitimate claims from people who want to get on with their life and want some degree of justice", he said.

"If the bishops' conference closes down that chink of light, then we will certainly walk away because it will mean there is no sincerity," he said.

A church spokesperson told the Guardian that, when it came to compensation claims, the church's hands were tied by charity commission rules that stopped it handing out money without first being lawfully entitled to do so. It is also a requirement for the church to be insured against indemnity and the spokesperson said it could not be responsible for the actions of the insurance company when it came to compensation claims.

Adrian Child, the director of CSAS, said: "The NCSC and CSAS have been in dialogue with representatives of a number of survivors' support organisations and others for the past 12-plus months. The aim is to develop a sensitive and just response to survivors of abuse within a church setting in order to promote healing for victims of abuse.

"Regret was expressed by the group that they [Macsas] had made that decision, but the decision was respected and they were thanked for their contribution to the work so far."

Chapter 10

Defectio mihi robur dat. Dolor est ratio mea.

'Failure gives me strength. Pain is my motivation.'

Shortly after the talks broke down, I received an email from Greater Manchester Police, telling me that their investigation into my complaints against the Salesians had come to a dead end. It was exactly a year since I contacted the child protection team at Cheshire police, and told them about the allegations I had been given by Eric and others, involving Fr George Williams. After some discussion with other police forces in the UK, they decided that they would ask Greater Manchester police to investigate, on the basis that Fr Williams now lived at the Salesian Headquarters in Bolton. To cut a long story short, their investigation was a fiasco, as is evidenced by the statement the investigating officer, DC Isherwood gave me – a year later!

'Mr WILMER. - Regarding your allegation of sexual abuse at the hands of Fr WILLIAMS. The matter was jointly investigated by the Child Protection Unit at Bolton and Bolton Social Services. All the information raised in your complaint has been passed to DC Mike HOBBS from Surrey Police, by DC PARKER of our unit. The reason for this was that the historical offences you outlined in your complaint were committed in the

Surrey area. The Salesian College has been visited and Fr Michael WINSTANLEY is aware of the allegations. Fr WILLIAMS is now house bound and has no contact with any vulnerable persons, and he is deemed currently not to be a danger to children. In respect of the Police at Bolton there are no further lines of enquiry to pursue. Regards. Keith Isherwood -Detective Sergeant – PPIU - Child Protection Unit'

DS Isherwood's response gives the clear impression that Bolton Police had carried out a joint investigation with Bolton Social Services, but I later discovered that the officer from Bolton Social Services, tasked with the investigation, was in fact a former governor of the Salesian College in Bolton, and had been involved with the school for many years. He was even was described by the Salesians themselves as 'a good friend of the school'. The evidence for this is contained in a report written by the then Rector of Salesian Community in Bolton on 30th August 2007. The report explains how the Salesians gave assurances that all was well, and there was no need to worry, as they had it all in hand. The report concludes that the officer, a senior social work manager, left after saying he was satisfied that everything was fine. The fact that this individual was so involved with the Salesians in his personal life raises a very serious conflict of interest. Did the police know of this conflict? I suspect not, as they would not have sanctioned his involvement if they had.

In any case, I hadn't asked them to investigate

my case – I wanted them to investigate the allegations made in the Baggaley document, which I had given to them, but somehow that had been lost in the way they had handled the information I had given them. I began to wonder if there would ever be a way to obtain justice for all the victims who had contacted me, but even as I thought about the next steps I might take, more allegations emerged from former Salesian pupils:

'Your description of Fr. Bamber's antics with you struck a chord. His rough beard rubbing on my neck was a painful recollection. I was never physically penetrated, but I was frequently exposed to Fr. Bamber masturbating and holding my hand so that he could place it on his genital organ.'

'When I was at Chertsey Fr Bamber held a post in charge of stores and uniforms etc., and he would sometimes call me out of class on some pretext so that he could be alone with me. He also took me on a bike ride into the surrounding country lanes and also took me to the cinema. In both cases he would masturbate me and make me masturbate him.'

Child abuse by Salesian priests is not, of course, only confined to the British Province of the Salesian Order, as a recent article by my friend and fellow Salesian survivor, Joey Piscitelli, explains: 'Fr. John Malloy, long-time San Francisco Salesian mouthpiece, known for his adamant shielding of accused Salesian pedophiles, has died. Malloy was also known for his selective moral stance of defending and harbouring clergy molesters, while voicing public bigotry concerning gay equality rights. Fr. Malloy, 91, died on Wednesday March 27, 2013, leaving behind a legacy typical of many Salesian Kingpins – a history of "no see, no hear, no speak" – regarding numerous accused Salesian abuser priests that surrounded him for decades.

Fr. Malloy was also a key organizer in San Francisco for the Defence of Marriage Rally, and was vehemently outspoken against equality in marriage. Concerning the controversial issue, Malloy was quoted in 2008: "To demand marriage as a matter of equality is fallacious".

At 13 years old, Malloy joined the infamous Salesian High School Seminary in Richmond California. The seminary was known to have housed numerous clergy rapists and pedophiles throughout its span from the 1930s through the 1960s. Malloy was cautiously silent to the press during the massive lawsuits lodged against the Salesians from 2002 through 2009 in California; despite the Salesians' schools record for the most clergy sex abusers clustered in an affiliated campus.

In 1952 he was principal of St. John Bosco in Bellflower, and was later principal of Bishop Mora Salesian High School in Los Angeles, Ca. Both schools have been riddled with lawsuits pertaining to sex abuse and molestation by Salesian clergy, named in the Southern California Clergy 2 Cases in 2003. Malloy, however, was quoted as saying he knew nothing about the conduct of the many Salesian pedophiles at the schools.

Malloy later became Salesian Provincial of the West Coast in San Francisco, during the 1960s. According to court depositions, several allegations of rape and abuse at the Salesian School in Richmond during the 1960s were forwarded to the Salesian Provincial at the time in San Francisco. Malloy also said that he was unaware of those alleged reports and accusations, regarding convicted Salesian priest Fr. Bernard Dabbenne, accused rapists Bro. John Vas, Fr. Lorenzoni, Fr. Presenti, Bro Billante, and several other Salesian clergy named in lawsuits.

Fr. Malloy became pastor at St. Peter and Paul parish in San Francisco in 2001. At the time Malloy was pastor at St. Peter and Pauls, the Salesians of San Francisco listed as staff accused pedophiles Bro. Ernie Martinez, Fr. Harold Danielson, and Fr. Steve Whelan. Fr. Malloy defended the accused molesters, stating as was usual, that he knew nothing concerning any misconduct by any of the named priests.

In 2003, Fr. Malloy's close friend, and Associate Pastor of St. Peter and Pauls, Fr. Steve Whelan, was sued in court for sexual molestation. Fr. Malloy stated that he knew nothing about the allegations against the priest who had lived with him for years, and stated publicly that the priest was innocent. Malloy kept Fr. Whelan in ministry with access to children until a court found the priest liable in a jury trial in 2006, and again in 2008.

During Fr. Malloy's tenure in the Salesian

Order in California from the 1960s to the present, the California Salesians have been inundated with lawsuits, convictions, and allegations for child rape, sodomy, molestation, sex abuse shielding, cover-ups and denial. The Salesian Order paid out 20 million dollars for lawsuits in California in 2009, which named many of Fr. Malloy's closest and oldest clergy comrades and roommates.

Malloy was constantly surrounded by countless, accused Salesian serial rapists and sex abusers, for over 60 years. He has always faithfully maintained he was unaware of any misconduct by any of them, regardless of his history of living with them for decades.

Some of Fr. Malloy's local fellow Salesians, who were accused of serial paedophilia, sex abuse, rape, and molestation – either in lawsuits or convictions were: Fr. Bernard Dabbenne, Fr. Larry Lorenzoni, Fr. Steve Whelan, Bro Ernie Martinez, Bro. Sal Billante, Fr. Richard Presenti, Bro. John Vas, Bro. Anthony Juarez, Bro. Ralph Murguia, Fr. Mario Blanco, Fr. Jim Miani, Mr. Sam Vitone, Bro. Jesse Dominguez, Bro Mark Epperson, Mr. Ricky Bonds, Fr. Harold Danielson, Fr. Al Mengon, Bro. John Verhart, and Bro. Dan Pacheco. Eerily, on April 1 2013, Fr. Malloy will be buried at the Salesian Cemetery in Richmond, at the school campus, where numerous accused Salesian serial pedophiles have been laid to final rest." (Posted March 31, 2013 by Joey Piscitelli - http://joeypiscitelli.com)

Child abuse in other Salesian Provinces also continues to be exposed, as is recorded in this news article from Australia:

'Salesian priest 'abused victim with pool cue'
BY: PIA AKERMAN The Australian April 26, 2013

'A CATHOLIC priest charged with child sex offences has been accused of assaulting one of his victims with a pool cue. A Salesian priest and former school principal Julian Fox, 67, today faced court for the first time since the Catholic church negotiated with Victoria Police to see him returned from Rome. He has been charged with 10 offences, including committing three counts of buggery against a boy under the age of 14 in 1980. It is alleged he indecently assaulted another victim with a shortened pool cue in 1981, and indecently assaulted another three times between 1976 and 1978. The fourth complainant was allegedly indecently assaulted in 1985. The Salesian Order has been accused of knowingly allowing Father Fox relocate to Rome after accusations were made against him by former students.' (Source: www.theaustralian.com.au)'

In other countries too, the child abuse scandal engulfing the Salesian Order, as recorded in Wikipedia, the free encyclopaedia, makes very sober reading, exposing a darker, criminal side to this corrupted and dysfunctional Catholic teaching Order:

Abuse in Australia (See also: Salesian College sexual abuse claims.)

In Australia, there are allegations that the Salesians moved a priest convicted of abuse in Melbourne to Samoa to avoid further police investigation and charges. In August 2008, the Salesian head in Australia, Fr Frank Moloney SDB, apologised to victims of a former priest Paul Evans convicted of a series of offences. Evans was a Salesian priest when the offences occurred at Boys' Town in Sydney in the 1980s. He was legally and canonically removed from the Order in 1991.

There have been a number of convictions related to sexual abuse by teachers and priests at the school, particularly in regard to offences committed in the 1970s and 80s, including: Michael Aulsebrook, gaoled for the sexual abuse of a 12-year-old student in 1983; Peter Paul van Ruth, who was sentenced to 28 months gaol in 2011 for indecently assaulting two 12 year old boys; and Frank Klep, a former principal of the college who "... was convicted in 1994 of four charges of sexual assault relating to incidents during the 1970s."

Other priests from the college reached settlements with substantial compensation payments paid to their victims, over allegations of sexual abuse, but were not otherwise convicted, while Father Jack Ayers, a teacher and gardener at the school, was moved to Samoa after accusations were made against him.

Abuse in Belgium

In 2007, a Belgian criminal court convicted Willem VC, a laicised Salesian priest, to 4 years imprisonment for sexual delinquency with multiple adolescent minors. During the criminal investigation by the police and judiciary previous acts of sexual delinquency were discovered that occurred during his membership of the Salesian congregation. He was expelled from this order in 2001 for these incidents.

Abuse in the Netherlands

In February 2010 the Salesians were accused of sexual abuse in their juvenate Don Rua in 's-Heerenberg. Salesian bishop of Rotterdam van Luyn pleaded for a thorough investigation.'

Chapter 11

SCCA – Stop Church Child Abuse campaign.

In 2011, the Lantern Project took part in the formation of a new national campaign: 'Stop Church Child Abuse'. The campaign, chaired by David Greenwood, a lawyer specialising in child abuse cases involving the clergy, is an alliance of clergy sexual abuse survivors, charities that support survivors, specialist lawyers and interested individuals, working in the field of child safeguarding. The campaign's objective is to investigate and highlight the serious safeguarding failures of church institutions, from 1954 to the present.

We launched the campaign at a press conference in London on 19th April 2012, at which we explained our purpose: 'We call on the Government to set up an Independent Commission of Inquiry into child sexual abuse perpetrated by clergy, religious and other church officials within all Dioceses and institutions of the Catholic Church in England and Wales and the Church of England and the Methodist Church in England and in Wales. Such an inquiry should have powers to compel the disclosure of all files of clergy, religious and other church officials containing reports and allegations of child sexual abuse. It should receive evidence, both oral and written from victims of child sexual abuse perpetrated by clergy and religious within parish communities and church institutions and also be able to compel those in positions of authority within Dioceses and religious orders to attend and give evidence.

The Inquiry should have the power to make recommendations concerning legislation to improve safeguarding in church institutions. For twenty years the leaders of the Catholic Church and the Church of England/Wales have repeatedly stated that they will respond appropriately to reports of child sexual abuse. Despite these assurances, many prosecutions have revealed that Church authorities have covered up past reports of child abuse and allowed clergy to remain in post despite allegations and in some cases past convictions for child sexual offences. In many reported cases further child abuse has taken place.'

At the press conference and on the campaign website, we published the following document (the appendices referred in this document are not included in this book, but can be found on the SCCA website):

STOP CHURCH CHILD ABUSE!

A call for a Public Inquiry into abuse of children and vulnerable adults by Clergy in England and Wales. For more details see: www.stopchurchchildabuse.co.uk

1. The Call for an Independent Inquiry.

For twenty years the leaders within the Catholic

Church and the Church of England/Wales have repeatedly stated that they will respond appropriately to reports of child sexual abuse, and numerous safeguarding/child protection procedures have been put in place. Despite these assurances and procedures produced there have been repeated court cases in which clergy and religious have been convicted of multiple child sexual offences often dating back and continuing for decades and involving a number of children. And repeatedly the prosecutions have revealed that Church authorities covered up past reports of child abuse and allowed clergy and religious to remain in ministry despite allegations and in some cases past convictions for child sexual offences. In many reported cases further child abuse took place. The James Robinson case in 2010 involving the Catholic Archdiocese of Birmingham, the recent convictions of monks and priests at Ealing Abbey, Buckfast Abbey and Downside and the subsequent Inquiries now being carried out, and the Cotton & Pritchard case in 2008 and subsequent CofE Diocese of Chichester Inquiries (2010, 2011 and ongoing 2012) are the latest examples.

The cases involving monks and priests at Ealing Abbey and Downside Abbey underline the fact that abuse has been happening very recently which could have been prevented. Clergy still have extensive access to children in church–run schools and this document sets out below why the safeguards are inadequate and are failing the current generation of children. All the evidence points to the conclusion that the cover up, denial and/or minimisation of child sexual abuse within Roman Catholic Church and the Church of England was widespread, and seemed to be most prevalent within a number of Dioceses and Church Institutions in England and Wales, and that abuse may still be going on. Victims of abuse perpetrated over the past six decades continue to report cases to Church authorities years after the abuse took place and they first reported: in cases where prosecutions are successful files continue to reveal what was already known by Church authorities, in other cases as seen in the MACSAS Survey 2010 reports continue to be ignored.

Until there is an inquiry which uncovers what was known about child sexual abuse by Church authorities and when, and what actions were taken when reports were made, these injustices will continue for decades to come. Justice requires that the truth is told; that victims are allowed to tell what happened to them and be listened to, and where it is proved that they suffered harm it is acknowledged. Church leaders and the heads of religious Organisations must accept responsibility for allowing sex offenders/abusers to continue in ministry and to continue abusing those they were placed in authority over. Only when the truth is known, when responsibility is accepted, will the institutional dynamics be changed. To date neither the Catholic Church in England & Wales nor the Church of England and in Wales has allowed such an inquiry to take place.

We call upon the Government to set up an Independent Commission of Inquiry into child sexual abuse perpetrated by clergy, religious and other church officials within all Dioceses and institutions the Catholic Church in England & Wales and the Church of England, and the Methodist Church in England and in Wales. Such an inquiry should have powers to compel the disclosure of all files of clergy, religious and other church officials containing reports and allegations of child sexual abuse. It should receive evidence, both oral and written from victims of child sexual abuse perpetrated by clergy and religious within parish communities and church institutions and also be able to compel those in positions of authority within Dioceses and religious orders to attend and give evidence.

The Inquiry should investigate how cases were handled by Church and religious authorities and should cover the period from 1954 to the present day. It should establish the extent of the abuse and the mechanisms employed by church authorities to cover up, deny and/or minimise the abuse. The Inquiry should also examine the impact the abuse and the response of Church and religious authorities had on the victims. The Roman Catholic Church, the Religious Orders and Church of England and in Wales should be compelled to pay for the cost of the Inquiry.

2. Outcomes sought from an Inquiry:

(1)   Mandatory reporting by church and religious leaders of all allegations of child abuse perpetrated by those in positions of trust and authority within Churches and Religious Institutions.

(2)   An independent statutory body to monitor and review safeguarding procedures within the Roman Catholic Church and its religious institutions and the Church of England and in Wales. Such a body to have powers to carry out regular and planned inspections, make recommendations for improvements and enforce compliance, as well as to inspect at no notice where substantive cause for concern arises.

3. STATISTICS, THE INTERNATIONAL SCENE AND COVER UPS

4. The statistics:

        As we can see (at appendix 1) a brief look into the numbers of allegations and convictions over the last 20 years reveals that 74 abusers have convictions. We know that abusers often abuse multiple times. To work out an estimate of the true number of abusers we have to relate these numbers to recognised research. We have to remember that our figures are incomplete as not all solicitors in England and Wales have contributed. Only specialist firms were asked to contribute. We must look at the figures themselves and extrapolate them against accepted research in this field.

To ensure that this document provides an under-estimate of the true scale of clergy abuse we have deliberately restricted the figures to cases where convictions have been achieved in the criminal court (the highest standard of proof). The issue of the standard of proof is examined below.

5. Surveys in other countries:

The incidence of adult sexual abuse perpetrated by clergy and has been widely researched in the USA, UK, Australia, and in international studies.

The John Jay Study commissioned by the USA Catholic Conference of Bishops in 2002 and published in 2004 found that of the estimated 4,392 priests (4% of the priesthood) in the USA alleged to have sexually abused more than 10,600 children between 1950 and 2002, only 6% had been convicted of child sexual offences. Only 1.5% of the reported cases in the study were deemed to be false allegations.

In the 5681 cases where the church investigated and reached a determination 80% were substantiated. The survey excluded cases where the priest was completely exonerated: (John Jay Study 2004 at www.usccb.org/nrb/johnjaystudy)

Conviction rates:

In Australia the General Synod of the Anglican Church commissioned a similar study of child sexual abuse perpetrated by clergy which was completed in 2009. Out of 191 allegations only 1.6% were deemed to be false or erroneous. Over half of reported cases were substantiated and another third were inconclusive and yet only 12% of reported cases resulted in a conviction. (The Australia Study 2009) at www.apo.org.au/research/study-reported-child-sexual-abuse-anglican-church

The failure of the criminal justice system to provide effective protection and redress for victims of child sexual abuse in the UK has been identified in numerous national surveys and studies, which have found that only 3-4% of reported child sexual abuse cases result in a conviction (Child Exploitation and Online Protection Centre figures 2010 at www.ceop.gov.uk; Cawson, P. et al. (2000) Child maltreatment in the United Kingdom: a study of the prevalence of child abuse and neglect. London, NSPCC).

A survey in the Netherlands of 34,000 people estimated that 10% of the population in Holland from 1945 have been the subject of some form of abuse from a member of the Catholic church. www.guardian.co.uk/world/2011/dec/16/thousands-children-abused-dutch-catholic Inquiries into abuse in Belgium have revealed widespread abuse of almost systematic proportions www.guardian.co.uk/world/2010/sep/10/belgium-child-abuse-catholic-church.

Research in the UK and the USA has also found that only 2 - 3% of allegations of rape and sexual offences have been shown to be false (Kelly, E., Lovett, J., Regan, L. (2005) A Gap or a Chasm – attrition in reported rape cases Home Office Research Study 293 CWAS Unit London Metropolitan University).

The reality we face in our society is that out of every 100 reported cases of child sexual abuse, on average 97 victims reporting abuse are deemed to be telling the truth but only 4 of the cases will result in the conviction of the offender. This leaves over 93% of sex offenders without a criminal conviction. As such 93% of suspected sex offenders working within Church communities and among clergy and religious organisations in the UK will not have been convicted of any offence.

It is clear from research across three continents that an allegation is not false just because the alleged offender is not convicted. 93% of sex offenders are never convicted. Those convicted represent only the tip of the iceberg and our view is that safeguarding is not applied adequately to these suspects.

If we are generous to church organisations and take the Australian figure of 12% of abusers being convicted this leaves 88% of them without sanction, police investigation or undetected. Relating this to our research shows that there are at least 513 abusers who have not been brought to justice. If the 4% figure from CEOP figures of 2010 is used the figure of un-convicted suspects rises to 1,680. The respected John Jay study found that 80% of its 5,681allegations had been substantiated. This leaves the alarming figure of between 542 and 1,776 abusers un-convicted and free to have contact with children or vulnerable adults.

6. England and Wales is lagging behind on child protection.

Despite the in depth research and inquiries commissioned by governments into church child abuse in other jurisdictions (most notably The Republic of Ireland, Australia, The Netherlands, Canada, Northern Ireland and the US), England and Wales has failed to explore the issue.

There is no credible reason to suggest the proportions of clergy who have abused in England and Wales are any different to other jurisdictions. The evidence gathered in this document is likely to be a small fraction of the full extent of offending. Unless there is an inquiry to establish the extent of abuse and to introduce effective legislation on child safeguarding in this jurisdiction, England and Wales will rank behind other countries in it's commitment to abuse prevention.

7. The Standard of proof:

At the heart of the difficulties faced in securing a conviction in child abuse cases is the standard of proof required, which is proof beyond all reasonable doubt. Where a child's evidence has to be relied on, or the evidence of a victim reporting decades after the offence took place it is very difficult to satisfy the standard of proof without corroborating, independent evidence and this is rarely available. This explains why the CPS often refuses to prosecute a case or the accused is found not guilty – the age of the victim at the time of the offence, the passage of time and the lack of independent supporting evidence, all weaken the chances of securing a conviction.

However the standard of proof required within Child Protection is on the balance of probabilities. The 'paramountcy principle' at the heart of child protection requires that the welfare of the child is placed above the lack of certainty of an alleged abuser's criminal guilt. If on the balance of probabilities a cleric or other person in a position of trust has or may harm a child based on all the information available, then he or she should not be allowed access to children or be placed in a position of trust that would enable him or her to exercise authority over children.

An examination of all allegations of abuse against priests and those working in church organisations will reveal numerous allegations which can be substantiated on the balance of probabilities test. At present church organisations do not appear to be applying this standard when assessing all cases and as a consequence are using this as an excuse to fail in their safeguarding responsibilities. This is an area in which the discretion of the decision maker has and continues to enable the church to "protect its own". Only legislation will remove the discretion. This is examined in detail below.

As a footnote to this section it is pertinent to make two further observations on the legal process. First the criminal legal system is reluctant to look into Bishops' failures to act. There is a general reluctance to prosecute for "inaction". Second since the 2001 case Lister v Hesley Hall Ltd [2001] UKHL 22 and the advent of vicarious liability in this field lawyers pursuing compensation for abused claimants are no longer forced to carry out deep enquiry into negligence and potential cover ups and it seems there is no-one looking into this important area of safeguarding.

8. Cover ups:

It is an instinctive and understandable reaction for an organisation facing challenge to defend itself against attack. It is however unacceptable for an organisation to cover up for individuals who it knows have abused children or vulnerable adults. At appendix 2 attached we can see that senior clerics have favoured protecting their organisation rather than the protection of children.

There is a growing realisation that this practice of cover up and bishops' failures to report allegations to the police is hard-wired into the Catholic Church (see appendix 3). The Anglican Church faces similar criticism as we are seeing a self preservation reaction having at best misguided senior clerics and at worst some senior clerics aided and abetted known sex offenders in the Anglican Diocese of Chichester.

The list of examples cited as potential cover ups are of course only the unsuccessful ones. Without an inquiry we will have no chance of finding out about cases of abuse which were easily preventable had senior clerics acted responsibly. It is hoped that an inquiry will have power to look into these issues.

9. THE DEVELOPMENT OF SAFEGUARDING IN THE ROMAN CATHOLIC CHURCH AND THE CHURCH OF ENGLAND FROM 1990

10. Church culture and institutional dynamics are standing in the way of effective child safeguarding measures.

The persistent mantra from Church Institutions when child abuse is raised is that since the Nolan and/or Cumberledge Commission (Catholic church 2002 & 2007) and since Protecting All God's Children (2004/2010 and the Past Cases Reviews (CofE 2010, CofW 2011) there are now Child Protection/Safeguarding policies in place that ensure that all allegations of child abuse are taken seriously and reported to statutory authorities, and that appropriate actions are taken to ensure that children are not put in danger of harm.

However the difficulty for the Churches is that the procedures they rely upon are neither sufficient nor effective in protecting children from harm. No independent or published review of the effectiveness of current or past procedures has ever been conducted. Whilst the Cumberledge Review on Child Protection in the Catholic Church in 2007 highlighted a number of gaps in the procedures within the Catholic Church; the lack of support for victims and a lack of procedures for complaints where criminal convictions are not secured, and also highlighted the failure of the Bishops to take ownership of the Procedures, it did not look at effectiveness in terms of whether children were actually being protected from harm posed by those alleged to have abused children. The Past Cases Reviews within the Church of England in 2010 and the Church in Wales in 2011 were never published, the findings remain unknown and the published summary reports of 1 ½ pages makes no reference to procedures.

Within the wider society it has been long acknowledged that safeguarding procedures developed since the mid 1990s and the 'Every Child Matters' agenda, have failed to have any substantive impact on the prevalence and extent of child abuse within our society. The detection rate remains lamentably low at an estimated 5%, and the conviction rates for child abuse remain stubbornly at around 3-4% of reported cases. Child Line celebrated its 25th Anniversary this year and reported a record breaking 600,000 calls received in the previous year, of which tens of thousands concerned sexual abuse. Child pornography and internet grooming are a growing industry and child trafficking for sex or slave labour is on the increase into this country and beyond.

What gives Church leaders the sense of security in their assertions that all is fine now they have procedures in place when we know that institutional dynamics, a culture of indifference and apathy and a lack of moral and professional courage have been found time and again to undermine even the best policies and procedures? There is now compelling evidence that the mainstream Churches are unable to recognise the institutional dynamics that continue to protect the institutions at the cost of the safety of children; they continue to deny that abuse has happened and/or that it was ever reported to them; they continue to deny and minimise the impact on the victims; and even reject and deny the victims themselves all in an attempt to maintain the power, reputation and resources of the institution.

11. The Current Safeguarding Procedures

A simple analysis of the main safeguarding procedures within the Catholic Church and the Church of England raises major cause for concern

12. THE CATHOLIC CHURCH

13. Catholic Safeguarding Procedures 1990 – 2011.

The Bishop's Conference of the Catholic Church

in England and Wales has had child protection policies in place since 1994 ("Child Abuse: Pastoral and Procedural Guidelines" ("the 1994 Guidelines")). However it soon became clear that the Guidelines were not being followed by Bishops, Archbishops and Cardinals. In 2000 the newly elevated Cardinal of England & Wales and former Bishop of Arundel and Brighton, Cormac Murphy O'Connor was put under pressure to resign following the mishandling of a clergy child sex offender who went on to abuse more children. The Cardinal was forced to respond by commissioning Lord Nolan to review how reports of child sexual abuse had been handled within the Catholic Church and to make recommendations.

New Guidelines were drawn up, taken from the recommendations of the Nolan commission (found at www.cumberlegecommission.org.uk) and announced to the press in June 2002 with a statement from the newly elevated Archbishop of Birmingham Vincent Nichols who was named Head of Child Protection in the Catholic Church. He stated that at the centre of the guidelines was 'the paramountcy principle' placing the welfare of children first. He stated that "from now on those priests cleared in court of child sexual abuse still faced a risk assessment and possible sanctions".

The Nolan commission did not discover or disclose the extent of abuse reported within the Catholic Church, or those cases held on file still waiting victims to come forward again and report to the police. It focused only on the 102 cases that had gone through the criminal justice system between 1995 and 1999. The Church leaders may know something of the scale of the abuse perpetrated but they have never been compelled to disclose the files of clergy and religious with reported allegations of child sexual abuse dating back to the 1950s. Neither the Nolan nor Cumberledge Commissions had access to those files.

From 2002 the Catholic Office for the Protection of Children and Adults (COPCA), set up following the Nolan commission recommendations, published an annual report setting out statistics for reported allegation of child abuse within the Catholic Church and the actions taken by statutory and Church authorities in response (www.csas.uk.net/document). However from their introduction the New Guidelines provoked controversy and misunderstanding within the Catholic Church. From the beginning the hierarchy and clergy within the Catholic Church took the view that when a priest was not prosecuted or convicted of a criminal offence the presumption was that he was innocent of any wrongdoing and that the allegation was false, and many considered the Guidelines to be optional.

In 2006 Baroness Cumberledge carried out a five year review of the Nolan Commission and the effectiveness of the procedures in place. The report was published in 2007 (www.cumberlegecommission.org.uk). Identifying that the Bishops had not taken ownership of child protection, which undermined the effectiveness of the procedures, the Cumberledge Commission recommended that the role of COPCA be transferred to the Bishops and Religious leaders so that they would have direct responsibility for Child Protection. The National Catholic Safeguarding Commission (NCSC) was established in 2008 with three Bishops and three Heads of Religious Orders included as members and was to be headed by an Independent Chair. In addition the Catholic Safeguarding Advisory Service (CSAS) was set up to advise the NCSC on safeguarding matters. New guidelines and procedures were drafted in 2008 having regard to the Cumberledge recommendations.

Many believe that it was a grievous mistake to place child protection back under the control of the Bishops who had shown themselves incapable of dealing with child sexual abuse in the past. The NCSC is made up almost entirely of Bishops, clergy and religious superiors. The so called independent chairs to date have include a former priest and friend of the Archbishop of Westminster, a Baroness who failed to meet with any victims and lasted just eight months (the post had a mere £30,000 annual budget half of which went on a part time secretary), and we are now we are on our third chair. The new chair of NCSC was chosen by a panel made up entirely of bishops, clergy and religious superiors, and he was chosen on criteria kept secret from the wider public.

14. Case Study – Ealing Abbey and St Benedict's School
The abuse scandal at Ealing Abbey and St

Benedict's School which it runs, first came to widespread attention in 2009, when Father David Pearce pleaded guilty to 10 indecent assaults and one sexual assault against 5 boys (all pupils of the school) over a period of 36 years from 1972 to 2007. He was sentenced to eight years, reduced to five on appeal. Pearce was placed on restricted ministry in 2006 following a civil action against him and Ealing Abbey, in which a former pupil of St. Benedict's claimed he had suffered sexual abuse at the hands of Pearce. The judge found against the Abbey and Pearce, and awarded the victim £43,000 plus costs. However, even after this, and although Pearce was placed on restricted ministry on the advice of the Diocesan Safeguarding Adviser Mr Peter Turner, Pearce was able to abuse another pupil of the school, who had been employed to come into the monastery at weekends to wash dishes.

Pearce "retired" as headmaster in 1993 following complaints from pupils and parents of abusive behaviour. It is likely that he would have been prosecuted at the time, except that the father of one victim died about then, and the mother understandably in the circumstances didn't feel able to sustain the complaint. Pearce was made Bursar of the school, and remained in contact with children through his continuing supervision of the Cadet Corps.

Father Stanislaus Hobbs was tried in 2007 on a charge of sexual assault of a pupil in the 1990s. He was acquitted, but under police questioning admitted to a similar assault against the same pupil on a school trip to Italy. As the law stood at the time, this admitted offence could not be prosecuted in the UK because it had occurred outside the country. He was subsequently placed on restrictive covenant with no public ministry. When he resigned as a Trustee following his arrest in 2005, the school had a statutory obligation to issue a notification to the DfE.

Mr. John Maestri has been convicted on three separate occasions, in 2003, 2005 and 2008, of indecent or sexual assaults against pupils at St. Benedict's when he was a teacher there in the 1970s and 1980s. On one of those occasions he was sentenced to 2 1/2 years in prison. Maestri was a teacher of mathematics at the school. In 1984 he was appointed Master of the Middle School, but departed very suddenly as a result of complaints concerning his abusive behaviour before taking up his new post. He was given a good reference by the school and went on to teach (and quite possibly abuse) elsewhere. Again, the school had a statutory obligation to report the circumstances of his departure to the DfE and they did not do so.

The previous Abbot of Ealing, Abbot Lawrence Soper, who has been residing in recent years at Collegio Sant'Anselmo in Rome, was requested to return to the UK to answer police questions concerning alleged sexual offences against boys at the school. He was permitted to retain his passport, and has since failed to attend a police bail appointment and his whereabouts are currently unknown. A European Arrest Warrant has been issued.

Complaints have been made against Father Gregory Chillman, both concerning sexual abuse of boys at St. Benedict's School when he was a teacher there in the 1970s and 1980s, and more recently in connection with his roles as Chaplain and Chairman of Governors of St. Augustine's Priory School, a nearby independent Catholic school for girls. As a result of these complaints, an investigation was carried out by Ealing Social Services. No charges have been brought, but following the investigation it was decided that Father Gregory posed a danger to children. He resigned as a Trustee of St. Benedict's on 29th March 2010, and was placed on restrictive covenant on terms which barred him from access to children and from any public ministry. Again, the school had a statutory responsibility to report his resignation as a Trustee, and they did not do so.

Mr Stephen Skelton, a lay teacher at the school for a short time in 1983, was convicted in 2011 of an indecent assault on a pupil in 1983. Like Maestri, he was sent on his way with a good reference when a complaint was made against him, and he did go on to abuse elsewhere. At the same trial in 2011 he was convicted of an indecent assault against another boy at West Hill Park School in Hampshire. Again, St Benedict's school had a statutory obligation to notify the DfE at the time of his departure, and clearly they did not do so.

Serious complaints have also been made against

Father Anthony Gee, a former headmaster of the school, and against Father Kevin Horsey (who died in 2006). The Charity Commission carried out two Statutory Inquiries into the school following the civil case against the school in 2006. Their report was highly critical of the Trustees for failing to ensure that restrictions against Pearce were not adequately enforced.

The Independent Schools Inspectorate (ISI) carried out a routine inspection of the school in November 2009, and found nothing wrong. As a result of information provided by a member of the public, the DfE ordered the ISI to make a further inspection in April 2010, which found severe shortcomings in the school's safeguarding procedures, and records of unreported incidents involving six different monks or members of staff. One of the recommendations of the ISI was to "Ensure that any staff or members of the religious community live away from the school, if they are subject to allegations of misconduct related to safeguarding or convicted of wrongdoing." At the present time, one of the monks against whom there have been allegations is still living at the Abbey under restricted ministry.

Ealing Abbey commissioned Lord Carlile to conduct an inquiry into the abuses that had occurred at the school. The inquiry took more than a year, and resulted in a recommendation for a change in the governance arrangements for the school, but no new recommendations concerning safeguarding. The school's safeguarding policy even now does not make a commitment always to report allegations or incidents of abuse to the secular authorities.

15. Current Safeguarding Procedures within the Catholic Church:

The current procedures (found at www.csasprocedures.uk.net) are constantly being updated by NCSC to keep up with the growing criticisms made of them by analysts, survivors groups and professionals working in safeguarding. This knee jerk response to criticism is itself a cause for concern however there are a number of serious concerns with the substantive procedures:

(i) The structures for Safeguarding include: four regional safeguarding commissions; a safeguarding commissioner for each Diocese; and within each Diocese there may also be a Safeguarding officer/advisor working under the Safeguarding Commissioner.

In recent years a number of safeguarding coordinators and advisors within the Catholic church have resigned or been pushed out following disagreement over how cases were handled within Dioceses. The most recent resignations come from Bristol and the Diocese of Clifton where the Safeguarding Coordinator, a retired judge on the Safeguarding Commission and the Safeguarding advisor all resigned in January 2012 after they were criticised/disciplined by the Bishop for treating a sex offender priest unfairly. The Bishop of

Clifton who led the criticism against the safeguarding team is one of the vice chairs of NCSC Bishop Lang and was also on the appointment committee for the new NCSCS Chair.

(ii) Laicisation/removal from access to children. Where a priest is convicted for a child sexual offence and sentenced to more than a year in prison the Nolan commission recommended that steps are taken for the priest to be laicised. However the Procedures make it clear that when a priest is convicted or cautioned for child sex offences consideration will be given to whether steps should be taken to laicise the priest, and no more.

Senior researchers, social workers and other organisations have repeatedly requested information from NCSC on how many priests who have been convicted and sentenced to more than a year in prison have been actually laicised to date. The simple truth is that no one at NCSCS is prepared to reveal this and all statements made in the media over the past two years now appear to be misleading.

(iii) Risk assessment, discretion and reliance on the criminal justice system. Whilst much is made of Independent Risk Assessments being the "cornerstone of the Church's commitment" to safeguarding Children the details within the Procedures makes it clear that not all those alleged to have abused children will be risk assessed either independently or at all. The Procedures state that Independent risk assessment may be carried out for those offenders who have been investigated, prosecuted, convicted or cautioned for child sex offences.

The published statistics from COPCA and NCSC for the period 2003 and 2007 there were only 22 risk assessments carried out for the more than 206 priests and religious with allegations of abuse made during that period, approximately 10% of cases. This very low level of risk assessments may be because the Procedures state that there is "no obligation in Canon Law for a member of the clergy to undergo an assessment that asks for an examination of conscience". Also "the informed consent of the clSimonis required in all cases".

The very fact that clergy are allowed to refuse to undertake a risk assessment under Canon law should raise very real concerns about what appears to be the paramountcy of Canon law in child protection matters.

If a risk assessment is undertaken, the procedures provide that the regional Safeguarding Commission must have regard to the recommendations from the Independent Assessment when determining the recommendations to make to the Bishop. If there is a dispute over the recommendations made by the Assessor, or the Safeguarding commission these must be resolved by reference to CSAS. It is also of concern that Diocesan and/or safeguarding authorities can challenge the recommendations from an Independent Risk Assessment; on what basis would they do this?

To date no information has been provided by

CSAS or NCSC on how many 'disputes' arise. Clearly in the Diocese of Clifton in January 2012 such a dispute led to the complete collapse of the regional safeguarding commission and a case being taken to the Employment tribunal. What happened to the Priest who was convicted on child pornography offences?

(iv) The Procedures say that where police/statutory authorities do not prosecute or the priest is not convicted then an independent risk assessment may be commissioned if concerns remain.

• Who determines whether there is sufficient concern for an independent risk assessment?

• How is the effectiveness of the ad hoc risk assessment by the regional safeguarding commission, diocesan safeguarding commissioner and/or the safeguarding officer/advisor being assessed?

The Procedures do not make it clear what if any effective actions should be taken to ensure that clergy and religious reported to have committed child sexual offences do not pose a risk to children either following conviction or following an allegation if there is no conviction.

This wide discretion on what to do with alleged sex offenders led to such cases as that of Father Michael Hill (above) and Fr David Pearce who both went on to abuse more children following in one case a clinical assessment that said he was an ongoing risk to children and in the other a civil court finding that he had abused a child. Clearly whatever risk assessment was undertaken in the case of David Pearce after 2004 it failed to identify the obvious risk posed by letting a known child sex offender live beside a school and remain a priest where children came into and out of the house on a daily basis.

(v) A curiously named Preliminary Investigation Protocol was introduced into the procedures in May 2011. This protocol is optional and is only engaged where there is no conviction or prosecution of a reported case, and where the safeguarding coordinator believes that such an investigation is necessary (May 2011). However this optional protocol is not sufficient to mop up the more than 95% of cases where there is no conviction and there are very real concerns about the independence and effectiveness of the protocol where the decision to have an investigation, the remit and scope of such and the investigation and the outcomes possible are entirely prescribed by lawyers, insurers and the Bishop.

16. THE CHURCH OF ENGLAND AND WALES – an Overview:

Whilst the press and public have focused on the failing within the Catholic Church a similar events have gone unreported in the Church of England. From its Cathedral Choir Schools and independent boarding schools to Dioceses across the country there have been many reported cases of multiple child sexual abuse perpetrated by clergy and other church officials within the Church of England.

No independent review has been conducted into child abuse within the Church of England or in Wales. However following two high profile convictions where failings by Bishops were revealed in 2007 the Archbishop of Canterbury ordered all Dioceses to conduct a Past Cases Review of child abuse allegations held within all Diocesan files. The review was completed in 2009 and the summary report published in early 2010 identified only 13 cases on record where allegations had been made and/or convictions secured and the offender was still in ministry and concerns were raised. Of these no substantive action was taken against any after reports and reviews had been completed. There were no figures given of how many people in ministry within the C of E had allegations of child sexual abuse, had been found guilty of such abuse and/or had been otherwise assessed or deemed to have abused children. The C of W Past case review identified only 5 cases in a similarly constructed report (2010). Some of the Dioceses conducted internal reviews run by senior clergy and in others independent consultants conducted the review. Whilst Bishops were urged to hand over all files, it is now known that some Bishop's chose not to do so which undermined the validity of the Past Cases Review. This review will be studied in more detail below.

The Joint National Safeguarding Advisor for CofE and Methodist Church is not informed of cases reported within Dioceses and does not collate statistics of cases reported either to the dioceses or to statutory authorities, or cases where prosecutions and convictions resulted. There are no statistics of the prevalence of abuse either now or in the past, no central record of risk assessment undertaken and no understanding of what happened to those against whom there were allegations of child abuse unless the cases are reported in the press.

Abuse in the CofE has taken place within parishes, in the Scouting movement and in youth work where vicars and other church workers are involved. Also choirmasters have been convicted of abusing choir boys where there have been numerous convictions involving choir masters: Chichester Cathedral Prebendal School in the early 2000s, and those identified and Peter Halliday in Diocese of Guildford in 2007 just two of many. Bishop Peter Ball, formerly of Lewis and then Gloucester accepted a caution for gross indecency against a 17 year old seminarian in the 1980s; this was only one of a number of allegations made against him and kept on file. Another vicar picked up runaway boys from the train stations in London and abused them. In Winchester in 1988 two vicars, a choirmaster, a solicitor and a convicted child sex offender were convicted of 22 specimen charges of child sex offences with boys which took place on church outings, at the YMCA and in the churchyard.

Something similar to Winchester appears to have taken place in Chichester and continued until the 1990s with Cotton now believed to have been abusing children up to 1996 from the latest victim to come forward.

17. CASE STUDY Diocese of Chichester - Roy Cotton & Colin Pritchard, Inquiries and Further Arrests:

Bishop Hind of the Diocese of Chichester apologised in March 2011 to the victims of Roy Cotton and Colin Pritchard for the sexual abuse they suffered and the failure of Diocesan authorities to recognise the danger posed by Cotton, a known and convicted child abuser at the time he was ordained in 1967 (see statement on www.macsas.org.uk ; and BBC South East report of 2nd March 2011 also available on www.macsas. org.uk).

In fact Cotton was convicted in 1954 whilst he was training for ordination and was told to go away and come back when he was 'more mature'. Cotton then set up a boarding school where he systematically abused children until he left in 1967 following allegations of child abuse being made against him. Despite church authorities knowing of Cotton's previous conviction and of the more recent allegations made against him, he was ordained in 1967.

In 1996/7 two brothers reported Cotton and Pritchard to the police for child sexual offences perpetrated against them in the 1970s. – 1980s. However following a three year investigation no charges were brought because of lack of independent evidence, i.e. another victim not related who had been abused. The Diocesan authorities did not disclose the information they had on file, nor the fact that Cotton had a previous conviction for child sexual offences. Although Cotton was immediately retired and told that he was permanently barred from ministry, he was granted a PTO in 1999 immediately after the police decided there was insufficient evidence to prosecute him. He kept his PTO up until his death in 2006. Pritchard meanwhile was allowed to remain in ministry and did not have any restrictions placed on him after 1999. When he too retired in the early to mid 2000s, he was immediately granted a PTO. Cotton worked regularly within the same church where Pritchard was parish priest until he went into hospital in 2003. The house Cotton and later Pritchard lived in which the Diocese had purchased, overlooking a primary school.

In 2006/7 Northampton Police investigated another allegation of child sex abuse made against Pritchard, who had been a parish priest in Wellingborough in the 1970s and 1980s. He was eventually charged with child sex offences. When a new Safeguarding adviser arrived in the Diocese of Chichester in 2007 she found a record of the prosecution of Pritchard in Northampton and told the Bishop of Chichester to hand over the files on Pritchard and Cotton to the Northampton police. Cotton had died in 2006. Pritchard was eventually sentenced to 5 years in prison in 2008.

Since the conviction of Colin Pritchard there have been two inquiries into the handling of these cases. Roger Meeking an independent consultant who conducted the Past Case review in the Diocese of Chichester reported in 2009 and his report was not published. The diocese did not agree with his findings and asked Baroness Butler-Sloss to conduct and inquiry and to recommend whether the Meeking report should be published. That report was published in May 2011 (www.diochi.org.uk) however despite recommending that the Meeking report be published it has yet to see the light of day.

Since the Butler Sloss report it has been discovered that Butler Sloss was not told the whole truth by the Bishop of Lewis and the now Bishop of Blackburn, former Archdeacon of Hastings and Brighton, and there is concern that there may have been an attempt to mislead both the Meeking's and Butler-Sloss inquiries by some within the Diocese of Chichester.

As a result of considerable concerns raised the Safeguarding Advisory committee in the Diocese of Chichester sent a report to Lambeth Palace in the Autumn of 2011 under the Clergy Disciplinary Measures 2003 complaining about the conduct of Bishop Wallace Benn and his failure to safeguard children. The committee recommended his immediate suspension from his post. Whilst no action has been taken by the Archbishop in respect of Wallace Benn he has ordered an Arch Episcopal visitation to the diocese to investigate into the handling of child abuse allegations led by Bishop Gladwin and Canon Bursell QC. This is the first such visitation in over 130 years and the first ever into the diocese of Chichester. Since being initiated the Investigation has broadened out in light of further recent developments and police investigations which are ongoing.

In latest developments in early March 2012 an Addendum to the Butler-Sloss report was made public, in which the Baroness sets out that she had been repeatedly be told misleading and incorrect information by Bishop Wallace Benn and Bishop Nicholas Reade former Archdeacon of Hastings and Brighton concerning the granting of a PTO to Roy Cotton in 1999. Bishop Reade, the Bishop of Blackburn, announced his early retirement the day the Addendum report was published.

The following week in March 2012 police arrested two more vicars of the diocese of Chichester on allegations of child sex offences; Canon Gordon Rideout and Rev Coles. It is understood that two other vicars in the Diocese of Chichester have been arrested and bailed in recent months. Also in Chichester Rev Noel Christian Moore was originally arrested in 1950 and convicted on 8 counts of indecent assault against minors in 1951. He was imprisoned until 1955 but then returned to working as a priest and chaplain. In the 1960s he and a lay teacher abused upwards of four boys in Warden House, a private school in Crowborough. Some of the abuse was committed by both men working together in the Chaplain's Lodge at the school. This involved alcohol and boys were abused by each man in separate rooms and then swapped. The Rev Moore died in 1973. The teacher and Moore were also working at a Church in Crowborough where one of the victims was an Alter Server.

Moore regularly took services there. The teacher appears to have had a role much like a curate and he was only in his 20s at the time the abuse took place, this man has yet to be identified and questioned. In 2003 Church officials re-launched an investigation to find out how two cases of child abuse went unnoticed at Chichester Cathedral. It was re-opened after David Bowring, 54, a maths teacher at the Prebendal School, which is linked to the cathedral, was jailed for three years for sexually assaulting four boys in the early 1970s. The case of Bowring came to light while police were investigating pedophile Terence Banks. Banks, 64, was jailed in 2001 for 16 years for abusing boys he met through the cathedral over 30 years. Church chiefs initially launched the investigation after Banks was put behind bars but it was halted while detectives worked on the Bowring case. The investigation was re-started and the Bishop of Chichester, the Right Rev John Hind promised to publish the inquiry's findings.

A child protection officer was employed by the diocese to carry out the investigation. Bowring pleaded guilty to six charges of indecent assault at Chichester Crown Court: (http://www.portsmouth. co.uk/news/local/church_probe_after_child_abuse_ case_1_1229594).

No report was ever published by the Diocese of Chichester. It is understood that a file containing the names of a number of ministers in the CofE Diocese of Chichester with allegations of child sexual abuse against them was handed to the police following a second secret report produced by Baroness Butler-Sloss. Some of these are or were in senior positions within the Diocese. More details can be found on www.macsas.org.uk.

Since the Butler-Sloss report was published last May (2011) there are now 16 victims of Cotton and 4 of Pritchard who have come forward. Cotton is now reported to have continued to abuse up to at least 1997. As of this week upwards of 50 victims of child sexual abuse perpetrated by clergy within the Diocese of Chichester have come forward and this number is believed to be the tip of the iceberg.

The damage caused to the victims, to the communities where these men served and to the wider population is incalculable. As the Diocese begins to settle cases before they reach courts, and vicars consider what options they have, faced with mounting allegations against them it is time for an independent public inquiry to establish what it was within the church, its institutional dynamics and its culture of secrecy that attracted these men into Church ministry, into the Diocese and enabled them to continued to abuse scores of children for decades, whilst seemingly at all times senior church officials knew about it.

See Appendix 4 for a list of cases concerning CoE/CofW vicars and other church officials. It is notable that a number of cases in the Appendix 1 also involve connections with the Diocese of Chichester.

18. Child Protection and Safeguarding Procedures within the Church of England 1990 – 2010:

The events unfolding in the Diocese of Chichester cut across official church statements that with child protection procedures now in place these things cannot happen again. But for the enormous courage of the victims in Chichester who refused to allow the Church to get away with bland apologies and worthless statements of intent there would not now be such intensive police investigations, media scrutiny and church inquiries going on.

So what of the Child protection/Safeguarding Procedures that are now in place, can these effectively change the institutional dynamics that have been exposed in the Diocese of Chichester?

The first guidelines in the Church of England concerned with handling child abuse cases were issued by the House of Bishops in 1995 following the publication of the Government policy on Child Protection 'Safe From Harm' (1993). The Guidelines stated that no cleric convicted of serious child sexual offences should be allowed to work with or close to children. It is clear from past cases where convictions have now been secured that this policy was not put into effect. It is also clear that the House of Bishops had no regard to the danger posed by the majority of offenders who are not convicted yet pose a considerable risk to children (see Chichester case above).

In 2004 the Church of England published their Child Protection/Safeguarding Guidelines and Procedures "Protecting All God's Children" which reflected the Government's new child protection agenda "Every child matters". However in 2007 two cases of child sexual abuse perpetrated within the Church resulted in convictions which caused considerable concern about the handling of child abuse cases within the Church of England. These concerns were similar to those found within the Catholic Church (see Halliday and Smith cases Appendix xx).

Following the conviction and imprisonment of Rev David Smith and Peter Halliday in 2007 the House of Bishops asked all Dioceses to review past cases/reports of child sexual abuse held on clergy and other church personnel files. It was clear from these two cases that Diocesan authorities were still sitting on files containing allegations of child sexual abuse and had allowed clergy and others in positions of trust to continue working with children, leading to further abuse of children.

In 2009 the Church of England completed the Past Case Review. It is understood from discussions with those involved in the Review that the Bishops were allowed to determine who should undertake the review within their own Dioceses. Some commissioned independent consultants to review the files and others decided to do it internally. Clearly issues of objectivity and transparency arise in respect of those Dioceses where reviews were undertaken internally. A number of the independent consultants called in asked Diocesan Bishops to sign letters to the effect that all files had been disclosed to those carrying out the review. It is not known how many Dioceses had an independent review done or how many Bishops signed such a letter. We now understand that in at least one diocese cases have been reported where allegations have gone back decades but the files were not disclosed to those undertaking the Past case review (Diocese of Chichester).

A less than 3 page summary of the Past Cases Review report was made available to the public. Of very real concern is that only 13 files were found to cause concern requiring any action to be taken, and of these 11 were sent to statutory authorities. From this brief note and from speaking to those involved with the Past Cases review MACSAS was able to clarify that the 13 cases referred only to ministers who had allegations of child sexual abuse in their files and were still working in active ministry at the time the review was conducted and for whom concerns were raised during the inquiry. It is not known how many files there are for ministers and other officials currently in post containing allegations of child sexual abuse nor how it was determined that these ministers/officials did not pose an ongoing risk to children thereby requiring formal action to be taken. The brief report makes no mention of clergy, and other church official who had died, retired, were ill, had left ministry, or those who had moved to other countries.

Given the Halliday case that triggered the review concerned a man who was no longer a church official, these are staggering omissions. The Church of England did everything it could to minimise the true extent of child abuse perpetrated within the Church. It is clear that the 13 cases stated are just the tip of the iceberg of child sexual abuse perpetrated within and reported to Diocesan authorities. This is evidenced by the fact that upwards of 12 vicars are on file in Chichester alone.

Also of concern was that only three of the thirteen cases were deemed to have required a risk assessment strategy to be put in place, whatever that means; and that only two cases have required formal disciplinary proceedings. No risk assessment appears to have been undertaken for the remaining cases identified or the other cases where allegations have been made and are on file. As we see in the cases within the Appendix to this report the lack of effective actions being taken when allegations have been reported in the Church of England has time and again led to more children being abused by the alleged offenders.

The report of the Past Case Review also failed to explain why Bishops in Dioceses across England have continued to allow clergy and other church officials to remain in active ministry when there are allegations of and even convictions for child sexual abuse on their files. Despite the past case review which was itself triggered by revelations of such practices, it is clear that this is still happening as evidenced from the outcome of the past case review where actions were only taken in two out of the thirteen cases identified (see also the Diocese of Chichester).

Of very real concern is that the Past Cases Review report appears to have been a serious attempt by Church Authorities to minimise and/or deny the true extent of child sexual abuse taking place within the Church of England.

If for no other reason than the now compelling evidence coming out of the diocese of Chichester we can safely say that the past cases review was a whitewash, and can give no comfort that the Church is any safer now than it was before the review was carried out.

19. Current Procedures in place in C of E (from 2010):

In 2010 the Child Protection Procedures for the Church of England were updated: "Protecting All God's Children" (www.churchofengland.org/clergy-office-holders/child-protection-safeguarding.aspx). The 'paramountcy of the child's welfare' is repeatedly referred to throughout and Words such as 'justice' are used, and statements about working with those who have suffered abuse, and the commitment to safeguarding children are liberally sprinkled about. However the substance of the Procedures raises a number of serious concerns.

(i)   Lack of Independence and transparency. The Procedures provide that every Diocese must appoint a Safeguarding Children's Adviser who is accountable to the Bishop and should have full access to church files and other confidential material. The Safeguarding Adviser should be a professional who has training and experience in child protection. However the Safeguarding Adviser can also be a member of the clergy or a relative of the Bishop/member of the clergy (Dioceses of London and Chichester). It is very difficult to see how there is no conflict of interest if the person investigating an allegation of clergy perpetrated child abuse is a colleague or friend of the accused. The Procedures also provide that there should also be a Coordinator in each parish to work with the parochial church council (PCC) who should be a member of the PCC. This person could be a volunteer and again could be either clergy or related to clergy.

As with the Catholic Church it is clear that the Safeguarding advisor is placed in a vulnerable position when a case comes up that puts him or her in direct conflict with the Bishop. In Chichester the safeguarding advisor at the time of the Pritchard conviction was forced out of post in 2010 when she raised serious concerns about the Bishops handling of allegations. It is now believed that a dispute about Rideout led to her leaving. She settled her employment case with the Diocese for an undisclosed sum and signed a confidentiality agreement. On another Diocese the Safeguarding Advisor has reported that she has faced repeated bullying from the Bishop and others working round him as she has tried to do her job effectively.

(ii)   Responding to Concerns. The Procedures provide that Diocesan authorities should respond to all reports where a child is at risk or may have been harmed however adults who report 'historic cases' are not mentioned in the Responding to Concerns section. This omission is of serious concern as most cases of child sexual abuse are reported when the victim is an adult (see the Australian Study 2009; John Jay Study 2004; NSPCC 2000 and 2011).

(iii)   Confession. The Procedures explicitly state that Canon law constrains disclosure of details of a crime/offence revealed in the course of formal confession. Whilst the Procedures note that this may be inconsistent with civil law, there is no attempt to set out what should happen in these cases.

Past cases such as the Halliday and Cranch (Appendix xx) illustrate that Bishops know about the offending behaviour of some priests yet they are still allowed to continue in ministry or to work with children and invariably continue abusing. The MACSAS Survey identified two more vicars who are believed to have confessed to their Bishops but are still in ministry as no conviction was possible. These men have multiple allegations against them.

(iv)   Managing Allegations against church officials - when clergy and others in positions of trust are accused of child sexual abuse it may be necessary to suspend the accused. If there is a 'prima facie' case of serious misconduct/abuse the accused should normally be suspended whilst the allegation is investigated. With such wide discretion allowed even in 'prima facie' cases it is little wonder that few if any of the alleged abusers were suspended in the cases reported in the MACSAS Survey 2010 (www.macsas.org.uk) . In past cases Diocesan authorities have even allowed priests to continue in ministry up to the day of the court hearing.

The Procedures warn of the dangers of providing character references in criminal matters. This may well reflect lessons learnt in past cases where serial pedophile clergy have been provided with glowing references from Bishops stressing the minister's 'outstanding and selfless pastoral ministry over many years'. Often priests got reduced on suspended sentences on the back of such references.

(v)   Where No Prosecution or Conviction. The Procedures do state that the fact that no prosecution is brought or there is a finding of 'not guilty' does not necessarily mean that no concern remains. However the language speaks of minimisation and denial. We know that the vast majority of reported cases of child sexual abuse will result in no conviction. Most will not even be prosecuted (9% John Jay Study 2004; 23% Australian Study 2009; COPCA/NCSC statistics 2003-2011).

(vi)   The Procedures go on to provide that "maybe" it "might be" appropriate to continue disciplinary actions; and "maybe" a risk assessment should be undertaken if well founded concerns remain. Such ambiguous wording ensures that it is highly unlikely that any risk assessment is carried out or any actions are taken against those not actually convicted of an offence.

(vii) Risk Assessment & Redeployment. Where a risk assessment is carried out the Procedures provide that it will be done by an outside agency normally professionally qualified. However by the time the procedures get to this point few if any of the accused will be considered. This provision is set in the context of those with previous convictions or cautions and with blemished CRB checks. Worryingly the Procedures state that where a person has old offences of child abuse this will not normally prohibit otherwise suitable people from working with children. The Church will always recognise reformed characters.

The Procedures as currently drafted bend over backwards to accommodate those with allegations of child sexual abuse made against them enabling them to continue in ministry, in positions of authority over children and invariably to continue to pose a risk.

(viii) Ongoing reliance on the Criminal Justice System. CRB checks are flagged up in all Church of England publicity on their Child Protection/Safeguarding measures, yet we know that less than 10% of child sex offenders have a criminal conviction. Many escape detection for years and even when they are discovered only 3-4% of reported cases result in a conviction.

20. CONCLUSION - THE CHURCH OF ENGLAND:

There is currently no consistency in the responses to allegations of child abuse in Dioceses in the Churches of England and in Wales, the National Safeguarding Advisor has no access to information on allegations raised in all dioceses and with no central overview it is very difficult to see how consistent responses can be developed. MACSAS worked with the National Safeguarding Advisor giving details of all cases reported in the MACSAS Survey 2010, which formed the first information held national on what was happening in Dioceses across the country.

The Diocese of Chichester is now undergoing a third church commissioned inquiry since the conviction of Pritchard in 2008. Further it is known that the Police in Sussex have an ongoing investigation into child abuse in the CofE in the Diocese of Chichester and it is believed that arrests will be made shortly.

In other dioceses there a vicars with multiple allegations of child abuse still in ministry including those who are believed to have confessed to their Bishops. The current safeguarding procedures do not protect children from risk of abuse by those already reported for such offences lets alone those who are unknown.

21. Note on Child Pornography:

There have been a number of convictions in recent years for child pornography which is also child abuse and must be taken seriously, yet time and again we read of Bishops etc., writing references of support for these men as if they had done nothing wrong. What we see in these illustrative cases is that often child pornography was just one of the ways the vicars/priests abused.

Recent cases include:

•   In 2000 Fr Joseph Jordan of the Archdiocese of Cardiff was convicted in two separate trials for sexual offences against boys in the 1980s and possession of child pornography, and was sentenced to a total of 8 years in prison. During the trials it was revealed that Jordan was subject to investigation following allegations of child sexual abuse when he lived in Plymouth in the 1970s before he became a priest. Although Jordan had been acquitted on that occasion the Bishop of Plymouth had warned the Archbishop of Cardiff, Archbishop Ward that he was investigating Jordan's suitability for ministry as a result. The Archbishop ignored those warnings.

•   In 2006 the Rev Richard Thomas former director of communications in the Diocese of Oxford was found guilty of making and possessing images up to the most severe level 5 which includes images of child rape. Quite extraordinarily the Bishop of Oxford gave a character reference for Thomas at the hearing, which ensured that he received a 3 year community order rather than a prison sentence.

•   In 2007 the Rev James Morrish pleaded guilty to child pornography charges in the Diocese of Hereford after his wife reported him to the police.

•   In 2008 the Rev Richard Hart parish priest

in Powys, Mid Wales was convicted of possession of 56,000 child pornography images including 44 images at category 5, depicting sex with children. He also took photographs of girls. He had been collecting child pornography for 16 years from 1991 to 2007. He was ordained in 1988 and was also the governor of a local primary school. He was sentenced to 3 ½ years in prison.

• In 2009 Rev Trevor Diaper of the Diocese of Chelmsford pleaded guilty to six charges of making indecent images of children including moving images and to the possession of 1,145 indecent images of children ranging in seriousness form level 1 to 4. Diaper had also been charged with seven counts of child sexual offences against a child which took place between 1999 and 2003; however the CPS decided not to proceed with the charges when he agreed to plead guilty to the child pornography offences to spare the victim further distress. Extraordinarily Diaper was only given a three year community order. However Diocesan officials indicated at the time that he would be subject to disciplinary procedures to ensure that Diaper does not minister in church again.

• In 2010 Rev Dominic Stone of the Diocese of Lichfield was found guilty of 16 charges of downloading indecent images of children after 600 child pornography images were found on his computer. He was given a nine month sentence suspended for two years and ordered to sign the sex offenders register for 10 years. Stone resigned from ministry following his conviction.

•   Also, in 2010 former senior vicar, Paul Battersby was convicted of downloading child pornography and sentenced to eight months in prison. This was the second offences, for which he was convicted. Battersby had been the Church of England national youth officer. In 2007 he was reported to police after his family found pornographic images on his computer. One of the movies was of a 10 year old girl being raped by her father. Battersby, then a parish priest in Leyland was given a 34 week suspended sentence, 200 hours community service and ordered to attend a sex offenders' programme.

•   A Roman Catholic priest John Shannon from the Diocese of East Anglia who was teaching at Durham Seminary was convicted in January 2011 on 16 counts of making indecent photographs of children. He was sentenced to 8 months for each count to run concurrently.

22. Note on safeguarding in church schools:

        Church organisations run many schools around the country. Priests and other church officials have free access to pupils. An effective safeguarding policy is more likely to deter abusers, as well as empowering parents and children to speak about any abuse, reducing trauma and preventing other victims from suffering. The government's statutory requirements do not ensure that an effective policy exists in all schools. There is no statutory obligation on the management of a school to report allegations or even known incidents of abuse to the authorities. Parents are mostly unaware of this, and trust that the safeguarding policy is adequate without checking it themselves. When they do check it, they find it is in education jargon and difficult to interpret.

Many Church of England and Catholic schools still do not have effective polices in place. The Department of Education's statutory guidelines, last updated in July 2009, state: "The local authority is required to take the lead role in ensuring the safety of children and young people but safeguarding is everybody's responsibility. Safeguarding should be of concern to the whole community. All public services, not just those directly providing services for children, have a role in safeguarding children and young people for example housing and leisure services."

For church schools to make their contribution to this, they need to report any suspected abuse to the Local Authority Designated Officer for Child Abuse (LADO), without delay. Unfortunately, this is merely guidance, and schools have no statutory obligation to follow it. Research has found that a large proportion of church schools do not commit to reporting all allegations or incidents of abuse (www.stopchurchchildabuse.co.uk).

This gap in safeguarding legislation in failing to make reports to the police and/ or social services or the LADO (Local Authority Designated Officer) mandatory is putting children at risk. The Downside Abbey case (Richard White – appendix 2 below) is just one example of how easy it is for church organisations to protect their own without compulsion.

The issue of clergy access to children in schools makes clear the importance of tightening safeguarding in church organisations as children are at risk today. Despite what we hear from churches it cannot be said that this is an old issue and that there is no urgency. (Appendices referred to in the text can be found on the SCCA web site www.stopchurchchildabuse.co.uk).

Chapter 12
A damning report

On 13th February 2013, the SCCA campaign's chairman, David Greenwood, published the following progress report:

Updating Report for SCCA Campaign:
  2012 proved incredibly important in raising public awareness of the institutional cultures and dynamics that hinder the effective implementation of Child Protection/Safeguarding policies and procedures. The Savile Inquiries, the Rochdale cases and the inquiries and police investigation into child sexual abuse perpetrated by clergy within the Diocese of Chichester all in 2012 raise considerable concerns about how those placed in positions of authority within institutions, local authorities and police services as well as within the wider communities respond to Child Sexual Abuse that is taking place in some cases quite literally before their eyes.
  The campaign and the Government's response:
The Stop Church Child Abuse ("SCCA") campaign was launched in March 2012. The campaign is an alliance of clergy sexual abuse survivors, charities supporting survivors, specialist lawyers and interested individuals working in the field of child safeguarding. The campaign aims to highlight the serious safeguarding failures of

church institutions. The campaign and many individuals have called on the Government to institute an independent inquiry into child sexual abuse perpetrated by clergy, religious and other church officials within all Dioceses and institutions of the Catholic Church in England & Wales and the Church of England and in Wales.

Many contacts and letters have passed between the campaign's supporters and the MPs. The Government response to this pressure has been (quoting from the Education Secretary's letter of 25th May 2012):-

1) "No child should ever have to tolerate abuse. I am not however convinced of the need for a public inquiry, as the key issues are already being addressed by reforms we have underway.

2) We are improving disclosure and barring arrangements that prevent unsuitable adults working with children. Any organisation (for example a school run by a church) with individuals who look after children has clear statutory duties with criminal penalties for non-compliance. For example, any organisation that has removed a person from work, due to the risk of harm they posed to children, or would have removed them had they not left first, must refer that person to the Independent Safeguarding Authority (ISA). The ISA will then consider barring that individual from working with children. It is an offence to fail, without good reason, to make such a referral.

3) It is also an offence for an organisation knowingly

to allow a barred person to work with children. Schools and a range of other bodies that are regulated by this department also have a duty to check that a new entrant is not barred.

4)   "…..we are committed to strengthening the role of statutory Local Safeguarding Children Boards (LSCBs). LSCBs coordinate the effectiveness of organisations' safeguarding activity, and they should also secure the involvement of faith groups in their arrangements"

5)   In the tragic event that a child is seriously harmed and there is cause for concern about how local professionals and services involved have worked together, then the LSCB will carry out a Serious Case Review.

6)   The office of the children's commissioner in 2011 also launched an in-depth inquiry into Child Sexual Exploitation in Gangs and Groups. Therefore we believe that we are already taking forward action that will broadly meet the outcomes that the campaign is seeking from an inquiry".

This response is inadequate for the following reasons:-

1)   Every single plan or initiative set out by Michael Gove will fail to catch a person suspected of abuse whose colleagues turn a blind eye either through misplaced loyalty to the individual or the organisation and/or conflicting interests.

2)   Barring arrangements can only catch individuals already convicted of abuse or already barred by ISA.

3)   Local Safeguarding Childrens Boards whilst

helpful have no power to take action to force organisations to implement policy.

4)   The lessons learned in serious case reviews whilst important are rarely translated into positive action.

5)   The inquiry into Sexual Exploitation in Gangs and Groups whilst important ignores abuse within established church organisations.

Overall the lack of compulsion to report to the police and social services is the key issue which has enabled many cover ups and scandals like the Archdiocese of Birmingham and Chichester to fester and be so harmful to children caught in these organisations.

A close analysis of the Diocese of Chichester reveals the dysfunctional dynamics and distorting attitudes and conflicting priorities that undermine child safety within Church communities and Institutions.

The Diocese of Chichester – The Dynamics of Abuse and Failures to Respond: At the beginning of 2011 Baroness Butler-Sloss was asked to conduct a review into child protection failings within the Diocese of Chichester in respect of two vicars, Roy Cotton and Colin Pritchard. The report was published in May 2011 and found the Bishop of Lewes Wallace Benn to have acted incompetently. Numerous recommendations were made for improving responses to reported allegations of child abuse, especially where allegations are made by adults reporting abuse when they were children. Within days of the report being published survivors and vicars within the diocese contacted Butler Sloss claiming that the facts given to her by Bishop Wallace and the former Archdeacon of Hastings and Brighton, now Bishop of Blackburn Nicholas Reade, were incorrect. The Bishop they said had allowed the convicted sex offender, Rev Roy Cotton, who had further allegations made against him, to continue in ministry within the parish run by his co-accused Colin Pritchard, where children attended and where he was allowed to work with children.

Bishop Wallace Benn was reported under the Clergy Disciplinary Measures by the Diocesan Safeguarding Advisory committee, the first Bishop known to have faced a CDM. In late 2011 the Archbishop of Canterbury commissioned an Arch Episcopal Visitation in the Diocese of Chichester to investigate and report on current Child Protection/Safeguarding failing within the Diocese. This was the first such Visitation in over 130 years in any Diocese in England.

Butler-Sloss wrote an addendum report to her review published in January 2012, setting out how she had been misled by Bishop Benn and Bishop Reade during her review. Whilst the Archbishop's Commissars held hearings in the Diocese of Chichester and took evidence from a range of agencies and professionals, survivors of clergy abuse and support organisations, files were handed over to the police containing reported allegations of child sexual abuse made against a number of clergy within the Diocese. Operation Perry was launched by the Police to investigate clergy abuse within the diocese and in late 2011 and early 2012 four arrests were made and as a result of upwards of a further 70 victims coming forward, four men have been charged with sexual offences against children and all face trials during 2013.

The accused include:

(i)   Canon of Chichester Cathedral, Rev Gordon Rideout who had been investigated by police on four separate occasions over the previous thirty years in relation to reports made to Police of sexual offences against children at the Bernardo's children's home where he worked in the 1960s. It has also come to light that Rev Rideout had been court marshalled out of the army whilst an army chaplain on charges related to child sexual abuse before he worked at the Bernardo's children home.

In 2003 when Rev Rideout was last questioned by police, he attended the police station with the Bishop of Lewes Wallace Benn. Following questioning no charges were brought and the Bishop appointed Gordon Rideout Acting Archdeacon of Hastings and Brighton in 2004 and then Canon of Chichester Cathedral.

During the Past Cases Review of all files containing allegations of child sexual abuse by church officers and ministers conducted across all CoE Dioceses in England and in Wales between late 2007 and early 2009 Gordon Rideout's file was not disclosed to the independent reviewer appointed for the Diocese.

It also came to light when Gordon Rideout was arrested

that until November 2011 he had been the Chair of Governors of Bishop Bell Secondary School, and as such was responsible for safeguarding at the school. He had been allowed to continue as Chair of Governors despite the Head teacher of the School and Bishop Wallace Benn having knowledge that Rideout had multiple allegations of child sexual abuse made against him and multiple police investigations and had a blemished CRB check since August 2010 as a result.

After events at Bishop Bell School unfolded in September 2012 it was discovered that during Rev Rideout's time as Chair of Governors a comprise agreement was signed between the school and a teacher, Robert Healy, who was reported to have had acted inappropriately with female pupils, this enabled the Healy to move to another school where he was arrested and convicted for grooming pupils. Gordon Rideout was also Chair of Governors when Jeremy Forrest was appointed to the school as a teacher. Forrest made news headlines and triggered a Europe wide police hunt in September 2012 when he ran away with a pupil from the school with whom he was having a relationship, and fled to France. Forrest has been charged child abduction. At all times the HT and Chair of Governors knew about the inappropriateness of the relationship and yet failed to take effective action and failed to protect the pupil from further harm.

Gordon Rideout is now charged with 38 sexual offences against 18 children and young teenagers alleged to have been committed between 1962 to 1973, he pleaded Not Guilty at a plea and directions hearing in December 2012 and faces trial in April 2013.

(ii)   Rev Robert Coles previously investigated by police in the 1980s and 1990s in relation to reports of sexual offences against children. In 1997 he was questioned by police after victims came forward. In the summer of 1997 Coles confessed to the Bishop of Lewes, Wallace Benn and the then Archdeacon of Hastings and Brighton, Nicholas Reade that he had abused a child in the church. This information only came to light during recent police investigations when the files of clergy with allegations of child abuse were handed over by the Diocese.   As a result the Diocesan safeguarding committee reported Bishop Wallace Benn and Nicholas Reade, Bishop of Blackburn under the CDM in the summer of 2012. In 2012 Coles was arrested and charged with multiple counts of sexual offences against children and at the plea and directions hearing in December 2012 he pleaded Guilty to eleven counts of sexual offences against children including buggery. On 14th February 2013 he was sentenced to 8 years in prison.

Following his conviction the former Bishop of Lewes, Wallace Benn issue a statement absolving himself of any blame or responsibility for the mishandling of the allegations that he had failed to disclose to police and/or the ongoing harm caused to the victims that resulted. We were also informed that the CDMs against him were dropped by the Archbishop of York for lack of evidence.

Police investigations are ongoing in respect of Operation Perry and evidence continues to be gathered.

Investigations into the former Bishop of Lewes and of Gloucester

Whilst the Archbishop's investigations continued in 2012 further allegations of sexual abuse and assaults were reported concerning the former Bishop of Lewes and Bishop of Gloucester, Peter Ball. The National Safeguarding Advisor to the Church of England commissioned and Independent review of Peter Ball's files held at Lambeth Palace to determine whether there were criminal offences recorded there that should be investigated by police. Following the recommendations of the independent reviewer the Peter Ball files were handed over to Sussex police. In May 2012 the police launched Operation Dunhill to investigate allegations of the sexual abuse of children and young men aged between 1980s and 1990s. Following publicity of the investigation more men came forward.

One of the first victims to report abuse back in 1992, when he was just 18 years of age was Neil Todd. It was his allegations to which Peter Ball pleaded guilty to gross indecency in 1992, in an appalling plea bargaining deal that meant far worse charges were dropped and Ball was allowed to walk away free. The CoE National Safeguarding Advisor's office contacted Neil in early summer 2012 and asked him to come forward and make an official report of the appalling sexual and physical abuse by Peter Ball that he had suffered. Neil agreed to do so, however shortly after in July 2012 Neil took an overdose of insulin in his home in Queensland and remained in a coma until he died after his life support machine was turned off in August 2012.

Bishop Peter Ball and Rev Vickery House were arrested in October 2012. Peter Ball was arrested on suspicion of sexual offences against eight boys and young men aged from 12 to their early 20s in the late 1980s and 1990s. However Peter Ball did not answer questions as he was said to be too ill. He has maintained ill health to avoid answering police questions since then. Some of the men who have now come forward reported abuse taking place when they were testing their call to ministry, and have since become ordained ministers. They hesitated in reporting to police for fear of reprisals from Church Authorities if they pursued their allegations: a number had previously reported Peter Ball to church authorities in the late 1980s and early 1990s and had been severely criticised and condemned by church officials up to and including Lambeth Palace.

Police investigations are ongoing in respect of Operation Dunhill and evidence continues to be gathered.

Upwards of 70 people are believed to have now reported that they were sexually abused by clergy within the Diocese of Chichester from the 1960s up to the late 1990s.

Arch Episcopal Visitation Report:

The Interim Report from the Arch Episcopal Visitation was published in September 2012 and was damning of the cultural and institutional dynamics that had failed to ensure that the welfare of children and vulnerable adults was paramount. Bishop Wallace Benn was heavily criticised for creating and contributing to the negative culture and dysfunctional dynamics within the Diocese, which undermined the power of the Diocesan Bishop and therefore the Diocesan child protections polices. The recommendations made by Butler-Sloss were endorsed and recommended for consideration and implementation across Dioceses in England and Wales.

Many questions remain however as there is compelling evidence implicating Bishops who up until this year were member of the House of Lords, in the cover up of a network of child sex offenders within the Diocese of Chichester. There is clear evidence that several Bishops with the permission of the Archbishop of Canterbury in the late 1960s circumvented the procedures to be followed when selecting men for ordained ministry in order to accommodated a convicted sex offender who would otherwise not be selected. There is compelling evidence of attempts to protect Bishop Peter Ball going to the top of the establishment in this country and including senior members of the royal family. And there is compelling evidence that Bishops and other senior clergy within the Catholic Church and the Church of England used their close ecumenical ties within the overlapping dioceses to moved sex offenders between denominations and across dioceses when allegations of sexual abuse of children and vulnerable adults threatened to become a public scandal. Internal inquiries such as those that have so far taken place fail to ask the questions that would get to the heart of what happened in Chichester.

Other cases within the Diocese of Chichester:

There had been a number of reported cases of sexual abuse by clergy within the Diocese of Chichester before 2011 as set out in the original SCCA report. The cases of Rev Roy Cotton and Colin Pritchard were the subjects of two reviews conducted by Roger Singleton in 2010 and Butler-Sloss in 2011. It was found that Cotton had first been convicted of child sex offences in 1954 in Oxford where he was in seminary training for ordination. He was told by the church to go away until he had matured. Cotton went off and set up a school with a friend in the early 1960s, Cookham Wood School. Multiple allegations of sexual misconduct with pupils were made against him and he left the school in 1967. Cookham Wood was the first school Esther Rantzen investigated as part of the ground-breaking investigations into child abuse with the That's Life team in the 1980s and managed to get the school closed down.

Despite all this information being passed to the

Diocese of Portsmouth where Cotton lived the Bishop asked for special dispensation from the then Archbishop Ramsay so that he could be ordained without the normal formalities and scrutiny. This was allowed. The Bishop of Portsmouth also persuade the Scouting movement to overturn its lifetime ban on Cotton working with scouts and he then persuade Bishop Simon Kemp of Chichester to take him into ministry there, his file went with him, with the conviction and the multiple allegations set down. Cotton proceeded to abuse boys for decades up to 1998, however when the reviewers checked his files in 2010 and 2011 they found all records from 1972 to 1997 had been removed.

The Johnson brothers reported extensive and prolonged sexual abuse by Cotton to police in 1996. Following a three-year investigation during which no corroborating evidence was found, no charges were brought against him or his co-accused Rev Colin Pritchard.

In or about 2006 Pritchard eventually pleaded guilty to sexual offences against the Johnson brothers in 2008 and was sentenced to 5 year after an interminable wait a report was made by another victim of Colin Pritchard and police were able to link this to the report by the Johnson brothers, new investigations into Cotton and Pritchard were opened and Cotton died shortly after. s in prison.

During protracted negotiations as the Johnson brothers settled their claims against the diocese evidence emerged of the Cotton conviction and previous allegations and of further allegations coming to light after previous police investigations were closed in 1999, none of which were reported to police. The Johnson brothers demanded a review into how Roy Cotton ever became a vicar, and how he was placed in a position of authority to abuse them. The Singleton and Butler-Sloss reviews followed in 2010 and 2011.

A review was also conducted into the handling of child sexual abuse allegations at the Prebendle Cathedral School in Chichester in 2003 after three men including a choir master and a vicar were convicted of child sex offences against choir boys. Although the Bishop of Chichester promised to make the findings public only a summary was ever made public. The 'Carmie Report' uncovered that files central to the inquiry were deliberately destroyed/burnt at the Bishop's palace.

In the early 2000s a murder trial took place in Eastbourne after a young man, aged only 16 was charged with killing and dismembering the body a retired vicar Rev Glazebrook. The young man, Christopher Hunnisett was found guilty of murder and sent to prison for life. In the Court of Appeal in 2008 Hunnisett had his conviction overturned after evidence was produce that Glazebrook had sexually abused him from the age of 10 and that he had killed him when he tried to abuse him again. Having already served a number of years in prison Hunnisett was released.

Upon release Hunnisett, by now the balance of

his mind seriously disturbed, set about finding other child sex offenders and having drawn up a list of over 900 he met with one on his list, Peter Buck and murdered him in 2010. Hunnisett was found guilty of murder and sentenced to life in prison in 2012.

Disturbing Evidence of Collusion and Abuse between Catholic and Anglican clergy:

Among the disturbing evidence to emerge over the past year have been reports from a number of people who have contacted survivor support groups including Eastbourne Survivors and MACSAS about clergy who seem to have worked together with priests from the Catholic Diocese of Arundel and Brighton which overlaps the Diocese of Chichester geographically to abuse children. Reports include that of a Catholic priest who had multiple reports for alleged child sex offences and who was moved by the Catholic Bishop over to the CoE diocese of Chichester and became an Anglican Minister. This man had abused children and teenage girls whilst a Catholic priest and had multiple allegations on his file. In or about the 1980s one of his victims became pregnant and in a deal with then Bishop Cormac Murphy O'Connor he agreed to marry the victim and become an Anglican minister. Within a few years the vicar's wife suspected that he was abusing their daughter and following a hospital investigation she left him. In 2001/2 when all files of Catholic priests with allegations of child abuse were being investigated by police the man confessed to the Archdeacon of Hasting and Brighton that he had abused many children including his daughter. This information was not passed to the police, the Archdeacon was Nicholas Reade who went on to become the Bishop of Blackburn and was found to have misled Butler-Sloss in her review into the Diocese in 2011. It also came to light that the offender had on occasion brought his daughter to meetings with Fr Michael Hill, a convicted sex offender and Rev Roy Cotton also a convicted sex offender.

The relationship between the Anglican and Catholic churches in the Dioceses of Arundel and Brighton and Chichester has been historically close. The Pope celebrated an ecumenical service in Arundel and Brighton in the 1980s at the height of that closeness, Bishops Cormac Murphy O'Connor and Peter Ball were close friends and it is now known that both sat on multiple reports of child sexual abuse by clergy and did nothing to protect children from further abuse.

In total upwards of 17 Anglican and 19 Catholic clergy have been reported to have abused children up to the late 1990s within these Dioceses. Most lived and/or worked within one small geographic area which adds to the concern that there was a network of sex offenders shoaling for victims within church communities, schools, cathedrals, youth groups and scouting groups. There has been no inquiry into the movement of these men across parishes, Dioceses and denominations and the harm caused to so many more children as a direct result.

Ongoing concerns within the Catholic Church and Religious Communities:

The recent issue of The Child Abuse Review (December 2012) is a special issue on Child Sexual Abuse within Religious Institutions in the UK with a particular focus on the Catholic Church. Philip Gilligan of the University of Bradford contrasts the narrative on responses to victims of clergy abuse in England and Wales and considered how the responses to victims of child abuse continue to be undermined by trying the serve conflicting legitimacy of communities and prioritising the financial interests and reputation of the Institution over the needs of victims.

This issue comes after three years of unprecedented focus on the abuse of children by clergy within the Catholic Church and institutions run by it Religious Orders. The Pope's visit the UK in 2010 provided the opportunity for survivors to publicise the failure of the Church to acknowledge the many thousands of children in this country who were sexual and physical abuse by priests and members of religious communities over decades.

MACSAS (Minister and Clergy Sexual Abuse Survivors) carried out a survey throughout 2010 asking victims/survivors about the responses they received from the Church (all denominations) when they reported cases of child abuse. The findings and analysis of the Survey were published in 2011 and provided compelling evidence that despite the rhetoric of the Catholic Church that it was prioritising responses to victims of abuse, the experience of victims was of being ignored, dismissed and re-traumatised when they reported cases. Even where clergy and members of religious communities were convicted for child sex offences their victims were ignored and forced to seek pastoral responses and restorative justice through the civil courts (eg. St Williams Children Home – Supreme Court Judgement Autumn 2012; and Archdiocese of Birmingham – Robinson Conviction October 2010).

The Ealing Abbey and St Benedict's School inquiries and reviews (Carlisle, Charity Commission and OFSTED 2011/2012) highlighted the institutional failings to protect children from a known sex offender who had previously been found to have abused children in a civil claim in the High Court in 2006. When interviewed by journalists in 2011/12 the current Abbot of Ealing Abbey appeared not to recognise the moral and personal culpability of the members of the religious community who had known for decades that the former head teacher of the school was sexually abusing boys. The Abbot continued to refer to 'rumours' of abuse as if these were something different in nature to concerns raised and reported allegations made by pupils past and current.

At no time did any member of the community

acknowledge how wrong they were to continue denying David Pearce had abused children right up to the day of his conviction for multiple sex offences against boys over a period of more than thirty years including a victim who had reported the abuse in 2004 and was told by the then Abbot that Pearce was well known to have abused children for decades. Yet from 2004 to 2008 Pearce was portrayed within the press and the school and parish community as a man falsely accused of sexual offences against children and was allowed to reside at the Abbey beside the school where he was able to abuse another child between 2006 and 2007. He was eventually convicted in 2009.

Pearce was only one of six teachers and monks who had allegations of sexual abuse made against them as revealed in the Carlisle review. Fr Lawrence Soper, a former Abbot of Ealing Abbey went on the run aged 80 in 2011 when he was faced with the prospect of police questioning. It is undoubted that his whereabouts it known to senior officials within the Benedictine order and the Catholic Church, he is believed to be in a monastery in Italy.

Buckfast Abbey and Downside Abbey and School and the safeguarding failings within the Diocese of Plymouth have also been the subject of multiple reviews and inquiries in 2011/2012 following the latest convictions of the Prior of Buckfast Abbey and a monk at Downside Abbey for the sexual abuse of pupils at their associated Schools, and the conviction of the Diocesan of Plymouth Safeguarding Advisor who was investigating Buckfast Abbey, for possession and production of images of children being sexually abused. There is no evidence that anything has changed within the Catholic Church with respect to its handling of child sexual abuse allegation made repeatedly and over decades. Many thousands of victims of sexual abuse perpetrated within the Catholic Church continue to struggle to be heard and for their cases to be taken seriously, or to receive any kind of compassionate response from Church leaders and the leaders of religious communities.

The Supreme court cases concerning the more than 150 victims of sexual abuse at St Williams Children's Home in Middlesbrough and the case of JGE and the Diocese of Portsmouth are evidence of the lengths to which the Catholic church will go to avoid any acknowledgement of responsibility and liability for the devastating harm caused to some many children whilst under the care of their officers and within their institutions.

How are the actions and inactions of the Catholic Church and the Church of England set out here and within the original SCCA report any different to those found within the Savile Inquiries and inquiries into Local Authority run children's services and homes?

Why smart policies and procedures for real people living in the real world are needed, rather than ones written for super heroes living in fantasy world.

Victims of child sexual abuse carry terrible suffering that cannot be resolved without processes of truth, justice and reconciliation being engaged with. In the Diocese of Chichester one victim murdered his abuser and another took his own life after a courageous life long battle to overcome the abuse he suffered. Yet it has been the tireless efforts of one man, a victim of sexual abuse by a vicar that he endured for over 9 years that uncovered a network of sex offenders within the Church of England who had been enabled to continue to abuse children for decades despite cases reported by victims from the 1950s onwards. Some victims reported cases multiple times over a period of more than thirty years, never forgetting what happened to them, some were in children's homes and social service care when the abuse took place, they were the most vulnerable of the vulnerable. Others were choir boys, boy scouts, pupils in schools; all were abused by men who wielded unquestioned power and authority over their communities and whose denials were believed by police, social services and church communities over the reports of victims who did not wield the same level of power or authority.

Church leaders express their shocked at the reports of the extent of the abuse perpetrated within the Diocese of Chichester, yet compelling evidence has emerged over the past ten years that church leaders knew about these cases, held files containing multiple allegations against the same men and did nothing to report what they knew to the police, bar the offenders from ministry or protect children from harm. At best church leaders were naive and incompetent and at worst they perverted the course of justice, aided and abetted the commission of criminal offences against children and colluded in the cover up of crimes.

Destroying files when inquiries are taking place, failing to hand over evidence of previous convictions and multiple allegations when police are investigating and failing to report to the police when offenders confess they have abused children, all has happened within the Diocese of Chichester.

Church communities and church leaders refused to look at what was happening and the terrible harm being caused to so many despite it being common knowledge within the Church that certain vicars liked choir boys, scouts, and little girls. There was no secret among the brotherhood of clergy about those among them who had particular 'weaknesses' for children or young men and women. Congregations preferred to believe the statements issued by Bishops and Archdeacons when cases did break into public knowledge often fearful of what it would mean if it was true that the parish priest was having sex with their children.

For what does it mean when leaders within communities betray and abuse the trust and authority that adheres to their office in the most horrendous way, to rape and sexually abuse our children? What does it mean that Bishops, Police and social services knew about the growing number of cases and allegations yet did little and took no effective actions against suspected offenders, thereby allowing them to continue abusing? What does it mean that parents of children abused preferred to believe the denials of prolific sex offenders over the truth told by their own children?

We must sit with these truths, the truth that power dynamics and conflicting priorities can and do distort our responses to the dangers of sexual predators attacking our children. Society needs to acknowledge that this is true, that despite the noble objective of wanting to protect children and place their welfare as paramount, children are vulnerable because they are not adults and they do not have the power and authority that would enable their experiences of abuse to be heard over the insistent denials and manipulations of the offenders who often do have power and authority and most crucially legal rights that do not accrue to children.

There is a need to be a reflective society not a reactionary one, a need to gather the evidence and research to understand how people actually respond to disturbing reports that all is not well within the community, that close to us are people who are abusing and harming children, women and the vulnerable.

Contrary to our perception of ourselves as brave and courageous in the face of evil, we are not, we shy away from costly confrontations and the more powerful the offender the more costly any engagement with reporting concerns and pursuing reports becomes. For it is costly to report a colleague, a family member, a husband, brother, grandfather, a teacher or Head Teacher, a doctor, judge, priest or Bishop. The uncertainty, the 'what if I'm wrongs', begin, then the 'what would it means', or 'how would this look', or 'what about the school, church, family reputation'. 'What about my job', so many get sacked for reporting concerns about colleagues especially if they are more senior. The Whistle Blowing legislations has not been well used not because there are not multiple concerns within institutions, hospitals, schools, children's homes etc, but because the cost to the whistle blower is still huge and often outweighs doing the right things.

Most people do not say to themselves "despite the consequences of reporting my concerns the welfare of the child and others come above anything that can happen to me as a result". We should not expect people to be heroes or martyrs: people have families, children, bills to pay, they have careers and aspirations for promotion, they have positions within churches and communities, they also have egos and fantasies and delusions and weaknesses, fears and anxieties. People often trust the people who are accused of abusing children and vulnerable adults and want to believe their friends, relatives and/or colleagues, because if what is alleged is true they too have been betrayed and abused. People invest themselves in relationships with others and they cannot help but be affected by and influenced by what others do. It is very difficult to set aside all these pressures and relational dynamics to engage with the objective principle that the welfare and safety of a child, even one we don't know very well is paramount; in many cases the child's welfare is not paramount within institutions where abuse is taking place. Paying the bills, maintaining a close friendship, keeping a family together, or a school running, protecting reputations, avoiding being called racist, are often more important at the time, in the instant when decisions have to be made.

"Why should I be the hero?"; "why me?"; "if I do nothing someone else will"; "I can't afford to get involved"; "I'm too busy";" I don't even know if it's true"; "the heck the child lies all the time"; "it's not that serious"; "she asked for it"; "he provoked him"; "he's disturbed"; "she's made a choice to be a prostitute".

These responses by real people in the real world have been said and reported when professionals and others were confronted with deciding whether to officially report concerns and allegations of child abuse. Why are we so devastated that these responses are common? Why do we continue to maintain that if we just get the training right people will suddenly find the personal courage to overcome all the cultural and institutional, personal and familial dynamics that stop them acting according to the objective principles within the safeguarding policies?

Mandatory Reporting and Smart Policies:

Instead of trying to change human natures and characteristics why not draft policies and procedures and legislation that acknowledge these human dynamics? Make the reporting of allegations and concerns of child abuse mandatory and so cut across many of the distorting dynamics. A bishop might want to protect his friend or church reputation but if he gets a criminal conviction for so doing and a hefty fine then he will think it a poor exchange to have his own destroyed. Within schools and hospitals a colleague would have no choice but to report or face prosecution, and so would be better protected from blame by others, as all are in the same boat. It cuts across friendship and loyalty when faced with prison or hefty fines. Also it takes away the perceived need to weigh up whether the concerns reported are true, or serious enough, or who to believe before deciding what to do, the person reporting is freed from having to make judgements about friends and colleagues or the child.

However mandatory reporting alone is not enough. There needs to be build into policies and procedures the understanding of how real people respond to disturbing events within their communities, work places and families. Making it explicit that people will feel conflicted, and how our decision making may be distorted by disturbing events which are so serious. We need to develop policies and procedures that acknowledge these dynamics yet remain effective.

Training is part of that, together with developing reflective practices within institutions and communities and professions, that question how things are being done and what is determining decision making on a regular basis to ensure that distorting dynamics are identified as soon as possible, engaged with and minimised.

We won't be able to do this whilst Governments and others continue to draft legislation, policies and procedures fit only for the few with the personal integrity and moral courage to transcend the distorting dynamics and conflicting interests within Institutions, communities and within ourselves.

The Need for a Commission of Inquiry:

There needs to be a Commission of Inquiry in order for the public, our society to understand why we continue to fail to safeguard children, why the prevalence of child abuse has remained stubbornly constant despite more than 20 years of Government policies, from Working Together to Protect Children to Every Child Matters, Safeguarding Children, Safer Recruitment and Dealing with Allegations of Abuse etc; inquiries such as Victoria Climbe', the Soham Murders and Peter Connolly, and the development of a profession and a multi-million pound industry dedicated to child protection and safeguarding.

Anecdotal evidence, serious case reviews and piecemeal research conducted within academic institutions and child protection organisations is not enough to bring about the shift in understanding that is required within society to enable the fundamental changes in attitude required to make real our stated objective to protect children.

A Commission of inquiry would set down what has happened to our children in the care of institutions in this country: Church and State, public and private, charitable, social care, education and health care services. A Commission would help us to understand why even today those tasked with protecting children are failing to recognise the harm being caused to them even when the abuse is happening before their eyes (including Rochdale, Oxfordshire, Hill Side First School, Ealing Abbey, Chichester Diocese and the Savile Inquiries). Only when the truth is faced, when victims have told what happened to them, those who knew and did nothing have answered questions, and when those who tried to report and were ignored are heard, will we be able to understand what it is that needs to happen next. Then the development of legislation, policies and procedures will reflect reality: fashioned by the knowledge of the dynamics and culture, attitudes and conflicting interests that distort responses and undermine the protection and safeguarding of children.

We need to have the courage to face the truth and acknowledge what undermines our best intentions if we are ever to effectively protect our children.

Let's have policies and procedures for real people living in the real world rather than for super heroes living in a fantasy world. Let's stop blaming people for being human and start working out how we can better protect our children together. [NB 1] 6th February 2013 – The report of the public inquiry into the Staffordshire Hospital Care scandal recommended inter alia that it should be a criminal offence if hospital staff and managers fail to report cases of poor care which is like to cause serious harm or death to patients. If it hospitals and patients why not institutions tasked with working with and caring for children?

[NB 2] 18th February 2013 – the look at improving the whistle-blowing legislation is in response to the understanding of the difficulties and conflicts of interest that stop people reporting concerns. Let's see something similar in terms of our statutory frameworks for safeguarding children.

Chapter 13
The lamp of hope

In December 2012, the Lantern Project published a book called 'Understanding and treating the life-long consequences of childhood sexual abuse', part of a new training programme we had developed with the help of our local Primary Care Trust and the Clothworkers' Foundation, who kindly donated £10,000 to cover the cost of printing 1500 copies of the book. Our aim was to help professionals and others working with survivors of psychosexual trauma gain a better understanding of the true impact of child abuse, to both the individual survivor, and to society as a whole, and how to enable the survivors they work with achieve what we call a sustainable recovery, without re-traumatising them in the process. The book, written by myself and fellow survivors, David Williams, Amanda Tietavainen and Jill Joynson, takes a much more pragmatic approach to treating survivors than is available on the NHS, as it is currently structured. Based on all that we have learned since the project began in 2000, we have been able to put forward a new theory; Psychosexual Trauma Disorder, and introduce the therapeutic recovery model we have developed to help survivors recover; Unstructured Therapeutic Disclosure (UTD), which we have been using with considerable success since 2008.

The tragic, and totally avoidable, death of survivor

Francis Andrade, in February 2013, is a stark example of the lack of knowledge among many professionals of the damage caused to children through sexual abuse. To make the point, we issued the following press release to our local newspaper, the Liverpool Echo.

PRESS RELEASE – 10 February 2013.

'Abuse victim's death was entirely avoidable,' says child abuse victim specialist.

Graham Wilmer, founder of Child Abuse Victims' support service, The Lantern Project, says the tragic death of Frances Andrade, the key prosecution witness in the trial last week of choirmaster, Michael Brewer, was entirely avoidable.

"There is a great deal of confusion among the legal profession when prosecuting child abuse cases," Said Wilmer, a survivor of child abuse himself, who has written a number of self-help books for victims of childhood sexual abuse, and who set up the Lantern Project 13 years ago in Wallasey, specifically to help victims deal with the enormous difficulties of seeking the psychological and legal help they need to help them recover from their trauma.

"The advice often given to vulnerable victims by prosecutors, not to seek counselling before a trial, as in Frances Andrade's case, is wrong, and is based on a lack of understanding of the balance between the needs of victims of psychosexual trauma and the needs of prosecutors to demonstrate best evidence practice.

"We have developed a comprehensive, holistic support service, which we have used to help hundreds of victims of childhood sexual abuse, long before they get anywhere near a court room, and then during any subsequent trial, and for many months afterwards, until they have reached what we call a 'sustainable recovery.'

"The recovery model we have developed is in line with the criteria set down by the government for ISVAs (Independent Sexual Violence Advisors), which meets the requirements of Best Evidence Practice, and enables the victims to withstand the rigours of being a prosecution witness in, what is a brutalising legal process, which is totally unfit for dealing with this unique group of witnesses, nearly all of who will be suffering from Psychosexual Trauma Disorder, and all of who will be vulnerable to secondary wounding, as a result of the prosecutors lack of understanding of how to deal with sexual abuse victims in the court setting."

The Lantern Project has just published a new book to help lawyers, doctors and other professionals, who work with victims of sexual abuse, have a better understanding of the subject. The book, entitled 'Understanding and Treating the Life-Long Consequences of Childhood Sexual Abuse,' and written by Graham Wilmer, David Williams, Jill Joynson and Amanda Tietavainen, provides a new approach to help victims of childhood sexual abuse recover from the impact of the abuse they suffered and repair the damage it caused. The book looks in detail at how the many complex psychological issues that develop over time can be resolved. This is a unique piece of work and is based on a wide range of interviews and therapeutic work with more than 1000 victims, carried out by The Lantern Project since its foundation in 2000.

"The purpose of this book," explained Wilmer, "is to contribute to a better understanding of the long-term impact of childhood sexual abuse, and to introduce more effective ways to help survivors recover from the damage they have inherited. The book is a combination of our own experiences, and knowledge we have gained through our work with hundreds of other survivors, male and female and of all ages, over the past 13 years, together with contributions from recognised experts and specialists in the UK, the USA, Canada and Australia, who work in the field of child protection and victim support.

"The book introduces a theory of Psychosexual Trauma Disorder, which we have concluded, from the evidence we have gathered, is a comorbid disorder, which all survivors of childhood sexual abuse seem to develop over time, regardless of the type and nature of the sexual abuse they have experienced."

Having recognised that there is an identifiable, comorbid psychological disorder that develops in survivors of sexual abuse, Wilmer and his colleagues at the Lantern Project, set about developing a holistic recovery framework that could be offered to survivors of all ages, which would help them reach a point that they call a sustainable recovery; a point from which they would not regress.

"We call this recovery framework Unstructured Therapeutic Disclosure (UTD), which we have been using since 2009, with encouraging results, and we are confident that UTD can be seen as an effective therapy for treating survivors of psychosexual trauma, and in particular adult survivors.

"We are not suggesting that it is the only therapy that can be successful, and we recognise that the model we have developed will always benefit from continuous development and improvement, over time. Consequently, this book should be seen as a 'work-in-progress', and we welcome any feedback from professionals and survivors alike," said Wilmer. ENDS.'

As if to underline the lack of understanding of what we were talking about, the newspaper did not even print the article, even though I had given an exclusive interview to one of their senior reporters. Their reason for not running the story was: "Lack of space in the paper that day." A more enlightened response came from Dr Anne Lazanbett, the NSPCC Reader in Childhood Studies at the School of Sociology, Social Policy & Social Work at Queen's University in Belfast: "I just wanted to say that I was delighted when I received a copy of your book, 'Understanding and Treating Lifelong Consequences of Childhood Sexual Abuse'. This training programme will be so beneficial for health professionals especially GPs and HVs and is a brilliant resource. The new therapeutic recovery model was an extremely interesting read."

Funding permitting, we will be able to continue the work of the Lantern Project for a few more years yet, although the current economic climate for charities like ours is not looking very good. However, a feint heart never won a fair lady, as the saying goes, and unless or until we are forced to close, we will continue to fight for a better understanding of child abuse and its impact, and for a better support services to help those who have been abused and those who are still being abused right now.

A significant part of our work is also aimed at bringing offenders to account, something that is not easy when fighting large institutions, such as the Churches, and in my case, the Salesians, but neither is it impossible. As I have grown older, the fear I experienced as a child, when I was threatened with 'catastrophic consequences' by the then Provincial of the Salesians, Fr George 'Gus' Williams, when he swore me to silence back in February of 1968, has been replaced over the years, originally with anger, but more recently with a growing sense of responsibility. This coupled with a deep routed feeling that this is something I should and can do something about. It is fair to say that I have never really believed in fate, or that somehow every we do was pre-determined, long before we were even born. However, I do believe that we all have the power to influence not just our own futures, but those who we meet along the way. The key seems to lie in not being daunted by the mistakes of the past when trying to evaluate the new opportunities that life presents to us every day, not all of which appear before us as blinding flashes of light!

In this case, it was a simple email from a former Salesian pupil, Sean, which started a remarkable chain of events. I never knew Sean existed before sent me the message to say that he had just found my story on the internet, and was raging with anger to read that the teacher who had brought about my destruction was none other than Hugh Madley, who had also taught him chemistry while he was at Salesian College Battersea, the year after Madley had been moved there by the Provincial after admitting that he had been abusing me. I'd had similar emails before from other Salesian pupils, but this one had a surprise in it that would prove very helpful! Sean said that after he left the Salesian College, he joined the Metropolitan Police Service (MPS), and, that, prior to a near-fatal road traffic accident later in his career, he had been working as a senior officer with Peter Spindler, now Commander Peter Spindler, the officer now leading the inquiry into the serial pedophile, Jimmy Savile. 'Sean said he could introduce me to Spindler, if it would be helpful in any way? I jumped at the chance, as I had been ignored by the MPS on a number of occasions recently, when I was trying to get them to respond to other cases of child abuse I had been working on.

One particular case involved an equally evil, serial pedophile, Fr Terence O'Brien, who I knew had been abusing children at the Salesian College in Battersea, and in other places, for decades, and who was one of the names listed in Eric Baggaley's disclosure document. Part of the work I was doing with two of his victims, a brother and sister, involved submitting a claim for both of them for compensation from the CICA (Criminal Injuries Compensation Agency), however, when the CICA had approached the MPS to ask for confirmation that they were aware that these two victims had come forward several years ago and made a complaint against O'Brien, they were told by the MPS that no such allegation had been made to them, so the CICA declined the application I had made.

I knew, however, that the Salesians were aware of the case, as they had made an out-of-court settlement of a measly £5,000 to each of the siblings, on the understanding that they would remain silent about it. If they had followed their own child protection procedures, they should have also informed the police about the allegations against O'Brien, so I contacted the Salesian Child Protection Co-ordinator, Fr Tom Williams, who, after a lot of pressure from me, finally sent me a copy of a letter they had sent to Battersea Police Station in 2008, confirming that these two former pupils had indeed made allegations against Fr O'Brien. Despite its rarity, the letter said nothing about the compromise agreement they had made both victims sign in order to be paid the pittance they then gave them for their silence, but the fact that it existed was enough for me to challenge both the MPS and the CICA, which I did, but I got no answer from the MPS. I wrote to them a second time, and a third, and still no response, and I was almost ready to give up, when Sean's email arrived! Here was my chance to get in at the very top of the MPS, so I grabbed it with both hands.

Within a matter of just a few days, I received an email from Commander Spindler himself, informing me that he would appoint an officer on his team to take up my concerns, which he did. But, rather than just use this fantastic opportunity to deal with the siblings' cases alone, I jumped in feet first and suggested to this officer that there were many more Salesian victims' cases I was working on, cases which I knew the police were totally unaware of, such was the nature of secrecy at among the Salesians. The reaction was swift! I got a phone call a couple of days later informing me that Commander Spindler had instructed that my concerns would be handed to the MPS Child Abuse Command, and I would be hearing from them soon, so I prepared a list of the 25 cases I knew about, and waited for the phone call. The phone call came, and a wide-ranging investigation into historical child abuse at Salesian schools in the 'Salesian Province of Great Britain', under the code name Operation TORVA, began.

A few weeks later, Pope Benedict XVI resigned, saying that he now "will simply be a pilgrim" starting his last journey on earth, followed shortly afterwards by the resignation of Cardinal Keith O'Brien (no relation) on 25th February 2013. Apparently, the Vatican knew of allegations against the Cardinal 'five months ago', it was later claimed. His resignation as leader of the Catholic Church in Scotland came after a priest lodged a complaint in October about "inappropriate behaviour" by the former Archbishop of St Andrews and Edinburgh in 2001.

On a wet evening in Rome, A new pope was elected. Calling himself Pope Francis, but emphasising that he will be known as the Bishop of Rome. The following morning, the dirt digging started, as the Guardian reported: 'The cardinals of the Roman Catholic church on Wednesday (13/03/2013) chose as their new pope a man from almost "the end of the world" – the first non-European to be elected for almost 1,300 years and the first-ever member of the Jesuit order.

Jorge Mario Bergoglio, the archbishop of Buenos Aires, becomes Pope Francis – the first pontiff to take that name – an early indication perhaps of a reign he hopes will be marked by inspirational preaching and evangelisation.

But the cardinals' choice risked running into immediate controversy over the new pope's role in Argentina's troubled history. In his book, El Silencio, a prominent Argentinian journalist alleged that he connived in the abduction of two Jesuit priests by the military junta in the so-called "dirty war". He denies the accusation.'

The following morning, in other news, the

Independent reported that the use of 'Compromise', or 'Hush' agreements in the NHS is to be banned: 'The Health Secretary has said so-called "gagging clauses" within NHS severance agreements will be banned following whistle-blowers being prevented from speaking out over alleged hospital failings.

'Jeremy Hunt last night said the "era of gagging NHS staff from raising their real worries about patient care" should end. He said departing staff should be given new legal rights to raise issues – including patient safety, death rates and poor care – that could be in the public interest even if they have signed severance agreements.

The move follows calls for a culture of "openness and transparency" in the NHS after the Mid Staffordshire scandal in which as many as 1,200 patients are thought to have died.

"There has been a culture where people felt if you speak up about problems in the NHS you didn't love the NHS," Mr Hunt said yesterday.

In the last three years some £14.7m has reportedly been spent on almost 600 "compromise agreements" for departing NHS staff.'

I will ask new pope if he intends to ban the use of such agreements by Catholic Bishops and Religious Orders, in their future response to victims of child sexual abuse, like the one I was asked to sign by the Salesians back in February 2001? Let's not forget that the agreement I signed was meant to buy my silence forever, under penalty of civil litigation, if I breeched it.

The agreement prevented me from taking any action against the Salesians or Madley, in any court – that includes a criminal court. The Salesians' solicitors had even asked me to if I would withdraw the allegations I had made against Madley to Surrey Police! I refused on the grounds that if I did that, I would be ensuring that if any other victims of Madley's were to come forward, my testimony would not be able to be used by the police as corroboration of new allegations. This was something I was absolutely not going to do, and I told them so. But, they did not give up, pressurising me to instead allow the following statement to be included in the agreement: 'Mr Wilmer agrees that in consideration of the above payments: (a) he will not hereafter commence or pursue any proceedings in any court or tribunal nor actively pursue any complaint to the police against SDB, Surrey County Council, or Hubert Cecil Madley ("Mr Madley") arising out of or in connection with any act neglect or default of any of them which occurred while he was a pupil at SDB's school at Chertsey or any subsequent effect or consequence of any such act neglect or default'.

What kind of arrogance was that? Did the Salesians really think that they were somehow above the law; or rather they could use the law to their own advantage against a very vulnerable victim, to save their precious reputation from being damaged by the exposure of their failure to protect children from abuse? Let us also not forget that a few days before the Salesians' lawyers presented me with the agreement, the

Salesians had referred to me as a 'disturbed individual', whose 'instability means he is not capable of sustained logical thinking', yet they thought it was still OK to ask me to ask me to sign this agreement, knowing that I was not legally represented, and I was clearly 'unwell'.

It is simply reprehensible for an organisation, any organisation, to attempt to use such legal instruments when responding to and dealing with victims of sexual abuse, which is something I put to the Salesian Provincial, Michael Winstanley, at one of our meetings. He responded by assuring me that the Salesians would 'not attempt to use such legal instruments in the future', but yet the Salesians were not willing to tear up the agreement they had used with me.

So then, what now? There is no doubt in my mind that I have restored my self-worth and my inner dignity. I am still, and will always be a survivor of childhood sexual abuse, but I no longer consider myself to be a victim. It is true to say, though, that there are times when the two states still merge for a while, and I feel the fear creeping back into my thinking, but it does not last long. I am also much less restless than I was, and much slower to anger, but, deep down, the monsters of my childhood still lurk, and they may emerge again at sometime in the future. Who knows? However, if they ever do, I know that I will face them this time as their master, and not as their victim, and I also now know that my toil over the past 13 years, since I set up the Lantern Project, and the patience and love of my family and friends, during these dark times, has also now been recognised by the State, as, on Friday 10th May 2013, I received a letter from the Cabinet Office, informing me that the Prime Minister had put my name forward to the Queen for her approval for an MBE. The citation reads: 'For services to survivors and victims of abuse.'

The door-opening value of such an award took a while to sink in, but when it had, I put it to work. The 'troublesome nuisance', the Salesians had once called me, now had a stick to beat them with, and beat them with it I would, just as my headmaster at Chertsey, Fr O'Shea, had beaten me with a cane when I was 13, only the marks he left faded in time, whereas the marks I was planning to leave would never fade!

A few days later, other rays of hope began to emerge, as representatives from the Catholic Church and the Church of England made contact with us. It seemed that the work of the SCCA campaign had been noticed! I took it as a very positive sign, as ever since the collapse of the meetings we had with the Catholic Church's National Catholic Safeguarding Commission (NCSC), back in October 2011, there had been no contact between us. But in May 2013, the newly appointed Chairman of the NCSC, Danny Sullivan, phoned my colleague Anne Lawrence and asked if he could meet with the SCCA team, curious, no doubt, to find out what exactly we were up to. Anne suggested we should all meet at the Lantern Project. So, on May 15th, I drove to Liverpool Lime Street station, and picked up Anne, Danny and his colleague, Denise Moultrie, also newly appointed to the post of Deputy Chair of the NCSC, and brought them to the project. We fed them coffee and Danish pastries, while we talked them through what the SCCA was all about, sparing no detail, to ensure that they could feel and fully understood the strength of feeling we all had, and our commitment to bring about a public inquiry into the years of rape and violation of children by priests, that has been going on in the Churches, unchallenged, for many, many years. It was a difficult meeting, but one gets tired of trying to soften the subject in order to appease the feelings and sensitivities of others, so we were forthright in what we said to them, which did not go down well, although they went away saying that they would think about what we had said. The door was not entirely closed.

A few days later, I received an email from Elizabeth Hall, the Safeguarding Coordinator for the Church of England and the Methodist Church. The contrast between the tone of her message and the tone of our meeting with NCSC could not of have been greater:

'Graham - Since speaking earlier this year, I have wanted to pick up the dialogue with you about a number of matters.

The survivor about whom we spoke long ago, but where I am left uneasy about the diocesan response. At the time I was very new into this world, but since then have learned a lot, so would welcome the chance to revisit the discussion.

Your model for therapy. I have watched your video clip and would be really interested to discuss. What you say makes intuitive sense to me as a former foster carer; we need to reflect further about how exportable it may be as a model.

Issues for the church, not only about facing up to our own failings, but how can we be supportive to anyone from a abusive background?

How can we better respond to our own survivors – recognising all the lessons from Chichester, but is there more to learn? I think there is.

I was interested in your ideas about some form of Truth commission rather than a public inquiry. Would be really interested to tease that out.

Would you be OK to meet with me if I travelled to the Wirral? A really good day for me would be Friday 14th June. Of course, I could come any other time but this is worth trying first! Am now off until 3rd June, but will be in touch on return. Best wishes - Elizabeth.'

So, here was a request from a senior officer of the largest

religious organisation in the UK, to talk to me about the work we had been doing at the project, and the ideas we had developed to help support survivors. If ever there was an open door, this was it. It was in every respect, the opposite of what Anne Lawrence had referred to a few days earlier as 'the collusive crap that continues to come from the NCSC, which they expect us to swallow!

Chapter 14
Mea Culpa - The Churches repent?

On June 12th, 2013, I received the following letter by email:

'Dear Graham

This letter is coming to you as part of the group from the Stop Church Child Abuse! Campaign, with whom we as the Church of England and the Methodist Church representatives met back in February. It is an invitation for you to attend the safeguarding debate at General Synod in York in early July.

This debate arises in response to the work of the Chichester Commissaries. In part, it is an opportunity for the Synod to hear from the safeguarding leads about the work we have already done in response to the commissaries' reports. Further, it provides the opportunity for members to wrestle with the pain of this matter – the fact not only of abuse within the church, but of the failure of the church to listen or to act properly. This failure, as you well know, relates not just to listening to the victims or trying to provide appropriate support. It also relates to a failure to actively pursue reports about anyone who may pose a risk, including passing all information to the statutory authorities.

The Synod will be debating the appropriateness of offering an apology to victims for these failures. The Synod has done this once before, in relation to slavery, and much of the debate there was not about the core issue, but about whether or not a body such as General Synod can sensibly offer an apology in circumstances like this. It is hard to predict what may arise on this occasion.

It will be important for us to stress at the debate, as we will in any surrounding publicity, that this is only a step along the road of engagement with victims / survivors. We valued the discussion in February and look forward to moving on with you around the issues raised. Synod, whilst an important step, will only be one step in that engagement. In particular, since only Synod members are allowed to speak, your presence would be as observers rather than as contributors. We hope to develop a more reciprocal dialogue with you at a later date.

Turning to practical matters, it may well not be possible for you to attend. If so, please feel free to pass this invitation on to someone else if you would like to do so. The debate is scheduled for 5-6.30pm on Sunday 7th July. Elizabeth Hall and I will be on the platform for the actual debate and so Elizabeth's colleague, Jill Sandham, whom you may already know, will host you. For security reasons, all attendees at Synod need a pass. Please send to Jackie, my PA at Jackie@southwell.anglican.org   a photo electronically, so that we can make up the pass.

The absolute deadline for this would be Thursday 20th June. We will cover any expenses i.e. standard train fare (or equivalent cost for mileage); meals on the Sunday; and overnight B&B on Sunday evening should you want to stay overnight rather than travelling back late. Please let Jackie know if you would like us to book trains in advance and post you the tickets. Also let her know about overnight accommodation.

Finally, there will probably be media interest about this debate. You may well wish to establish some direct connection with journalists but there will be logistical challenges in ensuring that this works well. Our communications centre at Synod will help you as much as possible with the practicalities – Rachel Harden (deputy director, national communications) and Elizabeth Hall can help with planning this so that it works smoothly for you on the day. I do hope that you may be able to accept this invitation and attend. I also look forward to working further with you after this particular event.

Yours sincerely

The Rt Revd Paul Butler
Bishop of Southwell & Nottingham'

One of the events that appears to have prompted this extraordinary, and totally unexpected development, was the conviction of Canon Gordon Rideout, in Chichester on May 20, 2013. The BBC reported the conviction thus:

'Sex abuse priest Gordon Rideout jailed for 10 years

An Anglican priest who abused children in the 1960s and 70s has been jailed for 10 years. Canon Gordon Rideout, 74, from East Sussex, who is now retired, was found guilty of 36 separate sex offences, by a jury at Lewes Crown Court. The attacks took place between 1962 and 1973 in Hampshire and Sussex. Most of them were carried out at Ifield Hall children's home in Crawley, when he was an assistant curate. The charges related to 16 different children. Rideout, from Polegate, had denied 34 indecent assaults and two attempted rapes. He was acquitted of one charge of indecent assault against a five-year-old child.

Rideout was the assistant curate at St Mary's Church in Southgate, Crawley, from September 1962 to September 1965. During that time he regularly visited the Barnardo's children's home, Ifield Hall, which has since been demolished. The majority of the offences took place there, although he was also convicted of four charges of indecent assault on two girls at the Middle Wallop army base, where he was a padre at St Michael's Church on the site. In 1972 he was accused of three indecent assaults at the base, but was cleared by a military hearing. He was also the subject of a police investigation in 2001. Nigel Pilkington, head of the CPS South East complex casework unit, said: "As an assistant curate and then chaplain, Gordon Rideout was in a position of trust which he systemically abused, indecently assaulting the vulnerable youngsters that he met over a number of years.

"He was able to wander through Ifield Hall and the gardens, even visiting children when they were sick and alone in bed. One victim recalled how the children would hide under their covers when he came into their dormitories." Mr Pilkington said a number of his victims attempted to speak out about the abuse, but were subjected to "brutal beatings" when they did. "Some of his victims told police in interviews that it simply 'wasn't worth complaining' because of the punishment they would receive in return," he said. "Instead the victims hid what happened to them for many years and none of us can begin to imagine the impact that has had on their lives."

Barnardo's director of children's services, Sam Monaghan, said: "We are extremely saddened by this case and our deepest sympathies go out to those who have suffered; it has taken great courage for them to step forward and relive their experiences. "We are glad that justice has been served and believe it is critical that abusers are held to account for their crimes, regardless of when they took place." Following the sentencing, the Bishop of Chichester, Dr Martin Warner, said Rideout had caused "immeasurable and destructive suffering over a long period of time". "He has also betrayed the trust and respect of many who have valued his ministry," he said.

But in a statement, Dr Warner noted that the Diocese of Chichester was left with the question of why it had taken so long for "these grave accusations to be taken seriously and brought to trial". "What lessons do we all have to learn from this terrible catalogue of abuse about the strength and effectiveness of our communication within and between agencies that have responsibility for the safeguarding of children and vulnerable adults? "In the Diocese of Chichester we shall continue to interrogate those procedures and to do our very best to ensure that we deliver the quality and standard that others expect of us."

From the Church of England's' point of view, the denial game was 'well and truly up,' and for the newly appointed Archbishop of Canterbury, Justin Welby, there could be no more hiding the fact that the Church of England was 'riven with child abuse,' as he put it. He was 'determined to act decisively,' so Elizabeth Hall told us, when we met at the Lantern project on June 14th. And so, on Sunday, July 7th, at the Church of England's General Synod, in York, the Church of England formally apologised for past child abuse by Anglican priests and its own "serious failure" to prevent it. The ruling General Synod, meeting in York, endorsed a report apologising for abuse in the Chichester diocese.

Members also unanimously backed an earlier apology issued by the Archbishops of Canterbury and York. The Archbishop of Canterbury said there needed to be "a complete change of culture and behaviour" in the Church. The Most Reverend Justin Welby told the Synod: "And, in addition, there is a profound theological point.

"We are not doing all this, we are not seeking to say how devastatingly, appallingly, atrociously sorry we are for the great failure there has been, for our own sakes, for our own flourishings, for the protection of the Church.

"We are doing it because we are called to live in the justice of God and we will each answer to him for our failings in these areas."

The cases of two priests - Roy Cotton and Colin Pritchard - who abused several children during the 1970s and 1980s, had prompted an inquiry by the Archbishop of Canterbury's office into safeguarding procedures in the diocese.

The ensuing report described a "profoundly unhelpful and negative culture" there, producing an "appalling" and "dysfunctional" record in handling allegations of abuse. Opening the debate, the Bishop of Southwell and Nottingham, the Right Reverend Paul Butler, said the Church had "failed to listen properly".

"We did not acknowledge the wrong done and we protected the institution at the expense of the person abused," he said.

"We cannot do anything other than own up to our failures - we were wrong."

He said the church's "failures were sin just as much as the perpetrators sinned".

The bishop read out a statement from victims of child abuse in the Church who called for a public inquiry to find out the number of victims, how the Church protected abusers and whether there was a cover-up.

In response to the report, the Archbishop of Canterbury, Justin Welby, and the Archbishop of York, John Sentamu, offered their own apology for the "individual wickedness on the part of abusers" and serious failures by the Church to protect children or listen properly to victims. They said the suffering inflicted on the victims would be a source of grief and shame for years to come.

The motion before the Synod endorsed the archbishops' apology and the contents of the report.

During the debate, Bishop Paul Butler read out the following statement from the SCCA campaign group: "It is an indication of where the Church of England is in hearing the voices of those who have been caused irreparable harm within the Church that Survivors are not allowed to speak for themselves. Survivors are not allowed to share their vision for safeguarding the vulnerable and responding to those who have been abused at this important debate. We have been told it's to do with 'other' debates taking place over the coming days and the danger of setting a precedent.

If this Resolution had been thought through at all, if survivors had been consulted and brought into discussions about its content and purpose, and plans had been made accordingly then there would have been no need for precedents. Why are the victims always the last to be consulted about how they are to be responded to?

Because of the lack of consultation, Survivors are confused about this resolution and this debate at this time; an apology normally comes after the truth is known, when responsibilities have been placed where they belong and the harm caused has been set down, reckoned and acknowledged. An apology made without the costly engagement of reaching out to the victims, listening to what happened to them and the suffering endured, would be meaningless.

Is this resolution for a general apology, a first step to something more? If so what? Is this apology the beginning of a process that will reach out to victims, so that they may at last set down the responsibility for the truth they carry: a truth that no one has wanted to hear, a truth denied and covered up and for which they have been vilified, judged and condemned if they spoke of it? Will this resolution and apology lead to truth and restorative justice for all who have been abused within the Church, and ultimately to reconciliation for the Church? For there can be no reconciliation without the truth, the whole unmitigated truth being revealed.

Or is this a game, another in the decades of games

played out in the public, to present a Church responsive to its past failings and moving forward in harmony with survivors; until the next time, the next case that reveals further abuse, cover up and denial, and the inadequacy of ineffective procedures?

Many victims of rape and abuse perpetrated within the Church have not survived: our brothers and sisters died in despair longing for compassion and justice. Many victims suffer with mental health difficulties directly attributable to the abuse they endured, many are in prisons, homeless, unemployed, in ill health and socially isolated. Many countless others continue to struggle to find a reason to survive each day. Many Survivors have not come forward through fear, shame and a deep mistrust of the Church - they too must be acknowledged and it is only through engaging with Survivors that they trust that their ongoing suffering can be really heard.

Whilst Survivors welcome this resolution and this debate reconciliation is not something that can be attained without engaging in the costly journey towards truth and justice, reaching out to the victims and listening to their stories and the truth of what happened in this Church in the 20th and 21st Centuries, and responding compassionately to the often unendurable and incomprehensible suffering they carry. Without this process any apology is inappropriate and seems, to many survivors merely designed to bolster the Church's public image.

If the Church is proposing to apologise for its failure to listen and to act properly then why and how the Church acted as it did must be investigated and the whole truth must be shared, acknowledged and then apologised for. Survivors believe that only an independent public inquiry will uncover the truth; of how many have been abused and continue to suffer; of the privileging and protection of offenders and the denial, silencing and vilification of the victims and their families; of the collusion and cover up and attempts to pervert the course of justice; and of the on going institutional and cultural dynamics within the Church that continue to enable abuse and to cover up and deny the abuse perpetrated by clergy and others, at the cost of safeguarding the most vulnerable within the Church.

Once such an inquiry has reported, once individual cases have been acknowledged, and once the Church has begun to learn how to respond appropriately, maybe then the apologies, general as well as to individuals and their families will carry some meaning. If the Church through this Synod is willing to walk with us on this costly journey then there may be a purpose and there may be hope for Survivors and for the Church in this resolution and this apology being debated today." The debate, which lasted about 1 hour 45 minutes, was approved by 360 votes to none.

Some weeks earlier, I had invited the current Provincial of the Salesians in England, FR Martin Coyle, to the Lantern Project to talk about our proposals for a

National Commission for Truth and Reconciliation for victims of sexual abuse. To my surprise, he accepted, despite the fact that a report about the Metropolitan police investigation into allegations of widespread sexual abuse at a number of Salesian schools in the UK, going back to the 1960s (Operation TORVA), had just appeared in the National Press, written by my friend David Henke, an award winning investigative journalist.

'Exclusive – By David Henke - May 25, 2013 : Met Police launch nationwide child abuse investigation into Catholic order.

Over the last two weeks the Met Police Child Abuse Investigation Command has been secretly running a new investigation into alleged child abuse involving former schoolboys who went to primary and secondary schools run by the Roman Catholic Salesian Order in England and Scotland.

Some 23 alleged victims have already been contacted in one of the biggest operations since Operation Yewtree, which involved Jimmy Savile and Operation Fernbridge investigation into sexual abuse at Elm Guest House in Barnes – including tracing people who had left the country for Thailand.

The full story is revealed today in The People: (http://www.mirror.co.uk/news/uk-news/paedo-probe-catholic-schools-20-1911825) and Exaro News(http://www.exaronews.com/articles/4979/met-investigates-catholic-order-s-schools-over-child-sex-abuse). It is known to involve at least 30 victims and 20 priests and teachers, some of whom are now dead, and stretching back some 50 years. Some of the figures were prominent members of the Order which was set up in London in the late nineteenth century and now stretches world-wide.

The impetus for the new investigation comes from one former pupil of a Salesian school, Graham Wilmer, who was sexually abused himself, and has tirelessly and heroically campaigned for a full-scale police investigation into the order for decades.

He now runs the Lantern Project (http://www. lanternproject.org.uk) in the Wirral, which counsels victims of child sexual abuse and has managed to pass to the police 50 names of victims and abusers, some of whom had left the country.

The extraordinary decision to launch the investigation was finally prompted – after three false attempts – by a former pupil of a London Salesian school who was a senior colleague of Commander Peter Spindler, now at HM Inspectorate of Constabulary. He knew of the abuse in the order and directly contacted Spindler. His intervention led to Spindler launching the inquiry and the contacting of victims.

(See http://www.exaronews.com/articles/4980/operation-torva-ex-pupil-joined-police-and-triggered-met-probe) The Scotland Yard codename for the exercise is Operation TORVA.

One of the schools where abuse by staff was

alleged to have taken place was a Salesian College in Battersea, south London. Famous pupils there include Catherine Tate, who attended the sixth form and Lord O'Donnell, the former cabinet Secretary, who was a head boy.

The Met Police said: "The Metropolitan Police takes allegations of sexual abuse very seriously regardless of when they took place. All allegations when reported will be recorded and investigated and where possible evidence will be put before the court in order that offenders will have to answer for their actions. Officers from the Metropolitan Police have been engaging with members of the Lantern Project in order to work in partnership to encourage those who have suffered abuse to come forward."

Graham Wilmer said: "It is a matter of great comfort to us that the response we have had, when talking to the police, has always been very positive, and no one should be concerned about how they will be treated if they report abuse to the police. I would urge anyone who has been abused in a Salesian school, or elsewhere, to come forward and make contact with the police in the first instant.

"It has always been a matter of real concern to me that, up until the Jimmy Savile case, it has been very difficult to get justice for victims of sexual abuse, as nobody really wanted to know. Now, everything as changed, and the police, the DPP and the CPS are actively encouraging victims to come forward and seek help.

However, there is still no sign from government that they will provide the funding necessary to support survivor groups, such as the Lantern Project, without which the support that victims who come forward desperately need, will simply not be there."

The police are taking calls from victims on 101 or 999 and victims can also contact the Lantern Project on 0151 630 6956 if they don't want to call the police to report child abuse in the Salesian Order."

The Liverpool Echo followed up the story a few days later, under the headline: Catholic religious order behind Bootle's Savio Salesian College facing child sex abuse claims.

The story was met with outrage by the head teacher of the school, wrote with indignation to the Echo's editor:

'Sir, I am writing with regard to your headline on page 7 of the ECHO, of May 29, which is misleading. The headline states 'Mersey school faces child abuse inquiry'. This is incorrect. There is not an investigation into Savio Salesian College. Your headline gives the impression that Savio Salesian College is being investigated. This has caused considerable upset and distress among parents and pupils. As far as I am aware, there are no allegations concerning the school and there has never been any allegation of inappropriate behaviour involving a member of staff at the school.

We have robust safeguarding procedures in the school and this is confirmed by OFSTED. We are committed to keeping our pupils safe from any form of harm. Fr. J. G. Briody, Head teacher'.

His outrage found sympathy with some chap called Michael Bennett, who also wrote to the editor: 'The ECHO should be ashamed that they even ran a story which singled out an very good school, who work extremely hard with its youngsters and who have never, ever, been under an investigations for such crimes.'

What Fr Briody should have said, of course, was that he was 'very upset at the distress that his fellow Salesian priests had caused by raping children at other Salesian schools in England and Scotland.' But he didn't, so I wrote to the editor myself:

'Dear Editor - Until myself and the other victims of abuse at Salesian schools came forward, which led to the current investigation into allegations of child abuse at schools in England run by the Salesians, (Savio High School is run by the Salesians), there had never been any 'investigations for such crimes' in any of the other schools run by the Salesians either. The current police investigations (as at 30th May) had recorded eleven new allegations from seven victims, naming eight suspects, and involving the Salesian schools in Battersea, Oxford and Farnborough. This is in addition to previously reported cases, including my own, at Salesian College Chertsey, and Salesian College Blaisdon, and the Salesian Seminary College (now closed) at Shrigley Hall, in Cheshire. The Liverpool Echo was absolutely right to publish this story. We (the victims) have been silenced for too long. We are now breaking that silence, and I encourage all victims to come forward and talk to the police.'

The Echo, rang me a second time to confirm the numbers of victims I had passed to the police, which I did. The journalist was obviously under pressure from the Editor, who was also under pressure from the Salesians, but my words of caution about the Salesians seemed to fall on stony ground, and they published the following clarification article:

'A MERSEY secondary will not form part of a child abuse inquiry into the religious order that runs its family of schools, police confirmed today. In May the Metropolitan Police confirmed it had received "a number of allegations" relating to the Salesians of Don Bosco (SDB) order. As the ECHO revealed, there is no suggestion the allegations relate to existing pupils and it is understood the probe relates to now deceased SDB officials with the allegations stretching back some 50 years. SDB, set up in London in the late nineteenth century, runs five UK secondary schools including Bootle's Savio Salesian College. It has more than 16,000 priests, including 80 in the UK. Today the Metropolitan Police said although it was still assessing the allegations received, any resulting investigations would centre within the Force's boundaries. And Merseyside Police today also confirmed its public protection unit had not been passed any allegations relating to the SDB order or its involvement with the Bootle school.

When news of the police inquiry surfaced the SDB confirmed it would "be working with" the Bootle secondary as it awaited more information from The Met. It also stressed its schools were "totally committed to the safeguarding procedures" set out by the Catholic Church. And after police confirmed Savio Salesian College would not be part of the child abuse inquiries, a spokesman said: "There has never been any allegations of impropriety on the part of any members of staff at Savio Salesian College in Bootle. Should the police at any stage require assistance in the investigation into any Salesians of Don Bosco school then we would cooperate fully with them." Asked about the SDB allegations, a Metropolitan Police spokesman said: "We are still assessing the allegations we have received" but added: "If the allegations are taken forward by us they would be those that fall within our jurisdiction." And a Merseyside Police spokesman said: "Merseyside Police can confirm that no referrals have been made by the Metropolitan Police to our public protection unit relating to SDB.'"

The Echo then deleted the original article from their on-line version of the paper, leaving the following message in its place: 'Sorry... We can't find the page: http://www.liverpoolecho.co.uk/news/liverpool-news/catholic-religious-order-behind-bootles-4026130

Needless to say, when the Provincial turned up at our office, he was not best pleased by the fact that I had 'exposed' the Salesians, yet again, as he made very clear to me when he described 'the problems' my article had caused them, as they were having an OFSTED inspection on the same day the article had appeared in the Echo! Like FR Briody, the Provincial made no mention of the allegations that HAD been made, which was the nub of the problem I have with the Salesians, i.e., they have never shown any remorse or regret about the abuse that has taken place in their schools, nor have they shown any willingness to change that position, as became clear in the letter Martin Coyle sent me after the meeting:

'Dear Graham

I was pleased to have the opportunity to meet you at the Lantern Trust on July 17th. I had hoped to follow up with this email rather sooner, but necessary visits to Italy, Ireland and Poland along with other matters have been occupying my time. The presentation of your proposal for a National Commission for Truth and Reconciliation (CTRUK) was very informative. Recent events such as the Jimmy Savile affair and a number of other high profile cases have certainly brought to public attention the extent and damaging effects of child abuse. As you stress, the need to support victims is considerable and ever increasing, and your MBE is recognition of your work and that of the Lantern Trust. The signs are that the government and police forces are now prepared to be more proactive in ensuring that action is taken to investigate cases, but as you point out the support structures for victims are limited in extent and funding.

Your report of increasing Church interest in your CTRUK proposal is encouraging for the project. If established it certainly needs to be set up in such a way that it can command widespread support from all parties: institutions, churches, professional bodies, Local Authorities and victim support groups alike - and as a result have a chance of securing central government approval and funding. As I said during the meeting, the Salesians will need to take our lead from the National Catholic Safeguarding Commission and the Bishops Conference, and any support for the project would be through them, but you have a strong case and we wish you well in your initiative.

At the meeting we spent a little time on specifically Salesian matters. I accept that if historical allegations arise not all those coming forward may wish to have direct dealings with us, but we would always wish any such persons to be encouraged to make such contact, since this is the only way we can respond. Fr Tom Williams, our Safeguarding representative, will always wish to deal directly with victims and meet with them where possible. I note your recently forwarded Australian email. It seems a classic case of the Church (in this instance, the Salesians) being accused of cover-ups and victim supporters being accused of exaggeration. I really do not know any of the facts of the situation. I wish you well in your continuing work to support victims of abuse. It is only when all parties can work together that progress will be made to respond to the issue of child abuse and support its victims. Yours sincerely - Martin'

The 'Australian' email he refers to was about the row that had broken out between the Salesians in Australia and the government of Victoria, who were conducting an investigation into church child abuse in the State of Victoria. The Australian newspaper, The Age, had reported the story on 10th August:

'The Catholic Salesians of Don Bosco order misled the Victorian inquiry into child sexual abuse about its attempts to suppress an independent report that criticised it, according to the report's author. Patrick Parkinson, professor of law at Sydney University, told the inquiry in a right of reply published on Friday that Australians could not have any confidence in promises by the church "if we are unable to believe that the truth will be told even to a parliamentary inquiry".

Meanwhile, the church has in turn attacked the inquiry for making "incorrect, unfair and misleading" claims, and savaged witnesses in a right of reply published this week. A former consultant to Towards Healing, the church's national abuse protocol, had claimed that the church's insurance company dominated its policies at the expense of victims, and destroyed 40 boxes of personnel records. Professor Parkinson, a child protection expert, told the inquiry last year that the Salesians of Don Bosco suppressed his independent report because he criticised them for removing three priests from Australia.'

http://www.theage.com.au/national/church-fights-back-amid-claims-of-blocking-report-20130809-2rngy.html#ixzz2e0b6iIMX

Earlier, in April 2013, another Salesian priest had been hauled before the courts, charged with multiple offences against children, as was reported in 'The Australian' newspaper:

Salesian priest 'abused victim with pool cue'
BY:PIA AKERMAN From: The Australian April 26, 2013

'A CATHOLIC priest charged with child sex offences has been accused of assaulting one of his victims with a pool cue. Salesian priest and former school principal Julian Fox, 67, today faced court for the first time since the Catholic church negotiated with Victoria Police to see him returned from Rome. He has been charged with 10 offences, including committing three counts of buggery against a boy under the age of 14 in 1980. It is alleged he indecently assaulted another victim with a shortened pool cue in 1981, and indecently assaulted another three times between 1976 and 1978. The fourth complainant was allegedly indecently assaulted in 1985. The Salesian Order has been accused of knowingly allowing Father Fox relocate to Rome after accusations were made against him by former students. The order is due to face the Victorian parliamentary inquiry into how non-government groups have handled child sex allegations on Monday, along with other Catholic officials. Father Fox is out on bail and was ordered to report to a suburban police station once a week. He will face court again for a committal mention in July.'

On August 31st, another Australian newspaper, 'The Mercury' highlighted the case of another former Salesian priest, David Edwin Rapson: 'A FORMER Hobart Catholic priest has been found guilty of sex offences against eight boys, including five counts of rape committed at two Victorian schools. David Edwin Rapson, who taught at Dominic College in the 1980s, abused the boys during his time at Salesian College's Lysterfield and Rupertswood campuses between the 1970s and 1990. He denied the allegations but yesterday a jury at the Victorian County Court found him guilty of all five charges of rape and eight counts of indecent assault. During his nine-day trial, prosecutor David Cordy said Rapson had abused the boys, sometimes with witnesses around, and thought he could not be held accountable. "You can imagine the relative power ... between the parties," Mr Cordy told the jury. "If anyone said anything, it was just going to be swept under the carpet that's the way it was back then." Rapson was a junior priest at Lysterfield in the 1970s before becoming a teacher and vice-principal at Rupertswood. His barrister Shaun Ginsbourg told the court Rapson had given some children cigarettes and alcohol but denied all the abuse allegations. He said the time since the incidents made it difficult to test the evidence against him. "The lapse of time should make you more careful in accepting that these allegations are true," Mr Ginsbourg told the jury. But Mr Cordy said it often took a long time for sexual abuse victims to tell their stories. Rapson was jailed for two years in 1992 after being convicted of the sexual abuse of a boy at Rupertswood. He was removed from the priesthood in 2004 after the Australian head of the Salesians travelled to the Vatican to personally ask Pope John Paul II to defrock him. Rapson showed no emotion as his verdict was read. He will face a pre-sentence hearing on October 9. The Catholic Church paid one Tasmanian victim $80,000 to compensate for repeated abuse he suffered while aged 13 and 14 during the mid-1980s at Dominic College in Hobart.'

Chapter 15
'Nihil mali cum bonis triumphis'
'when good men do nothing evil triumphs'

A couple of times in this book, the name of Fr Terence O'Brien has been mentioned. He was a Salesian Catholic Priest, based for a number of years at the Salesian College Battersea, towards the end of his teaching career. In Chapter 7, his name appears in the testimony of one of his victims, but nowhere in any document or history of the Salesians will you find any negative mention of him, let alone an apology for his behaviour. So, let us compare what they do say about him, and what the Metropolitan Police say about him, following their investigation Operation TORVA.

Firstly, this is how the Salesians describe themselves: 'The Salesians are an international Roman Catholic order, founded in Italy in the 19th Century by St. John Bosco. We are dedicated to being signs and bearers of the love of God for young people, especially those who are disadvantaged.'

And this is how the Catholic Herald talked about O'Brien and his work running his 'Guild':

YOUTH GUILD WITH A DIFFERENCE
(Originally printed in the 3rd September 1965 issue of the Catholic Herald)

'ON September 8, Fr. Terence O'Brien, S.D.B., will be leaving the solitude of a Moorland village in Cheshire for the hurly burly of London. The move is designed to allow him more time to concentrate on youth work, in which field he enjoys a high reputation.

For the last 13 years he has been at Dominic Savio House, Bollington, which stands high on the Pennine slopes near Macclesfield. When he first arrived there it was a house of studies for the Salesian Order but nine years ago it became a retreat house running courses aimed particularly, but not exclusively at youth.

This transition coincided with the inauguration of the Dominic Savio Guild. There is no other organisation—if you can use that term—quite like it in the world. It is not a society in the generally accepted sense for it exists solely for the benefit of the individual who is not called on to participate in any corporate activities. There simply are none. In the words of Fr. O'Brien it sets out "to make boys into apostles and leaders among their own companions—in the parks and the sports fields". The whole concept of the Guild is based on the life of St. Dominic Savio whose motto was "Death, rather than sin". As this is not something that can he achieved by a mass approach the Guild focuses its attention on the individual.

Members are recruited not through advertisements but through contact with their friends who are members or through teachers who are interested. On enrolling a boy makes four promises-to obey his parents, to try to do the right thing, never to indulge in bad talk and to keep himself and his friends busy doing something useful.

He is expected to say a special prayer to St. Dominic daily and to recite the Rosary and to receive Holy Communion regularly. For his help there is "The Companion of Youth", a book of guidance for the young including prayers and spiritual exercises originally composed by St. John Bosco but modernised as recently as 1961. As for the man behind this scheme Fr. O'Brien has been responsible for running the Guild during the last nine years. This involves sending a letter to each of the 4,000 members who are scattered throughout the British Isles, Asia and Africa. Regular replies are not expected but boys are encouraged to write to Fr. O'Brien if they feel that they need further guidance or have special problems. All such letters are answered personally by Fr. O'Brien.

Naturally, many of the members have never seen either Dominic Savio House or Fr. O'Brien although from time to time boys living not too far away assemble there for a few days to escape from activity of the world. These are not organised retreats but more in the form of personal spiritual development courses geared to the needs of each individual. By moving to Battersea Fr. O'Brien hopes to have more time to devote to the work of the Guild, He also hopes to be able to spread his wings further/or he has several schemes in mind, all connected with youth. By being free of the responsibilities of running the retreat house he hopes to be able to formulate his plans and put them into action. Among these is a national crusade of prayer for youth. This will take some time to sponsor for it will necessitate enlisting the help of lay people and directing them in ways where their services can be of most value.'

Now consider what the Metropolitan police Child Abuse Investigation Command said about Fr Terence O'Brien, following their investigation Operation TORVA: 'Fr O'Brien was a prolific pedophile, who would subject children to strip naked, and be massaged, masturbated and physically penetrated, under the pretext that they were being rid of bad spirits that had made them behave badly. The children were brought to Fr O'Brien by their parents in the belief that he was a child psychotherapist, and could treat them for their behaviour. This abuse was practiced on children on a weekly basis, sometimes for years. The victims were instructed never to inform anyone of their treatment, or it would not work. Fr O'Brien was not a psychotherapist at all, yet he was allowed to practice his trade upon the grounds of the Salesian school without question, on a regular basis.'

Fr O'Brien's abusive history was, of course, already known to the police, following complaints made by a number of other children in 1996. He was arrested and charged with the sexual assault of three children, but was not prosecuted, as the CPS decided he was too old and too frail to instruct a defence. He died on the 11th August 2000. The police concluded that O'Brien's victims would most likely have numbered in the multiples of ten. To date, the Salesians have never made any public comment about Fr O'Brien, let alone apologised to any of his many victims.

On 10th September 2013, I received a phone call from an individual who asked me if I knew anything about the St John Bosco (Approved) School in Aberdour, Fife? I said no, but thirty minutes later, I knew a great deal about them, and the appalling regime of physical and sexual brutality they had metered out to children, as young as six, who had been sent to the school for a range of reasons, from behavioural problems to learning difficulties, or, in the case of this individual, the terrible offence on 'truanting'!

Over the next few days, the story he had told me was evidenced by documents he sent me from his time at the school, including extracts from the 'punishment' ledger, which bore the title: 'Return of Punishment for the quarter ending March and June 1963.' Against his name, and the names of other children, were the handwritten records of the 'punishments' and the 'offences', together with the signature of the priest who administered the punishments, and the signature of the priest who witnessed the punishment: '6 straps on the buttocks for lies and evasion over a period of 3 months regular incontinence,' '4 straps on the hand for disfiguring books,' '6 straps on the hand for smoking in school.' The sexual offences he described, committed against himself and other children, ranged from 'fondling of genitals' to 'rape'; assaults, he claimed, which were carried out on a regular basis, often in the showers, in full view of other children.

All this took place between 1960 and 1968, when the Salesians ran the school. The school, which is now called Hillside School, was categorised at the time as a 'List-D' approved school, and was managed by Glasgow Education Authority, although there is little evidence so far to suggest that they knew what was going on at the school. What we do know, however, is that in 1959, the United Nations published a resolution; designed to enshrine in international law the way all nations should treat children. This is what the United Nations said:

United Nations Declaration of the Rights of the Child

Proclaimed by General Assembly resolution 1386(XIV) of 20 November 1959

'Whereas the peoples of the United Nations have, in the Charter, reaffirmed their faith in fundamental human rights and in the dignity and worth of the human person, and have determined to promote social progress and better standards of life in larger freedom,

Whereas the United Nations has, in the Universal Declaration of Human Rights, proclaimed that everyone is entitled to all the rights and freedoms set forth therein, without distinction of any kind, such as race, colour, sex, language, religion, political or other opinion, national or social origin, property, birth or other status,

Whereas the child, by reason of his physical and mental immaturity, needs special safeguards and care, including appropriate legal protection, before as well as after birth,

Whereas the need for such special safeguards has been stated in the Geneva Declaration of the Rights of the Child of 1924, and recognized in the Universal Declaration of Human Rights and in the statutes of specialized agencies and international organizations concerned with the welfare of children,

Whereas mankind owes to the child the best it has to give, now therefore, The General Assembly proclaims this Declaration of the Rights of the Child to the end that he may have a happy childhood and enjoy for his own good and for the good of society the rights and freedoms herein set forth, and calls upon parents, upon men and women as individuals, and upon voluntary organizations, local authorities and national Governments to recognize these rights and strive for their observance by legislative and other measures progressively taken in accordance with the following principles:

Principle 1

The child shall enjoy all the rights set forth in this Declaration. Every child, without any exception whatsoever, shall be entitled to these rights, without distinction or discrimination on account of race, colour, sex, language, religion, political or other opinion, national or social origin, property, birth or other status, whether of himself or of his family.

Principle 2

The child shall enjoy special protection, and shall be given opportunities and facilities, by law and by other means, to enable him to develop physically, mentally, morally, spiritually and socially in a healthy and normal manner and in conditions of freedom and dignity. In the enactment of laws for this purpose, the best interests of the child shall be the paramount consideration.

Principle 3

The child shall be entitled from his birth to a name and a nationality.

Principle 4

The child shall enjoy the benefits of social security. He shall be entitled to grow and develop in health; to this end, special care and protection shall be provided both to him and to his mother, including adequate pre-natal and post-natal care. The child shall have the right to adequate nutrition, housing, recreation and medical services.

Principle 5
The child who is physically, mentally or socially handicapped shall be given the special treatment, education and care required by his particular condition.

Principle 6
The child, for the full and harmonious development of his personality, needs love and understanding. He shall, wherever possible, grow up in the care and under the responsibility of his parents, and, in any case, in an atmosphere of affection and of moral and material security; a child of tender years shall not, save in exceptional circumstances, be separated from his mother. Society and the public authorities shall have the duty to extend particular care to children without a family and to those without adequate means of support. Payment of State and other assistance towards the maintenance of children of large families is desirable.

Principle 7
The child is entitled to receive education, which shall be free and compulsory, at least in the elementary stages. He shall be given an education, which will promote his general culture and enable him, on a basis of equal opportunity, to develop his abilities, his individual judgement, and his sense of moral and

social responsibility, and to become a useful member of society. The best interests of the child shall be the guiding principle of those responsible for his education and guidance; that responsibility lies in the first place with his parents. The child shall have full opportunity for play and recreation, which should be directed to the same purposes as education; society and the public authorities shall endeavour to promote the enjoyment of this right.

Principle 8
The child shall in all circumstances be among the first to receive protection and relief.

Principle 9
The child shall be protected against all forms of neglect, cruelty and exploitation. He shall not be the subject of traffic, in any form. The child shall not be admitted to employment before an appropriate minimum age; he shall in no case be caused or permitted to engage in any occupation or employment which would prejudice his health or education, or interfere with his physical, mental or moral development.

Principle 10

The child shall be protected from practices, which may foster racial, religious and any other form of discrimination. He shall be brought up in a spirit of understanding, tolerance, friendship among peoples, peace and universal brotherhood, and in full consciousness that his energy and talents should be devoted to the service of his fellow men.'

Were the Salesians above the law? No, of course not, but who was to challenge them? They believed that they could treat all children in any way they saw fit, using the special 'Salesian method of teaching' to brutalise children into submission, on the pretext that the 'saviour of their souls' was their paramount task, and how they achieved that was not up for discussion, let alone challenge. So, after telling me his story, the survivor asked me if I would help him 'expose' what he and many others like him, had suffered at the hands of the Salesians in that terrible school in Scotland, and to help me, he gave me the names of three of the Salesians who had abused him and his friends at the school, one of who I already knew was a child abuser, as he had been convicted in September 2008:

Priest who molested teenagers caught through Friends Reunited.

A Roman Catholic priest who molested seven teenaged girls was caught more than 30 years later through the Friends Reunited website.

By Richard Savill 5:52PM BST 22 Sep 2008

Two of his victims, one of whom is now a solicitor, and another a professional singer, began talking on the website about their school days and discovered they had both been abused by Fr Peter Carr nearly 40 years ago. Carr denied nine charges of indecently assaulting the six girls. They recalled he would make them strip naked before using a sponge to apply make up to their bodies for annual pantomimes at a Roman Catholic school in Blaisdon, near Gloucester, where he was a teacher.

The two women reported Carr to his Roman Catholic order, the Salesians, who launched an investigation, which led to four other women making similar allegations. Later, a seventh woman came forward independently to report that she had been molested by the priest in similar circumstances at pantomimes five years after the other victims, At Gloucester Crown Court Carr, 73, of Battersea, South West London, was bailed for pre-sentence reports after he admitted two indecent assaults on his final victim between June 1975 and June 1979.

He had already been convicted after a trial last December of indecently assaulting six girls in the late sixties and early seventies. However details of the case could not be reported until now. Carr denied nine charges of indecently assaulting the six girls during pantomime productions at the school.

The jury convicted him of eight of the charges and cleared him of the other. The court heard Carr applied make-up over the girls' bodies while they were naked, and then washed it off. "They were then 11 or 12. They were of an age when they were quite capable of washing themselves," said Ian Dixey, prosecuting. "They found what happened very, very uncomfortable. They were all at a Catholic school and priests were viewed as God's messengers on earth. You simply did not question something you were asked to do by a priest."

Mr Dixey said the offences came to light after two girls made contact through Friends Reunited. "One of the first subjects that came up was Fr Peter Carr," he said. "Both of them felt he had behaved very wrongly towards them."

One of the victims, the professional singer, told the jury she was picked for a leading role in the school production.

"In my twenties Fr Carr became a monster in my mind," she said, "When my marriage broke up at the age of 32, I went to counselling and she told me that it was all down to this." The other woman, a solicitor, said she had always been reluctant to tell anyone about the abuse. "Even now, as old as I am, whatever stopped me telling then, stops me now. My mother thinks I am on a law course, not giving evidence here today."

Original Source: http://www.telegraph.co.uk/news/uknews/3057825/Priest-who-molested-teenagers-caught-through-Friends-Reunited.html

A quick Google check on the Salesians web site

showed me that one of the other named individuals was now dead, but the third was still alive, so I phoned my contact at the MPS Child Abuse Command and asked them for some guidance. They advised that I should inform Police Scotland ASAP: 'This is a child protection issue, and they will want to talk to him.' I phoned Police Scotland and gave them all of the information I had. They then made contact with the victim, and interviewed him. I will tell you more about this in another book.

So, what does the government say about all this? And, more particularly, what does the Secretary of State for Education say about it? Earlier in the year, I had written several times to Michael Gove MP, asking him to investigate the Salesians, and I gave him documents to evidence the seriousness of the situation. He did not respond initially, but one of his officials did, telling me that, while she was 'saddened to hear what had happened to me,' they were not going to investigate, as 'it was too long ago'. What planet were they on? Some of the offences I had told them about pre-dated those of Jimmy Savile, but his offences were certainly not deemed to be 'too long ago'! It was only when I asked my MP, Angela Eagle, to help me, that Gove responded, not to me, but to her – another direct snub by this arrogant, ineffective minister.

Gove made it very clear to Angela that it was not his job to investigate, so that was the end of the matter, as far as he was concerned. So, I wrote to him one last time, not because I thought it would make any difference, but so that the record would show that he had been told about the extent of child abuse at Salesians schools, and, one day, he would be asked to account for his inaction:

3rd June 2013
Mr Michael Gove MP
Department for Education
Sanctuary Buildings
Great Smith Street
London
SW1P 3BT

'Dear Secretary of State,

Police Investigation of child abuse at Salesian Schools in England

Further to my earlier letters to you, and the recent letter to you from my MP Angela Eagle, I can now confirm that on Thursday 30th May, the MPS Child Abuse Command, informed me that their investigation (Operation TORVA) has so far recorded eleven new allegations from seven victims naming eight suspects, with one suspect remaining unknown. The allegations relate to three Salesian Schools: Battersea, Oxford and Farnborough. They have also noted four previously reported cases, relating to six other victims, and they are aware of other cases where the suspects have been charged and convicted. Over the weekend, two further cases were presented to the MPS, who have confirmed that their investigation will continue and is not time limited.

In view of this, and the likelihood that many more victims may still come forward, will you now instigate an investigation yourself into the Salesians to find out how many other cases the Salesians are aware of, going back to the 1950s, and why they moved priests around from school to school whenever an allegation was made, rather than inform the police and protect other children from abuse? It is a gross failure of your department to continually refuse to investigate what was evidently widespread, systematic and tolerated sexual abuse of children in Salesian schools in England, going back many years, with multiple offenders abusing hundreds of children with impunity.

We need to know the full extent of what has occurred in these schools, otherwise, we cannot be sure that they are no longer dangerous to children, and I am looking to you to provide that assurance, based on an independent Investigation, rather than on the 'say so' of the Salesian Order, about who, clearly, there are now very serious concerns. I look forward to hearing from you on this very serious matter.'

Michael Gove MP did not respond. So, there we have it. The three wise monkeys are still at work: 'Malum non audi, non vide, non loquere malus',

Chapter 16
A new nightmare

At the beginning of October 2013, I received a telephone call from a former Salesian priest, who asked me not to name him in any subsequent discussion I might have as a result of what he had to say. I agreed, thinking he was about to tell me something that I probably already knew, but when he started to speak, I felt the dark hand of evil grip my very soul:

'Graham – in your book, Conspiracy of Faith, you say that the priest who interviewed you at Chertsey in 1868, after you had disclosed what was happening to you, was Fr George Williams, who was the Salesian Provincial at the time. I have to tell you that it was not. It was in fact Fr Terence O'Brien, who had been sent by George Williams to speak to you, and silence you.' I asked him how he knew, to which he replied that he had been talking to another Salesian priest, also a former Salesians Provincial, who had said that it was wrong that I should continue to labour under such a falsehood. He felt strongly that the truth should be told, and now it had been, the impact of which took a while to sink in, but when it did, I felt physically sick, yet, at the same time, a kind of calm filled my mind, as the pieces of the puzzle settled into place. Finally, I had the full picture, but there were many questions still to be asked.

A few days later, I emailed the current Salesian

Provincial to explain my concerns: 'Dear Provincial, I received a telephone call earlier this week from a Salesian colleague, informing me that he had recently had a conversation with a 'senior member' of the Salesian Order about me, who had stated that my recollections about Fr George Williams, in my book Conspiracy of Faith, where I talk about the prurient way I was interviewed by a Salesian priest at Chertsey, in February 1968, who I thought was Fr Williams, following my disclosure to Fr Madden and Fr O'Shea, were wrong. It was not, in fact, Fr George Williams who had interviewed me, but Fr Terence O'Brien, who had been sent by Fr Williams to interview me, and instructed to tell me not to tell my parents.

The priest who interviewed me was introduced to me on that day by Fr O'Shea, who described him as 'a specialist in these matters', who had come down from Battersea, but I could not remember his name. It was not until I had the mediation in 2001 that I was told that the priest who had interviewed me would have been Fr George Williams, who was the provincial at the time.

The reason they gave at the mediation was that such a serious matter would have only been dealt with by the provincial. Well, it now turns out that there is some real doubt about that, and I am, as you will appreciate, profoundly distressed at the thought that Fr O'Brien, who the police have recently stated was 'a prolific pedophile', was the priest who interviewed me on that day, and who had asked me all those prurient questions about my sexual thoughts and behaviour, questions which have bothered me ever since, as I could not understand why I was being asked such humiliating and distressing questions, given that I had just disclosed that I was being sexually abused by Hugh Madley.

You will understand that I need to get to the truth of who it was who interviewed me, and why, so I would be grateful if you could investigate your records, and let me know what you discover. I am sure Fr Fox may also have something to say about the matter, as he looked into my case some years ago. I appreciate that Fr Fox is no longer with you, but I'm sure you will know where to contact him. I look forward to hearing from you soon, on this matter and the other matters I wrote to you about recently.'

The Provincial replied a few days later, with more questions than answers: 'Thank you for your email with your request for help in getting to the truth of who interviewed you in 1968. I will ask Fr Mervyn Williams to check our records while he is dealing with your recent subject access request, though I would imagine that what is in our records was part of the processes you mention and therefore already known to you.

You say that your real doubt comes about from having 'received a telephone call earlier this week from a Salesian colleague, informing me that he had recently had a conversation with a 'senior member' of the Salesian Order about me, who had stated that my recollections about Fr George Williams, in my book

Conspiracy of Faith, where I talk about the prurient way I was interviewed by a Salesian priest at Chertsey, in February 1968, who I thought was Fr Williams, following my disclosure to Fr Madden and Fr O'Shea, were wrong.'

If you were able to, it may be helpful to tell me who the 'Salesian colleague' and 'Senior member of the Salesian Order' are, as a starting point for me to try to discover what they remember or know or understand, and thus help you to get towards the truth about who interviewed you.'

A couple of weeks before this bombshell discovery, I had asked the Salesians to re-open the cases of a number of O'Brien's victims, which the Salesians had settled out of court, but the payments they had given the victims was derisory. His response was, as I had expected it to be; totally without compassion: 'As the cases have been settled, it would be considered an unjustifiable expenditure of our charitable resources. I realise that this is not the decision that you want to hear but we have to consider the matter as closed.' The letter ended with a, reprimand: 'For information, I note the reference to Terence O'Brien repeats the often erroneous statement that he operated 'on Salesian school grounds for many years'. He operated from Salesian community property at Battersea, but he was never associated or connected with the school, nor did he ever operate from the school property or grounds.'

The lack of acknowledgment of any responsibility on the part of those who allowed this monster to rape and violate children for many, many years, is another example of the Salesians' abject failure to understand the scale and long-term consequences of child abuse. I replied, even though I knew my words would not change a thing, but at least they would have been be said: 'As for Terence O'Brien, you mention the 'often erroneous statement that he operated 'on Salesian school grounds for many years'. He operated from Salesian community property at Battersea but he was never associated or connected with the school, nor did he ever operate from the school property or grounds.' The distinction you make is of no consequence, given the structure of the Salesian Order, and how priests are sent from one place to another by their Provincial.

To be 'sent to Battersea' could and did mean all sorts of different things at different times, for different Salesians. For example: to work in the Printing Press, to be on the College Teaching Staff, to be a member of the Sacred Heart Parish Clergy, to work in the Provincial Office, to be a student, lodging there, to be a School or University Chaplain, to hold an Office in the Community (Rector, Bursar, Catechist, etc.,), or to work in the Salesian Missions Office. But, what it always meant, for all SDBs, however, was that they were sent there to be a member of the Salesian Community, and to carry out the Salesian work they had been appointed to do, by the Provincial and his Council.

In Fr Terence O'Brien's case, he had rooms in Orbel Street, and was doing what he had been sent to

Battersea to do i.e., to carry on his Salesian work ('St John Bosco's apostolate, caring for young people'), in his case, 'counselling young people'; work which he was to continue to do, uninterrupted, undisturbed, unchallenged, for many, many years. So, to make such a distinction is to attempt to separate the school from the community, and by doing so, presumably to divert the responsibility from successive Salesian Provincials for the failings of the Salesian Order to protect vulnerable children from O'Brien's predatory actions. In reality, there is no such distinction. O'Brien was sent to Battersea by a Salesian Provincial, and he could not have operated as he did without the full support of the Salesian Order.'

As the days went on, the nightmares I had experienced back in 1989, started to reappear, not with quite the same intensity, but enough to make me realise that the discovery that I too may have been a victim of Terence O'Brien, was re-triggering my depression. This time, however, I knew what it was, and, more importantly, I knew how to deal with it; I would take my nightmares to the Salesians. It was time the whole world was able to see for themselves just what the Salesians were really like, evidenced by how they had dealt with, not just my case, but with many others, which, very few people, other than the Salesians and the victims themselves, knew about. My time of being a victim is over; I am a survivor, but, so far, only my account of what had happened was in the public domain. What was needed to expose the complete story was to publish the Salesian's internal account, which they had never shared with me, but first I had to prize it out of them, which is why I had earlier sent them a Subject Access Request, asking for a copy of every record they had about me. I would like to have been a fly on the wall when that request landed on the Salesians' doormat, as they must have been dreading the day I might exercise my right to see what they had said about me behind closed doors. But, to be fair to them, they responded with good grace, saying that they would be 'pleased to respond' to my request, but it would take them a little time to collect and collate all of the records from their archives, which told me that there must be a lot of documents! The wait was almost unbearable, but, on Tuesday 14th January, 'Pandora's box' was delivered to the Lantern Project by a chirpy-faced DHL courier. I think it's fair to say that most people have heard of Pandora's box, and, like me, understood it to have contained all the evils of the world. Well, in fact, Pandora's box was not a box, it was actually a jar, but it did contain all the evils of the world. However, it also contained something else, the Spirit of Hope, which remained in the jar when Pandora opened it, and all the evil spirits escaped. Inside my Pandora's box were letters, documents, reports, hand written notes, internal memos, faxes and e-mails – everything that had been written about me by the Salesians, and their lawyers, as they tried to defend their reputation, limit the possibility of wider scrutiny, and paint me in the worst possible light.

In all, the box contained some 2,000 pages, covering a period from September 8th, 1999 to December 20th, 2013 - 14 years of constant struggle by me, against one of the largest Catholic Orders in the world. Hardly a fair fight, but one I was never going to give up on, because there can be no peace until the truth is exposed. I have included some examples at the end of this book, which demonstrate the mind-set of the Salesians, as they struggled to deal with their failure to protect me from abuse, and their incompetence in supporting me, when I reached out to them for help. Let us not forget that, despite the size of the Salesian Order, they are not a Church, they are not a nation state – they are just a group of Catholic priests who run schools!

Here is one example of the secrets contained in my Pandora's box, which, as you can see, when I challenged the Salesians about it, they try their best to minimise the issue, as they have done on every issue involving my case, for the past 14 years. This is simply unacceptable, and will be challenged further:

05 February 2014
Subject: Hugh Madley

Dear SDB I have discovered in the documents you sent me recently that, on 16th August 2000, you were advised that Wandsworth Personnel Department had received an anonymous telephone call about Hugh Madley, alleging that 'his activities were continuing – that he was coming into school and taking boys away. The local police will be in touch.' This advice was in a letter from the Headmaster at Battersea.

Subsequently, Fr John Gilheney sent you a note saying: 'The discussion changed as to how Wandsworth should respond to the telephone call, and the new slant it gave to the investigation that had ben suspended by the Surrey team. It was felt that this could develop into a 'major investigation'. They used the phrase "a text book case".' This information came from a Police and Wandsworth Child Protection Team meeting, on 18th September 2000, at which Fr John Gilheney was present.

Apart from the obvious, this also raises the question of the position SDB adopted at the mediation with me the following year, on 12th February 2001, at which you (SDB) maintained that you had no knowledge of any issues relating to child abuse and Hugh Madley, other than those I had raised in my complaint to Surrey police. John Gilheney was very instant about this, and, indeed, you used this same 'lack of knowledge' in you original opposition to my conspiracy charge in my book, Conspiracy of Faith. Well, on the face of it - it looks very much as if I was right! You held back from me at the mediation this vital piece of information, which would have resulted in a very different outcome, had I known of its existence at the time. Could you consider these issues, please, and let me your thoughts on the matter.

With best wishes, Graham Wilmer MBE

15th February 2014

Dear Graham

I am now in a position to reply properly to your email
of February 5th and apologise for the delay in doing so.
I will respond firstly to your view that at mediation in
February 2001 the Salesians stated that they had 'no
knowledge of any issues relating to child abuse and Hugh
Madley, other than those I had raised in my complaint
to Surrey police' and that this position was untrue. Your
reason for saying this is the documentation you refer to
in your email from August and September 2000, with
particular reference to an anonymous 'phone call.

For clarity I will respond in point form:

1.   Hugh Madley had retired from the staff of the
Salesian College in Battersea in August 1999. In section
4.1 of the official minutes of the First Strategy Meeting
convened by Surrey County Council Social Services
on March 3rd 2000 it is recorded that Hugh Madley's
personnel file held at the College in Battersea covering
his time at the school contained no allegations against
him.

2.   Section 5.6 of the same minutes states that the
headteachers of both the Salesian School in Chertsey
and the Salesian College in Battersea would be asked
if any children had made any allegations against Hugh
Madley or if he was in current contact with any children.

Neither headteacher reported allegations of abuse in response to these enquiries.

3.   In section 2.1 of the minutes of the Second Strategy Meeting of May 25th 2000 it is recorded that at police interview Hugh Madley denied the allegations of Graham Wilmer. The same section of the minutes also states that 'The police have received no other allegations'

4.   Section 2.4 of the same minutes of the Second Strategy Meeting confirmed that, in relation to Salesian College, Battersea, 'No allegations were made against Mr Madley to the school whilst he was a member of staff'. But the minutes state that names were given to the police 'of 4 young men now ex-pupils with whom Mr Madley had close contact whilst he was at school and maintained contact with once they had left'. The police did not later report any allegations against Hugh Madley from these four young men. It was agreed that Hugh Madley would be asked not to visit the school again.

5.   Section 3.1 of the minutes of the Third Strategy Meeting of July 14th 2000 records the Police Child Protection Team as stating that 'Graham Wilmer's friend could not provide corroborative evidence to support his allegation' against Hugh Madley from his time as a pupil at Chertsey.

6.   Section 3.6 of the same minutes of the Third Strategy Meeting deals at some length with the 4 young men named at the May 25th meeting. No evidence or allegations of abuse by Hugh Madley had emerged in relation to these or any other past pupils of Salesian

College, Battersea.

7.   Section 3.12 of the same minutes of the Third Strategy Meeting records that there had been no allegations from the staff of Salesian College, Battersea, in relation to Hugh Madley. Staff will have accompanied Hugh Madley on residential school trips (though probably not on any unofficial trips).

8.   Section 5.1 of the minutes of the Third Strategy Meeting states that 'Investigation has now been completed and as no further allegations have come to light, no further action to be taken'. But section 5.7 records that Hugh Madley will not be allowed on the site of the Salesian College, Battersea, again.

9.   On August 8th 2000 Stephen McCann the headteacher of the Salesian College, Battersea, wrote to Fr John Gilheney to state that 'about two weeks ago Wandsworth Personnel (Glenys Lawrence in fact) received an anonymous phone call re H.M. No names of pupils were given, but it was alleged that his activities were continuing – that he was coming into school and that he was taking boys away. The local police may be in touch in September'.

10. At a meeting with the police and Wandsworth's child protection teams on September 18th 2000, with Glenys Lawrence present, the minutes state the following in relation to the anonymous 'phone call: 'The call came from a lady who called herself a friend of a mother of a pupil at the school. It was alleged that HM took pupils of the school away – with parents' permission, gave them

sums of money, visited them in their homes and invited them to his house. (the age of these pupils was in the 14-16 year bracket)'. The minutes then say 'This call and its implications need to be followed up'. The minutes also record that towards the end of the meeting discussion considered 'how Wandsworth should respond to the telephone call and the new slant it gave to the investigation that had been suspended by the Surrey team. It was felt that this could develop into a major investigation. They used the phrase 'a text book case' but there is no record that any further investigation prompted by the 'phone call produced any evidence or allegations of abuse by Hugh Madley of Salesian College, Battersea, pupils or anyone else.

You suggest that the events summarised in points 9 and 10 above mean that the Salesians made a false statement at the mediation of February 2001 that they had 'no knowledge of any issues relating to child abuse and Hugh Madley, other than those I had raised in my complaint to Surrey police'. But the anonymous phone call made no allegation that Hugh Madley was abusing anyone. The allegations in that call were that he went into school, took pupils away with parental permission, gave then money, visited them in their homes and invited them to his. This in itself is not evidence that abuse was taking place. In summary none of the investigations or unfolding events that I have summarised in points 1 to 10 above provided any evidence that Hugh Madley had actually abused any Battersea Salesian College pupil, or anyone else, after his time at the Salesian College at Chertsey and the Salesians would have been perfectly in order to say this at the 2001 mediation.

Best wishes - SDB

This response from the Salesians is a typical example of the unchanged mindset that lies behind the lack of progress made by the Catholic Church and Catholic religious orders, 13 years after the Nolan Report was published. The report was commissioned by the English Catholic Church in 2000 to investigate sexual abuse in the Church, and make recommendations to prevent abuse happening again in the future. It also made recommendations on how to support the victims of past abuse by clergy, but little, if any, real progress has been made by the Church and religious orders, in the way they behave towards victims and survivors of clergy abuse. The Salesian order is, of course, not alone in its defiant defence of its 'good name' at all costs. The Benedictine order operates in exactly the same way, as indeed does the English Catholic Church itself, when challenged by victims. Richard Scorer's brilliant new book, 'Betrayed – The English Catholic Church and the sex abuse crisis' contains many more examples of the failures of the Church and religious orders in the way they have tried to distance themselves from scrutiny by covering up abuse and denying victims a voice. In his conclusion, Richard argues that there is now some hope, under Pope Francis, that the Catholic Church 'may yet become a place of safety for children'. He is right in as much as, while there is hope, everything is possible. But it will take more than hope to bring about the massive changes to the mindset of the Churches and religious orders, if we are to bring about lasting reform to such inward looking organisations. However, it would be wrong to give up on the spirit hope, which exists in many forms. The Spirit of Hope in my Pandora's box, for example, comes from finally being able to see the complete story in my case. The threats Madley placed on me when I was a child and the methods used by the Salesians to keep me quiet can harm me no longer, and I am now able to move forward as master of my past rather than its servant. So, I will finish this part of my story here but, in spite of all I have said, it would be wrong of me to leave you with the notion that all priests are evil men. They are not. However, to all those priests, be they Catholic priests, Methodist priests, Anglican priests, or priests from any other religious order, who have harmed children, or adults for that matter, I say this to you: If you thought your crimes would go undetected and unchallenged, you are very much mistaken. Your work is not the work of God. You are not 'good men of the cloth', you are corrupted, dysfunctional, amoral men in black, and I will continue to expose you, for my work is not yet finished. I am not just playing Devil's advocate; I am the Devil's advocate.

The End.

356

Sit ex se loquatur.
let the evidence speak for itself.

To put the evidence into context – here is what Lord Nolan said about the way victims of child abuse by clergy should be treated:

Extract from Chapter 3, Nolan Review – Final Report 2001

'Recommendation 69. It is important to treat current allegations about abuse that took place some years ago ('historical allegations') in exactly the same way as allegations of current abuse.

Recommendation 70. Bishops and religious superiors should ensure that any cases which were known of in the past but not acted on satisfactorily ('historic cases') should be the subject of review as soon as possible, reported to the statutory authorities wherever appropriate, and that there is appropriate follow-up action including possibly regular continuing assessment.

Support for the victim

3.5.22 A number of the responses to our consultation have suggested that the Church could and must do more, following an allegation of abuse, to give support to the victim and his/her family. Clearly an event of abuse or a decision to disclose one is a very difficult time for victims and their families. We have no doubt, having regard to the Church's mission, that it should provide all available help.

3.5.23 We believe the most helpful approach would be to make a 'support person' available to those who have, or may have, suffered abuse and their families. Such a person would be, first and foremost, a focal point for the victim and his/her family to turn to for help and advice. They could assist those wishing to make a complaint, facilitate them in gaining access to information and other more specialised help, and represent their concerns on an ongoing basis. (The family liaison officers now being developed and used by the Metropolitan Police may be a helpful parallel.) They must, above all, be acceptable to the victim and his/her family while also, once appointed, being completely independent of the CPC and his/her Team. It may be that they would often not be called on (because victims may well prefer to turn to others outside the Church to take on this role). Nonetheless, it seems desirable that such a person should be available if wanted and we so recommend. The CPC should be responsible for ensuring that they are available, and for appropriate training.

3.5.24 One further and substantial point has been made

to us about support. The need for victims/survivors to be given support may last for very many years and is not simply something for the weeks or months after disclosure. We agree with this and believe the Church should do whatever it can to support and foster the development of support services to meet the needs, including the spiritual needs, of survivors and their families. The National Unit should compile and maintain a database of such services.

Recommendation 71. A 'support person' should be available to those who have, or may have, suffered abuse and their families, to assist them in making a complaint, to facilitate them in gaining access to information and other more specialised help, and to represent their concerns on an ongoing basis.

Recommendation 72. Support may continue to be needed long after the allegation has been dealt with. The Church should do whatever it can to support and foster the development of support services to meet the needs, including the spiritual needs, of survivors and their families. The National Unit should compile and maintain a database of such services.'

Now compare those recommendations to way I and other victims have been dealt with the Catholic Church:

PRESS STATEMENT by the Salesians of Don Bosco.

January 2007

'Conspiracy of Faith' by Graham Wilmer.

The Salesians of Don Bosco became aware in 1999 of Mr Wilmer's allegations of indecent assault by a teacher in one of their schools in the 1960s. The alleged offender, who denied the allegations at that time, was a layman and not a priest or member of the Order. Some 30 years later, in 1999 there was no recollection or remembrance of the allegations among the surviving Salesians who taught at the school at the time, and the police could find no supporting evidence. Nevertheless, in the light of Mr Wilmer's clear distress, the Salesians of Don Bosco offered him support and assistance following current guidelines and legal advice at all times, and this support and assistance was accepted by him. The offender's admission of his guilt came much later, in April 2004.

None of the events about which Mr Wilmer made allegations took place on the teaching premises of the School or in circumstances which the School could have prevented in advance, and accordingly neither the Salesians nor the Catholic Church were in any way responsible for the actions of the alleged offender in Mr Wilmer's case. The way the matter was handled in 1968, when it came to the attention of the School, would now be regarded as seriously inadequate in the light of current knowledge and standards. The Salesians regret that Mr Wilmer did not receive appropriate support at the time.

Despite the absence of independent corroboration, and whatever Mr Wilmer may now allege, in 2001 the Salesians treated Mr Wilmer's account as truthful, fully recognised their earlier shortcomings and fully compensated Mr Wilmer for any claim he might have been able to advance. Any suggestion that in so doing the Salesians were guilty of some sort of conspiracy against Mr Wilmer is totally false.'

Memo to Salesian Provincial
From Graham Wilmer - 15 October 2007
SUBJECT: Moving Towards Closure

'Dear Michael - I am looking forward to seeing you again on the 18th, here in Wallasey, and I said last week that I would write you a briefing note for you to consider before we met, so here it is! I have thought about where we are now in relation to where we were before Seamus appeared in the equation, and what needs to be done to reach a point that we can all accept as closure. We are, in reality, much closer towards that point than may, at first, appear, so I thought I would try and summarise my position.

1. Firstly, let me deal with the 'conspiracy', given what we know now, that we did not know when I met with Mervyn and SDB's lawyers in London on 28th July 2006,

to discuss the manuscript of my book, Conspiracy of Faith.

1.1. Up until this time (28 July 2007), the position over whether SDB had, from our dealings in 1999 onwards, deliberately kept silent over what they knew about what I had disclosed in 1968, was an issue over which we were fundamentally divided; my position being that I had disclosed to Fr Madden on Wednesday 21st February 1968. I know this because Martin Allen died on Monday 19th February. His father Dr Michael Allen phoned me at home on Tuesday evening 20th February, to ask me if I would serve on the Altar at Martin's funeral Mass, which was held at St Joseph's in New Malden on Friday 23rd February, giving me only two days to make my confession to Fr Madden, so as to be free from mortal sin (as I thought at the time), so I could take Communion at the funeral mass, which I did, Fr O'Shea spoke to me the morning after my disclosure, Wednesday 22nd February, and I was interviewed by Fr Williams the same morning. In April 2004, having originally denied (on the advice of his NASUWT lawyer) that he had abused me, Madley informed me that, in fact, had also disclosed to Fr Gaffney some time after the 25 February, and then repeated his admission to Fr Williams on 18 June 1968, at Fr Gaffney's funeral, when he was offered the job at Battersea. As a consequence, I did not believe that the Order 'knew nothing about the matter', which was the position offered by SDB's Solicitors, following the so-called 'thorough investigation' carried out prior to the mediation in February 2001.

1.2. On 18 August 2007,I was presented with the bundle of documents prepared by the CICA Appeals panel, at a hearing in London, at which I represented myself. In this bundle was a copy the witness statement given by Fr O'Shea to WPC Sarah Harris from surrey police on 27 March 2000, in which he made his now famous remark "....if any such allegation had been made, I would have remembered." This document had not been seen by SDB when they carried out their 'thorough investigation'. Instead, they relied on Fr O'Shea's subsequent verbal version of what he told the police, which was that, he simply 'could not remember'. The difference between the two statements, one written, one spoken, is pivotal to understanding why the conspiracy, at that moment, exposed itself for what it really was – a conspiracy of silence; not between SDB as a whole, and me, but between Fr O'Shea, in support of Fr Williams, both of whom were determined at all costs to deny what they had also kept from the Provincial Council in 1968, and subsequently from Fr Eddie Fox, when he became Provincial after Fr Williams.

1.3. It was not until I met with you, Michael, in March 2007, that the significance of Fr O'Shea's words and the new revelations about Fr Williams, became clear, and the true nature of the conspiracy emerged, which was why I was able to write to you after that meeting and tell you that I was now settled in my mind that the Order itself had not conspired against me, the reason being that Fr O'Shea and Fr Williams had never told anyone, within the Order, still alive, what had happened, and, therefore, the Order could not have known, unless you had interviewed Madley in the 'thorough investigation' in 2000, which you did not. The fact that you did not interview him then was not a deliberate attempt to hide the truth, as I had originally thought, rather it was seen as unnecessary by SDB's Solicitors, given the voracity of Fr O'Shea's denials, which they took at face value. You, the Order and SDB's Solicitors were not in a position, then, to know that there lay a deeper secret, involving Fr Williams.

1.4. So, to summarise on this first point: I am totally satisfied that the Order (in what ever form others wish to construct it') did not know what had happened, for the reasons explained, and, as a consequence, the Order did not conspire against me from 1999 onwards. However, I am fully satisfied, given what we know now, that Fr Williams and Fr O'Shea remained silent, deliberately, but, or course, they were not 'the Order', merely retired Salesian priests. Therefore, I intend to explain this fully in the forthcoming second edition of my book, which will expunge any suggestion that the conspiracy begun by Fr Williams, continued through the years as a matter of policy within the Salesian Order in the UK, when dealing with allegations of child sexual abuse. I will, however, make it quite clear that the real culprits in my case were Williams and O'Shea, both of whom had the opportunity to do the right thing, but chose not to, Williams because he was an incompetent, and O'Shea because he was a weak man; his refusal to respond to the letters I wrote to him in 2004 being the evidence upon which I will base my case about him.

2. Secondly, the current issues about Fr Williams being considered by Steve Landy and his CP team are part of a process that has to run its course to allow a fair judgment to be made. I, for my part, have done what I was advised to do by Surrey police and others, and am happy that the process is fully engaged. Obviously, I will have a view on the outcome, whatever it may be, which will also be included in my new book, but, for now, there is no further involvement required from me. I have, as you know, put a number of questions to Steve, and he has agreed to seek further guidance from you and others, including COPCA, before he responds to me, all of which I see as part of the overall investigation. In the past few days, I have received messages from a former Chertsey pupil, who left in 1951, who has given a graphic account of the sexual abuse he suffered from Fr Bamber, who was subsequently moved to Battersea, and then back to Chertsey, while I was there. The account contains details which cause me considerable distress, as they describe things Fr Bamber used to do to me when I was

12. It appears that, for some reason, Fr Bamber did not progress with me beyond holding me in a bear hug from behind, pressing his body into me and rubbing his rough face against the back of my neck, a grooming technique X also describes, which, in his case, then progressed to sexual abuse over a prolonged period. Fr Bamber, or course, also appears in the list Seamus submitted to me, as being one of the priests other boys have disclosed sexual abuse about, and, given the cases about to be heard in the LA Supreme Court, set for trial on November 5th, involving Salesians Fr William Schafer and Father Nicholas Reina, I have asked Steve Landy to look at my case, not in isolation, but one of many that have now emerged (earlier hearings last year saw 12 Salesian priests/clerics named in lawsuits in San Fransico Bay Area, involving the Salesian High school in Richmond - Fr Steve Whelan, Fr Bernard Dabbene, Bro Sal Billante, Fr Richard Presenti, Bro Ernie Martinez, Fr Jim Miani, Fr Al Menon, Mr sam vitone, Fr Harold Danielson, Fr Larry Lorenzoni and Bro Dan Pachesco, two of whom have also been convicted. What I want to know from Mr Landy, and from you, of course, is to what extent were cases of sexual abuse known about within the Order, not just here in the British Province, but in Australia and the US, and how were they dealt with. I have been told by the solicitor acting for a female pupil at Battersea, that an 'hush' agreement was offered to her for the abuse she alleges too place at the hands of Fr O'Brien at Battersea, during his famous 'counseling' sessions.

3. Finally, there are some other details that need to be addressed, which can be done over time, rather than at one and the same time, that I want to achieve by way of bringing closure to my case. I will deal briefly with these now, but we can expand on them over time as necessary.

3.1. The 'Agreement'. As you know, the agreement I signed, after the initial mediation in February 2001, has always been a bone of contention for me, following the revelations that came with Madley's admission in April 2004 and the subsequent police interviews and legal arguments that took place in August and December of 2005 at Guildford Crown Court. The Order has not sought to enforce the technical breaches of the agreement that I have made in my pursuit of justice since then, yet the agreement still stands, and remains a festering sore because of its very existence. Therefore, a part of the instruments that will bring closure, I want the agreement to be withdrawn.

3.2, The CICA damages award. The CICA are about to reconvene the appeals panel to review my case, following their consideration of the psychiatric assessment I underwent in May of this year. As you know, in August of last year, the appeals panel awarded me £18,000 for the offences Madley committed against me, but then deducted the £20,000 the Order gave me in February 2001, on the basis that, despite what Mervyn Williams had said to the panel about the payment not being related to Madley's offences, but rather as compensation for the Order's failure to support me after the offences were brought to their attention in February 1968, the panel did not accept that argument, the consequence of which being that I was £18,000 worse off. Therefore, once the panel has made its final decision, which should be within the next few weeks, I will expect the Order to rectify the situation by either persuading the CICA appeals panel to pay me the £18,000 they originally calculated, in accordance with the CICA scheme tariff (this would require a legal argument submitted by Solicitors on behalf of the Order), or make me a personal award of the same amount, which would be over and above the £40,000 donation to the Lantern Project already agreed. Otherwise, it means in reality that the £40,000 donation has a real value of only £22,000, which was not what the Provincial Council had intended when it made the grant.

3.3. Recognition of our healing journey: In recognition of the healing journey we have almost completed, I would like Michael to publish something in the Salesian magazine, Don Bosco Today, which removes the PNG tag which I currently carry, particularly at Salesian College Chertsey, who continue to keep my name out of their past pupils register. I would like Michael's statement to talk about the second edition of the book, in which he will make a significant contribution, and, once the book

has been published, I would it reviewed in the magazine, and in the wider media through a press statement. Such a statement should also carry a message of apology from the Rector Major, addressed to all children who have suffered sexual abuse at the
hands of Salesians.

4. Overall summary: I am relaxed about the timing of these items, but I am confident that by agreeing to the above, we will have achieved a lasting closure that others will judge to be fair and acceptable, which is just as important to reaching a closure that you and I feel is fair and acceptable!

With all best wishes
Graham'

The Salesians' response to these requests was a simple 'no, we can't do any of that.' Whatever their reasons, they had turned down the opportunity to work with me, not just to resolve my case, but to help other victims, and to show leadership in the way victims should be treated in the future. Their decision would inevitably ensure that I would continue to dig away at their foundations for a long time to come, as is evidenced in the memo they issued on 15th January 2012, in response to an article about me in the Times Educational Supplement.

'TES Article by Francis Beckett 'Gove must act to clean up the Church' including G Wilmer's allegations against Salesians (Jan 13th 2012)

The attached article by Francis Beckett (who has written hostile articles before) appeared in the January 13th 2012 edition of the Times Educational Supplement. The article includes the following: Graham Wilmer, who founded the Lantern Project to support adult victims of childhood sexual abuse, wants the government to set up a truth and reconciliation commission.....Mr Wilmer's only real hope of getting his commission is the government and he has written to education secretory Michael Gove. He has also asked Mr Gove to investigate schools run by the Salesian order of priests. "We have about 60 cases of abuse in Salesian schools and we have instituted two police inquiries. There ore six state-subsidised Salesian schools in the country," he says.

This and other comments in the article about his own abuse by Hugh Madley at Chertsey are typical Graham Wilmer - slanted and misleading. He has previously said that he has written to Mr Gove so I do not think this is a recent action and I do not think we need worry that Michael Gove will get involved. This is Graham Wilmer seeking to present himself as having a high profile - as is his comment about having instituted 'two police inquiries'. This means that on two occasions he reported allegations to the police, something we also do as a matter of policy.

On the matter of '60 cases of abuse in Salesian schools, from our records, as far as I can ascertain, the facts are as attached - we have received 24 school related allegations covering the 1940s to the 1970s involving 11 Salesians (20 allegations) and three lay teachers (4 allegations). We have not received any allegations relating to school incidents occurring after the 1970s. Other than for Peter Carr all are unsubstantiated allegations without any corroborating evidence. Graham Wilmer may have information about other school allegations (but hardly 40 more!) in which case he should report them to the police. We do not have 'six state-subsidised schools'. We are the trustees of two voluntary aided schools (Bootle and Bolton) and joint trustees of one other voluntary aided school (the new school in Battersea).

The TES article may not get noticed and the 'Salesians' are not really news, but I would suggest that our safeguarding representative email our secondary head teachers [including Farnborough (independent) and Chertsey (diocesan trusteeship)l to alert them to the article and say that any media enquiry they might receive should be referred to you as our spokesperson on safeguarding matters.

Possible text for this email: Dear.......The January 13th 2012 edition of the Times Educational Supplement in its comment section on pages 52/53 contained the attached article about abuse in Catholic schools. lts references to the Salesians and Salesian schools are erroneous and seriously misleading. lf you should receive any inquiries in relation to the article from the media or from local or national press please refer them to our press spokesperson.'

United Nations Convention on the Rights of the Child Committee on the Rights of the Child - CRC/C/OPSC/VAT/CO/1

Distribution: General 31 January 2014 Original: English
ADVANCE UNEDITED VERSION

Concluding observations on the report submitted by the Holy See under article 12, paragraph 1, of the Optional Protocol to the Convention on the Rights of the Child on the sale of children, child prostitution and child pornography*

1. The Committee considered the initial report of the Holy See (CRC/C/OPSC/VAT/1) at its 1853th meeting (see CRC/C/SR 1853) held on16 January 2014, and adopted at its 1875th meeting, held on 31 January 2014, the following concluding observations.
I. Introduction

2. The Committee welcomes the submission of the Holy See's initial report and its written replies to the list of issues (CRC/C/OPSC/VAT/Q/1/Add.1). The Committee however regrets that the report was submitted with a 6 year-delay and that the Holy See did not respond to questions relating to the implementation of the Optional Protocol by persons and institutions placed under its legal authority. The Committee welcomes the dialogue with the multisectoral delegation of the Holy See.

3. While fully aware that bishops and major superiors of religious institutes do not act as representatives or delegates of the Roman Pontiff, the Committee notes that subordinates in Catholic religious orders are bound by obedience of the Pope in accordance to Canons 331 and 590. The Committee therefore reminds the Holy See that by ratifying the Optional Protocol, it has committed itself to implementing it not only on the territory of the Vatican City State but also as the supreme power of the Catholic Church through individuals and institutions placed under its supreme authority.

4. The Committee reminds the Holy See that these concluding observations should be read in conjunction with its concluding observations on the Holy See's second periodic report under the Convention on the Rights of the Child (CRC/C/VAT/CO/2) and on the initial report under the Optional Protocol on the involvement of children in armed conflict, both adopted on 31 January

2014 (CRC/C/OPAC/VAT/CO/1).

II. General observations Positive aspects

5. The Committee welcomes the measures taken by the Holy See in areas relevant to the implementation of the Optional Protocol, including:

(a) The Vatican City State laws No. VIII on Complementary Norms on Penal Matters, Title II: Crimes Against Children and No. IX containing amendments to the Criminal Code and the Criminal Procedure Code and issued Motu Propio by the Roman Pontiff, on 11 July 2013;

(b) The creation of a pastoral Commission for the Protection of Minors, with the aim of proposing new initiatives for the development of safe environment programs for children and improving efforts for the pastoral care for victims of abuse around the world, on 5 December 2013; and

(c) The establishment within the Governorate of Vatican City State of a special Office to oversee the implementation of international agreements to which the Vatican is a party on 10 August 2013.

6. The Committee further notes with appreciation the ratification of the United Nations Convention against Transnational Organized Crime on 25 January 2012.

III. Data

7. The Committee is concerned that the Holy See did not provide the data requested by the Committee on cases of sale of children, child prostitution and child pornography dealt with by the Holy See over the reporting period and by the Congregation for the Doctrine of the Faith (CDF) since 2001. The Committee is also concerned that the Holy See has not established a comprehensive data collection system to enable the recording, referral and follow-up of all cases covered by the Optional Protocol and to analyse and assess progress in the implementation of the Optional Protocol.

8. The Committee recommends that the Holy See develop and implement a comprehensive and systematic mechanism of data collection, analysis, monitoring and impact assessment on all the areas covered by the Protocol. The data should be disaggregated, inter alia, by sex, age, national and ethnic origin, geographical location, indigenous status and socio-economic status, with particular attention to children in the most vulnerable situations, and include information about the follow-up given to these cases. Until such a data collection system is established and effectively used for information sharing with States where offences are committed, the Committee urges the Holy See to ensure full and immediate disclosure of all the information on cases of sale of children, child prostitution and child pornography gathered by the Holy See and the CDF since 2001 to competent national judicial authorities for

appropriate follow-up.

IV. General measures of implementation General principles of the Convention on the Rights of the Child (arts. 2, 3, 6 and 12)

9. The Committee is concerned that in dealing with cases of child pornography committed by members of the clergy, the Holy See has failed to ensure children's right to express their views and have them given due weight, and that the Holy See has given precedence to the preservation of the reputation of the church over children's rights to have their best interests taken as a primary consideration. The Committee is concerned that in doing so, the Holy See has undermined the prevention of offences under the Optional Protocol and the capacity of child victims to report them and therefore contributed to the impunity of the perpetrators and created further trauma for child victims of offences.

10. The Committee reminds the Holy See of its obligation under article 8 1) (b) and (c) and 3) of the Protocol and recommends that the Holy See take all necessary measures to ensure that the rights of child victims of sale, prostitution and pornography to express their views and to have their best interests taken as a primary consideration are protected and respected.

Legislation

11. While welcoming the adoption of Vatican City State laws No. VIII and IX on 11 July 2013 which penalize

offences under the Optional Protocol, the Committee is concerned that the application of these laws is restricted to the territory of the Vatican City State and therefore do not apply to all individuals and institutions placed under the supreme authority of the Holy See. The Committee is also concerned that the Holy See has still not amended and continues to apply Canon Law provisions which breach the Optional Protocol as regards notably the legal definition of these offences as crimes and the procedure to address them.

12. The Committee urges the Holy See to bring all its norms and regulations, including Canon Law in line with the Optional Protocol and ensure that the same laws apply to the Vatican City State and to individuals and institutions placed under its supreme authority. The Committee also urges the Holy See to amend without delay all Canon Law provisions which contradict the Protocol and in particular the 1962 Crimen Sollicitationis and Sacramentorum Sanctitatis tutela of 2011.
Coordination and evaluation

13. The Committee is concerned that the Holy See does not have a coordinative body providing leadership and effective general oversight for the monitoring and evaluation of activities under the Optional Protocol.
14. The Committee recommends that the Holy See create a coordinative body capable of monitoring and evaluating activities for the implementation of the

Optional Protocol.

Dissemination and awareness-raising

15. While welcoming the publication and distribution to educators of materials on children's rights and the Optional Protocol by Catholic specialized institutions, the Committee is concerned that similar measures have not been taken by the Holy See to raise awareness about the Protocol to children, their families and the public at large and in particular to inform children on how to protect themselves and to report these offences.

16. The Committee recommends that the Holy See makes full use of its moral authority and adopt a comprehensive approach for the Optional Protocol to become widely known to the public at large, including to children, their families and communities, and to this aim develop, in close cooperation with civil society organizations, the media, the private sector, communities and children themselves, awareness-raising programmes, including campaigns, on all issues covered by the Optional Protocol. The Holy See should also ensure that individuals and institutions working under its authority worldwide, including Catholic schools, play an active roll in this regard, including in translating the Optional Protocol into local languages of the countries and in disseminating it in child-friendly formats.

Training

17. The Committee notes as positive the programmes developed by Catholic institutions at national level, such as the Catholic Pastoral Awareness Programme developed in Kenya to train teachers of Catholics Schools to detect and address situations of children at risk of abuse and exploitation. The Committee is however concerned that the Holy See has not developed similar programmes and disseminated them to all individuals and institutions placed under its authority but continues to refer exclusively to the 2011 Circular Letter to assist episcopal conferences in developing guidelines for dealing with cases of sexual abuse of minors perpetrated by clerics, which has revealed inefficient in protecting children and in providing individuals and institutions with appropriate guidance on how to deal with these offences.

18. The Committee urges the Holy See to provide appropriate guidelines and training material on the prevention, detection and appropriate handling of offences under the Protocol to all individuals and institutions placed under its authority. The Holy See should ensure that teachers and personnel of Catholic schools and institutions systematically receive this training and earmark the necessary resources to conduct such training.

Allocation of resources

19. The Committee is concerned that the Holy See has not allocated a budget for the development and implementation of programmes aimed at preventing offences under the Optional Protocol, protecting children and providing child victims of offences committed by individuals placed under its authority with physical and psychological recovery and social integration. The Committee is also concerned that the Holy See has no specific allocation for promotional activities of the Optional Protocol at the international level.

20. The Committee recommends that the Holy See accord high priority to allocating sufficient human, technical and financial resources for the development and implementation of programmes aimed at the prevention, protection, and rehabilitation of victims.

V. Prevention of the sale of children, child prostitution and child pornography (art. 9, papas. 1 and 2)

Measures adopted to prevent offences prohibited under the Protocol

21. The Committee welcomes the various initiatives developed by Catholic congregations and organisations around the world to support children in vulnerable situations and the indication that the Holy See employs

its moral leadership worldwide to address contributing factors of offences under the Optional Protocol. The Committee is however concerned the Holy See has not applied a similar approach to individuals placed under its authority and has not taken timely appropriate measures to prevent priests and nuns from committing offences under the Optional Protocol. The Committee is particularly concerned about cases of priests producing, possessing and diffusing child pornography who have knowingly been kept in contact with children.

22. The Committee urges the Holy See to ensure the immediate removal of all priests suspected of child pornography and other crimes under the Optional Protocol and adopt without delay regulations, guidelines and mechanisms to effectively prevent children from becoming victims of offences under the Protocol. The Committee urges the Holy See to ensure that the Pastoral Commission for the Protection of Minors created in December 2013 undertake a comprehensive assessment of policies and practices applied by the Holy See to cases of child pornography committed by individuals placed under its authority and ensure that the outcome of this assessment be made public and accessible, especially to the victims.

Sale of children / Adoption

23. The Committee expresses deep concern about the discovery in 2011 that thousands of babies had been removed from their mothers in maternity wards in Spain and sold by networks of doctors, priests and nuns to childless couples who were considered as more appropriate parents. The Committee is also concerned that similar practices were also carried out in other countries such as in Ireland where girls detained in the Ireland Magdalene laundries had their babies systematically taken away from them.

24. The Committee urges the Holy See to ensure that individuals and institutions placed under its authority who have organized, participated and assisted in the removal of babies from their mothers and their transfer for remuneration or any consideration to childless couples, individuals or institutions be held accountable. The Committee urges the Holy See to ensure a full disclosure of all information gathered by the institutions and individuals involved in these offences in order to facilitate victims' access to information on their biological filiation.

25. The Committee is concerned that although many Catholic institutions and organizations are involved in inter-country adoptions, the Holy See has not taken the necessary measures to ensure that Catholic institutions do not engage in unlawful adoption.

26. In light of article 5 of the Optional Protocol, the Committee urges the Holy See to adopt as a matter of priority appropriate legal and administrative measures to ensure that all individuals and institutions under its authority that are involved in the adoption of a child, act in conformity with applicable international legal instruments. The Committee recommends that the Holy See consider ratifying the 1993 Hague Convention on Protection of Children and Cooperation in Respect of Intercountry Adoption.

VI. Prohibition of the sale of children, child pornography and child prostitution and related matters (arts. 3; 4, paras. 2 and 3; 5; 6 and 7)

Existing criminal or penal laws and regulations

27. While welcoming the adoption in July 2013 of the Vatican City State laws No. VIII on Complementary Norms on Penal Matters, Title II: Crimes against Children and No. IX containing amendments to the Criminal Code and the Criminal Procedure Code, the Committee is concerned that:

(a) Laws VIII and IX apply only to the Vatican City State and do not address offences committed by individuals and institutions under the authority of the Holy See, which continue to be subject to Canon Law provisions; and (b) The 2011 Circular Letter to assist episcopal conferences in developing guidelines for dealing with cases of sexual abuse of minors perpetrated by clerics gives precedence to Canon law proceedings over national penal proceedings to deal with offences under the Optional Protocol.

28. The Committee urges the Holy See to: (a) Extend the application of laws No. VIII and IX to all individuals and institutions under its authority; and (b) Adopt clear rules for the immediate referral of all suspected cases of offences under the Optional Protocol to national law enforcement authorities even in cases where national laws do not make reporting of these crimes compulsory.

Prosecution and impunity

29. The Committee is deeply concerned that the vast majority of priests and clerics who have committed acts of child pornography as well as those who have concealed these crimes have benefited from impunity. The Committee is particularly concerned that:
(a) Canon Law provisions and proceedings which have allowed perpetrators to escape justice by imposing an obligation of silence on victims, prevented the reporting of cases to national law enforcement authorities and provided punishment with no relation to the gravity of the offences committed, are still in force and applied;
(b) On numerous occasions, the Holy See has refused to cooperate with law enforcement authorities and to disclose information requested by prosecutors and

national commissions of inquiry; and (c) The Holy See has signed treaties with certain States, notably Italy, which guarantee areas of immunity from prosecution to Vatican officials, including for bishops and priests accused of offences under the Optional Protocol.

30. The Committee urges the Holy See to repeal without delay all Canon Law provisions, which have created an environment favouring the impunity of perpetrators of crimes under the Optional Protocol. The Holy See should also amend its internal guidelines and ensure a transparent and effective cooperation with national law enforcement authorities. The Committee further urges the Holy See to revoke parts of any treaty it has signed with States, which would contribute to the impunity of perpetrators of child sexual abuse according to art. 22 of the Lateran Pact based on the double criminality rule.

The Extradition

31. The Committee notes that the Holy See does not seek extradition of persons for the purposes of prosecution and extradites persons to the Italian authorities Committee is particularly concerned that the Holy See in January 2014 refused the requests of a Polish prosecutor to extradite an Archbishop from the Vatican to Poland to face charges, including child pornography.
32. The Committee urges the Holy See to take the necessary measures to ensure that all the offences

referred to in article 3, paragraph 1, of the Optional Protocol are extraditable offences, and that the requirement of double criminality for extradition and/or prosecution of offences committed abroad is repealed. The Committee also urges the Holy See to use, where necessary, the Optional Protocol as a legal basis for extradition, in conformity with article 5 of the Protocol, and to proceed with the extradition of any clerics facing charges of child sexual abuse abroad.

VII. Protection of the rights of child victims (arts. 8 and 9, paras. 3 and 4)

Measures adopted to protect the rights of child victims of offences prohibited under the Optional Protocol

33. The Committee is concerned that in spite of the many obstacles encountered by child victims of crimes prohibited under the Optional Protocol to report the offences they were subject to by Catholic priests, the Holy See still does not consider the creation of a child-sensitive mechanism for children to make complaints as a legal requirement under article 8.1 of the Optional Protocol. The Committee is also deeply concerned that:
(a) Canon laws which have been and continue to be applied to offences under the Optional Protocol do not contain any provision on the protection of rights and interests of child victims; and
(b) In many cases, child victims and their families have

been re-victimized by the Church authorities, as noticed by several national commissions of inquiry.

34. In the light of article 9, paragraph 3, of the Optional Protocol, the Committee urges the Holy See to take all necessary measures to protect the rights and interests of child victims of all offences under the Optional Protocol and to ensure that the best interests of the child are a primary consideration in the treatment afforded by the criminal justice system to child victims. The Committee urges the Holy See to:

(a) Establish without further delay child-friendly mechanisms and procedures for complaints, remedy or redress in relation to all offences under the Protocol;

(b) Develop guidelines on child protection for all individuals and institutions working under the authority of the Holy See and ensure training on such guidelines;

(c) Establish mechanisms and procedures for the early identification of child victims of the offences under the Optional Protocol, including by establishing cooperation mechanisms with national law enforcement authorities; and

(d) Ensure that child victims are no longer victimised by church authorities when they denounce crimes under the Optional Protocol.

Recovery and reintegration of victims

35. While noting that the Holy See seeks to inspire States parties to the Optional Protocol to provide assistance

to child victims and that the Catholic church provide assistance to children victims of sexual exploitation, the Committee is concerned about the absence of appropriate measures taken by the Holy See to provide child victims of clerics with assistance for their physical and psychological recovery and social reintegration. The Committee is also particularly concerned that:

(a) Canon Law provisions which have been used to deal with cases of child pornography committed by Catholic priests contain no provision on the recovery and reintegration of the victims;

(b) The Holy See has not directly cooperated with States Parties in assisting children, as indicated in its written responses to the Committee; and

(c) Confidentiality has been imposed as a condition of financial compensation to child victims of abuses under the Optional Protocol.

36. The Committee urges the Holy See to take all appropriate measures for the physical and psychological recovery and social reintegration of child victims of all offences under the Optional Protocol, and ensure that those measures take place in an environment that fosters the self-respect and dignity of the child. The Committee also urges the Holy See to fulfill its obligation to provide compensation to victims of offences committed by individuals and institutions under its authority without imposing any obligation of confidentiality on the victims. To this aim, the Holy See should establish a

compensation scheme for victims of offences under the Optional Protocol committed by clerics.

VIII. International assistance and cooperation (art. 10) Multilateral, bilateral and regional agreements

37. In the light of article 10, paragraph 1, of the Optional Protocol, the Committee encourages the Holy See to strengthen international cooperation through multilateral, regional and bilateral arrangements, by strengthening procedures for and mechanisms to coordinate with law enforcement authorities and improve prevention, detection, investigation, prosecution and punishment of those responsible for any of the offences covered under the Optional Protocol. In this context, the Committee urges the Holy See to exclude offences under the Optional Protocol from any immunity agreement with States. The Holy See should also consider ratifying the Council of Europe Convention on the Protection of Children against Sexual Exploitation and Sexual Abuse.

IX. Follow-up and dissemination

38. The Committee recommends that the Holy See take all appropriate measures to ensure the full implementation of the present recommendations by, inter alia, transmitting them to the Pope, the Curia, the Congregation for the Doctrine of the Faith, the

Congregation for Catholic Education, the Catholic Health Care Institutions, the Pontifical Council for the Family as well as bishops conferences, individuals and institutions functioning under authority of the Holy for appropriate consideration and further action.

39. The Committee recommends that the initial report and written replies submitted by the Holy See and the related concluding observations adopted by the Committee be made widely available, including (but not exclusively) through the Internet, to the public at large, civil society organizations, youth groups, professional groups and children, in order to generate debate and awareness of the Optional Protocol, its implementation and monitoring.

X. Next report

40. In accordance with article 12, paragraph 2, the Committee requests the Holy See to include further information on the implementation of the Optional Protocol and the present concluding observations in its next periodic report under the Convention on the Rights of the Child, in accordance with article 44 of the Convention. – ENDS

Appendix i
Letters from a child abuser

These are the letters referred to in Madley's police interviews.

1 April 2004
Dear Hugh,

An appropriate date to write! You probably thought that you were in the clear following the CPS decision back in 2000 not to bring charges against you due to what they said was 'a lack of evidence,' for the sexual offences you committed against me when I was a child. There was, of course, plenty of evidence - my evidence - the evidence of the child who you groomed and then sexually abused.

Since then, much has changed. The support, albeit limited, that you originally enjoyed from the Salesians has now been completely eroded by my continuous efforts to educate them about the nature of child sexual abuse, its impact and its legacy. They now, finally, accept that I was telling the truth, and you were lying. This is, of course, the one thing that you always said to me would never happen. Well; it has. They now accept that you are a child abuser, a pedophile and a liar.

I have now gained the full agreement from the Salesian Order in the UK and their lawyers, that they will not stand in my way if I bring a private prosecution against you for what you did to me; what you did to me at the Salesian College in Chertsey, in my bedroom, at your mother's house and at the derelict cottage in Wales. Consequently, I have written to Surrey Police and instructed them to begin a private criminal prosecution against you. Obviously, you will remain in the eyes of the law innocent until you can be proved guilty, but I will do everything in my power to bring you in front of a judge and a jury; of that you can be assured. I am looking forward to seeing you again, but this time I will face you as a man, not as a child. We will see then who is telling the truth.

Yours sincerely
Graham Wilmer - Victim No Longer

5 April 2004
Dear Graham,

I wondered if you would be prepared to meet me some time in the near future? I hope you are well. I do not have your phone number, but mine is xxx, if you wish to speak to me to make arrangements.

Yours sincerely

Hugh - P.S. I have an answer phone if I am out

10 April 2004

Dear Hugh,

Thank you for your letter of 5 April 2004. You will understand that the thought of meeting with you fills me with very considerable apprehension after everything I have been through. I have discussed your request with my counsellor and been advised that now is not the time. However, I am prepared to exchange correspondence with you so if you want to write to me to explain what it is that you want to say to me, I will respond.

Yours sincerely
Graham Wilmer - Victim No Longer

14 April 2004

Dear Graham,

I appreciate your reply to my letter of the 5th. I am sensitive to your feelings and assure you of my best intent. I hope a meeting when you feel appropriate will help us both. One thing I have realised is that I accidentally misled you in '68. We were talking but were interrupted. I did not complete what I was saying to you and I believe this caused you grief.

I hope to help you in possible. I remember you came to see me the year after I left when I brought a cricket team to Chertsey. I was pleased to see you and you seemed well. I think you told me you were working in a hospital. We went for a drink after i gave you a lift home. We were going to arrange another tour of Wales but circumstances prevented me. I believe we parted as friends and it is my wish to regain at least something of that friendship if at all possible.

All the best
Hugh

15 April 2004
Dear Hugh,

Thank you for your letter of 14 April 2004. What do you mean when you say that you have realised that you 'accidentally mislead' me in '68? I don't understand what you are talking about. What happened between us is quite simple. You befriended me at school and overtime ensnared me into a sexual relationship with you when I was under 16 years of age, i.e. still a child. You did this to me at two of the houses in Station Road owned by the school. You also did it to me at my house in Pyrford and in the cottage in Wales when you took me on holiday.

You swore me to silence and you told me that no one

would believe me if I told anyone, but I did tell Fr Madden in Confession, and he then told Fr O'Shea. They closed ranks against me to protect themselves and the school. They too swore me to silence. Not surprisingly, I subsequently failed all of my 'O'levels and was chucked out of the school. You, on the other hand, were protected by the Salesians and moved to Battersea where you spent the rest of your teaching career. The psychological damage that I suffered as a result of what you did to me ruined my education and brought chaos into my life that endured for the next 30 years, leading eventually in 1999 to a complete mental breakdown.

When I eventually found the courage to disclose to the police in 2000 what you had done to me all those years ago, they came looking for you, arrested you and asked you to account for what had happened. You lied to them by saying that nothing had happened, and because it was your word against mine, they were unable to bring a prosecution against you for lack of evidence. These are the facts, and until you admit that you did this to me, you will never be able to 'help' me as you claim you want to do in your letter.

We never parted as friends as you claim. We were never friends. I hated you then and I hate you now. What you took to be my friendship was nothing more than a terrified child trying hard to deal with something that he did not and could not possibly understand - being used by an adult for sexual gratification.

However you try and justify to yourself that we shared a 'friendship', you know in your heart that it was much much more than that. You used me, and when you were finished with me, you moved on without giving a second thought to what might become of me. That was not friendship, it was abuse.

Yours sincerely
Graham Wilmer - Victim No Longer

17 April 2004
Dear Graham,

I suppose I should have guessed your feelings about me but it still was a bit of a shock. I am truly sorry that this is the situation. Nevertheless I still want to do my best to help in the only way I know how at this late stage. I understand your reluctance to meet with me but I hope you will give me a chance at least to put things right.

I hope you understand what I am trying to say as I am too nervous to put it in writing. If you do not wish to meet me on your own, would it help if your counsellor was present, or perhaps I could speak to him/her alone. I hope you believe that I am sincere in my offer - I do want to help! Please let me try!

Yours sincerely
Hugh.

20 April 2004
Dear Hugh,

Thank you for your letter of 17 April 2004. I think I do understand what you are trying to say, even though you are 'too nervous' to put it in writing, but to be sure that I fully understand, I have asked my counsellor to talk with you, as you suggested. Accordingly, he will telephone you and ask you what it is that you want to say. His name is Stephen Wilde and he has been supporting me for the past five years, so he knows everything about the case.

Yours sincerely
Graham Wilmer

28 April 2004
Dear Graham,

Sorry for the delay in replying to your letter of 20th April. I will be pleased to speak to Stephen or meet him if he thinks that would be better. Did I give you the correct number? It should be 0208-201-0244. I wondered as there have been no messages. To help Stephen contact me, I am always out Tues-Sun between 11:30 - 2:30 approx, and Mondays 11- 8:30. If I am out any time I will phone him if he leaves his number and contact times

Yours sincerely - Hugh.

8 May 2004
Dear Graham,

Thank you for putting Stephen in touch with me. It was a very emotional talk but Stephen helped me to realise the harm I did to you and I sincerely hope it will help you. I hope you and your family can find it in your heart to forgive me. I had no idea of the damage it caused then or more recently - I am so sorry. I wish I had been more sensitive to your emotions when we last met in '69. Until recently I did not know how badly you had done in '68, or that the Salesians had refused you the chance to repeat your exams. Had I been aware that you were having problems I would have wanted to help you with your education - if you would have allowed me. I told Stephen I would send all the old Battersea photos that I could find in case you recognise any Priest you spoke to. Does the name Fr Colin Hamer seem familiar? He is not on the '69 photo but I understand he was a psychology/philosophy expert. He left the Salesian Order some time in the 70's - I hope these will be some help.

Yours sincerely - Hugh.

15 May 2004
Dear Graham,

Last Saturday I sent a tube containing some old school photographs as I promised Stephen. Did you receive them? If not, please let me know and I will chase them up as I sent them special delivery. I hope to be away from next Saturday to visit some old friends in Scotland but it is not fixed yet.

Yours sincerely
Hugh.
P.S. You may spot Roy Fairs on the most recent photo - he taught with me for several years.

17 May 2004
Dear Hugh,

Thank you for your letter of 8 May, together with the school photos, and your letter of 15 May 2004. I don't recall the name Fr Colin Hamer, but he may well have been the priest who interrogated me back in 68 after I disclosed to Fr Madden and then Fr O'Shea what was happening. I can't remember Roy Fairs either. Did he teach me at Chertsey?

I am glad you were able to talk to Stephen about what you did to me. What you told him has certainly helped me in my recovery, although there is still a long way to go. I have just finished writing a survival guide for victims of sexual abuse. It is called 'Proud To Be Me', and it describes exactly what childhood sexual abuse does to people. It does not, of course, mention you or the school, as that is not its purpose. It should be printed by the end of May. I will send you a copy and I would appreciate any feedback you have once you have read it.

Now that you have been able to recall the events of 66/68 in more detail, I wondered if you might have been able to recall anything else. I am particularly interested to know what exactly was it that you told the Rector the evening you resigned, and what did you say in your resignation letter?

When I left the school, the Rector was Fr Harris. When did Fr Gaffney come into the picture? I don't remember him. There are still parts of the events of 68 that I have blanked out so completely, it is hard to recall them. However, other memories are so deeply burned into my mind that I cannot erase them. It was these memories that plagued me in nightmares and flashbacks when I had my breakdown in 1998/9. The most vivid memories are of the cottage, lying naked on the grey leather seats from your Ford Anglia, and what you did to me that night. I also recall very clearly the cardinal-red candlewick bedcover on your bed in the house next door to the school entrance. There are many other memories, but I won't repeat them here. They are just too painful.

I have forgiven you Hugh for what you did to me, but I can never forget. It is something I will have to live with for the rest of my life. What worries me more than anything else at the moment is your statement that I was the only one? What was it about me that made you do what you did? Think about it and write to me again with any thoughts you have. If you would like to talk to Stephen again, let me know and I will ask him to call you at a convenient time.

Yours sincerely
Graham Wilmer

19 May 2005
Dear Graham,

Thank you for your forgiveness and letting me know that the talks with Stephen have helped you feel better. It is important to me that this should continue and I will be glad to speak to Stephen at any time. I don't think Fr Hamer is on the '69 photo, he did not last long at the school - A nice chap, but a hopeless teacher. Roy Fairs was in form 5, when you were in 5A. On the '67 Chertsey he is 14th from the left in the 3rd row from the back (in glasses). I think he was wearing a brown/tan suit on the most recent Battersea photo.

When I joined Chertsey in '66 Fr Ford was Headmaster and Fr Harris the Rector. Fr Ford left in Summer 67 and was replaced by Fr O'Shea. Fr Gaffney was (I think) parish priest and became Rector when Fr Harris left some time before Christmas '67. The night you told me that the Salesians knew what was going on, I went to see Fr O'Shea after supper but he was not there. I asked Fr Gaffney if I could speak to him and he took me to his office - I knew at once that he was aware about what I had to say. He helped me through it, (like Stephen) and I admitted my offences. I told him that I had not set out that first time to offend, that it had just happened and I assured him that I would never offend against a child again. He said he believed me about the first time but what about the other times? - I had no answer to this. After a while, he told me I must resign which I did on the spot. He did not ask me to do this in writing but he said he would see Fr O'Shea in the morning. To the best of my knowledge, Fr O'Shea never mentioned anything about what had happened.

It seemed only a short time after that he died and I met and spoke to Fr George Williams after the funeral at the school. I repeated what I had said to Fr Gaffney. Fr Williams questioned me for some time and I repeated my promise that I would never offend again. After a while, he asked me what I was doing next year. I had nothing fixed up and he told me of Fr Perla's move to be Parish Priest at Battersea and he would not stand in my way if I applied for the post. I was gob-smacked at this but on reflection think they wanted to keep an eye on me! One thing that I think I have remembered since I spoke to Stephen is about the night you told me. I think you said "The Salesians want you to resign." Did they get you to say this to me when they should have questioned me themselves?

Graham - I have kept my word to both Fr Gaffney and Fr Williams that I would never offend against a child again. Even when we met in '69 and you were no longer a pupil, I did not want to risk breaking my word and risk offending again. You cannot know the terror that I felt that night or for years after. I did not know you had been sworn to silence by the Salesians. I assumed that your parents would have been told and might have wanted further action. I worked very hard at Battersea and have always done my best to help my pupils - I think successfully. In one year from a three form entry school, I had 32 pupils doing 'A' Chemistry and most passed well. I am very much engaged now with helping neighbours and friends and especially my uncle who helped me so much when my mother was dying. I cannot remember who became Rector after Fr Gaffney died - possibly Fr Harris came back to plug the gap. I will be pleased to speak with Stephen again as to why/how it happened. I am very concerned that it might reawaken memories best forgotten and may make things harder for you - This is the last thing I want to do - I had hoped to speak to you personally on this matter so I might know if it would be best to shut up! I am sure Stephen will be experienced enough to know what is best.

I hope your progress continues and pledge you my help.

Yours sincerely
Hugh.

P.S. I will now be going to Scotland on the 22nd, provided my car lets me (2 weeks) (It has done 234.000 miles so far!) Another 12K and it will have reached the moon!
P.P.S. I will be pleased to receive a copy of your book.

14 June 2004
Dear Hugh,

Thank you for your letter of 19 May, which was helpful. I hope your trip to Scotland was a relaxing time for you and your car did not let you down. There are a couple more questions that you could help me with if you don't mind. I have listed them numerically for ease of reply.

1. What was the name of the headmaster at Battersea when you joined the staff there?

2. Did he ever talk to you about what had happened, and, if yes, what did he say?
3. Did Fr Golding ever talk to you about what had

happened, and, if yes, what did he say?

4. Was Fr Golding the deputy head, and was he the same Fr Golding who taught me physics at Chertsey?

5. Can you remember what month it was when Martin Allen died?

6. In December 2000, the Salesians say they questioned Fr O'Shea and Fr Williams about me. Both Fr O'Shea and Fr Williams said that not only could they not remember me, but also they had no recollection of any incident involving you or me either. They maintained this position when questioned by the police, and they maintained it when they met with me at the mediation. Given the detail of the confession you made to both of them, and the subsequent actions involving your move to Battersea, would you not have expected them to remember your discussions with them?

7. Did anybody from SDB, or their lawyers ever talk to you about me in 2000 or 2001, and, if yes, what did they say?

8. Did you know that your union (NASUWT) had shut down two of my web sites in 2000 when I was trying to find out more about what had happened to you at Battersea? Had you instructed them to do that?

9. Did you know that your union's lawyers (Thompson's) had threatened to sue me if I continued to speak about what you had done to me?

10. When Thompson's informed you in February 2001 that I had signed an agreement with the Salesians, what exactly did they tell you?

If you could answer these is as much detail as possible, it would be a big help. I am trying to piece together everything that happened so that when I go back and face the Salesians again, I have a much better case than I had when I faced them before. They betrayed me Hugh, not just when I first went to them for help back in 1968, but when I went back in February 2001 and met with them at the mediation. At that time, I did not know that you had also told them what had happened and that you had resigned. All they would tell me was that they had no idea what I was talking about, other than what I was saying at the time. What I now know, of course, is that they had known all along, because you yourself had told them! This means they conspired to keep silent based on the fact that, as you had denied my allegations when the police interviewed you in April 2000, all they had to do to avoid any trouble was to deny any knowledge if it either, knowing that the case against you would collapse due to lack of evidence, which is what happened. I hope you are well and I look forward to hearing from you again soon.

Yours sincerely
Graham Wilmer

17 June 2004
Dear Graham,

Thank you for your letter of the 14th. My first week in Scotland was excellent. I visited Sky, Mull (much better) and most places North and West. My friend in Pooleve has been in hospital for a month so I visited her in Raigmore Hospital (Inverness). Her son hopes she will be out by this weekend (she is 84).

In the second week I was gold-panning in the Kildonan Burn near Helmsdale but a combination of too much sun and food poisoning knocked me up for three days so I cut the holiday short.

Q1. In answer to your questions, it might help if I list Headmasters and Deputies till the mid 80's.
- Approx. 75   Fr J Foley (HM)
- Approx 73 Fr M Blackburn (DH - became Head at Farnborough) 73 - 75 (Fr Douglas DH)

Fr Foley died in 75 and Fr Douglas became Headmaster. Fr Barrett became D. Head. Fr Douglas retired in 85 (approx) and Fr Blackburn came back as Headmaster.

Q2. Fr Foley called me into his office during the 1st week of term in 1968 and told me that he was aware of all that had happened at Chertsey, also that a 'close eye' would be kept on me. Fr Blackburn (D. Head) was the other Chemistry teacher at Battersea working in the Lab. but never made any reference to what had happened.

Q3+4. Fr Golding was never at Battersea in my time, but at Chertsey he was Deputy Head and my Line Manager as Head of Science. I suspect he had been told (in his position) but never said anything. I visited Fr Golding between 98-99 but although he did not seem very well, he seemed to have a good memory.

Q5. I cannot remeber the exact month Martin died but I think it was between Nov 67 and Jan 68. I used to have an 'In Memoriam' card to 'Martin Bayliss Allen'. I have searched my house but had no luck so far. I will keep looking and send it to you if I find it. I think I remember that Martin's father performed the surgery to try and save his life. I just cannot begin to think what he went through.

Q6. What happened in 66-68 cannot have been a 'run of the mill' incident, so I would have expected one or both of them to remember what happened. It is possible they think they are/were protecting either me, or the Salesians or possibly a combination of both. I now know from personal experience, the effect of trauma on 'memory', this might account for their 'loss of memory' - but both!?

Q7. No one from SDB contacted me to see what I had to say. This upset me at the time leaving me isolated. At the time I still did not accept your allegation and had expected their contact and support. I believe now that they knew all along and did not want to confirm it.

Q8. Yes I did know. One day I got home to find a message on my answer phone from the school saying that the allegation had been published on the Net. I have never had access to the Net and spoke to my Union Rep. He down loaded it, sent copies to me and the solicitor who advised them that as I could be clearly identified, it broke some charter or other.

Q9. Yes again. I was in a very bad state mentally at the time. I was receiving both psychotherapy and visited the Redhill Unit for Psychotherapy' weekly. I was offered 'in patient' treatment but could not face that. My solicitor knew how bad I had been, the antidepressants I was (and still am) taking. I had the crisis team come to my house when the doctors felt I was in danger of self harm. My solicitor would say to me at the end of any conversation 'now you are not going to do anything silly are you?' It was only my determination to be around to help my uncle that gave me the strength to resist. I realise you must have been offended by his action but I am sure he feared for my safety.

Q10. I was told that the Salesians had offered you a sum that enabled you to accept and not pursue your claim against them and that you had decided not to press charges against me.

Back to no. 8 again. If you had not put out the stuff about me on the Net and I had not read it again in Dec 03 and had flashbacks and nightmares I would not broken through the mental barrier I must have erected.

Can you remember what the Salesians said to you in 68 after I resigned? Was it before or after this that they swore you to silence?

When we went to Wales, did we either climb Snowdon or go up the mountain railway? Quite a lot of missing from my memory but every so often things seem to flit into my mind.

I hope this will be of further help. Please contact me if I can do any more.

Yours sincerely
Hugh.

P.S. If necessary I will go with you to the Salesians and repeat what I have said if you think it will be helpful.

P.P.S. Are you in contact with any old boys like Simon Beer, Michael Canning, Ralph Brown? I often wonder what has become of my old pupils.

Finally P.P.P.S. Did you recognise any of the priests on the photos that I sent you.

18 June 2004
Dear Hugh,

Thank you for your letter of 17 May, which was very helpful. If you could find the card about Martin, it would be very special to me. I was very close to the Allen family.

You asked a couple of questions in your letter, which I will try and answer. Firstly, the Salesians never told me that you had resigned. They swore me to silence on the same day that I was interviewed by Fr Williams, the Provincial. This would have been a couple of days after the day I had told Fr Madden what was going on. That day was only a few days before Martin's funeral, which was why I had to confess.

What you may not know is that Martin's father, Dr Allen, asked me to serve at the requiem mass along with Martin's brother, Paul. Ever since you had begun to abuse me, I had stopped going to communion because I thought I was in state of mortal sin, but I was too afraid to go to confession and confess what I thought were my sins. Ever since you first touched me, which was actually in your car on the way home, not in the lab as I think you told Stephen, I had been totally traumatised by what you were doing to me.

You might recall that the mass was actually celebrated by the Bishop of Leeds. He was a close family friend of the Allen's, and godfather to Veronica, one of Martin's sisters. The Bishop knew me well as I had met him many times at the Allen's family home.

The dilemma I faced was that I could not accept communion on the alter during the mass unless I had first gone to confession; that being what I believed at the time, having been so indoctrinated into the Catholic faith by the Salesians for the previous three years.
The idea of refusing communion at the mass, in front of Martin's grieving family, was something I just could not contemplate, so, the only was out for me was to confess what I thought were my sins. I went to see Fr Madden, he was my housemaster in year 5, and asked him if he would hear my confession. He did, but he was so disturbed by what I had said, he coerced me into repeating outside of the confession what I had told in the confession, which I did. He then went and told Fr O'Shea.

When I told you, I had literally just left the confession with Fr Madden. I was walking back from the main house towards the classrooms. You were bowling in the nets that were near the stairs that led up to the chemistry lab. I told you that I had told them. You just smirked at me and said that you would deny it and that they would never believe me. Fr Williams interviewed me a few days later. He asked me very detailed questions about my sexuality. I had no real idea what the bastard was up to, but it is clear now that he was trying to see if I was in any way to blame! The fact that I was a child under 16 and you were an adult and my teacher, seemed to be of little consequence to him. He just wanted to know if I had ever done anything like that with anyone else., which, of course, I had not. Incidentally, it seems Fr Madden was also himself an abuser. Two other boys came forward in 2000 with allegations about what he had done to them at Chertsey. His death prevented any prosecution.

I can't really remember what happened after I had been interviewed by Fr Williams, but I presume that you stayed on at the school working out your notice period until we broke up after the 'o' levels in June 1968. When in fact did you leave the school? You also mentioned to Stephen that you returned in 1969 with a cricket team from Battersea, and that you met me again and took me for a drink in a pub. I don't remember that. How did you make contact with me, and why did you not tell me then that you had resigned? What did we talk about?

I cannot remember if you took me up Snowdon or not. I recall vividly the time you turned up at the youth hostel I was staying at near Chepstow when I was on a school trip with Brother John and a group of lads from my class. You persuaded Brother John to let you take me home on the back of your bike. All the lads thought that was very strange. Before we made the journey back, you took me part-way up Sugar Loaf Mountain on the bike. It was a Matchless 500. On the way home, we stopped in Reading and had a meal. I had an egg curry. I have never forgotten that.

As for my old classmates; I see Paul meek regularly. We have remained close family friends ever since we left school. Michael Canning lives in California, but he visits our family regularly and stays for a couple of weeks each time. He was here with us last in April this year. Ralph Brown also lives in the USA. I spoke to him a couple of months ago via e-mail. I have never seen Simon Beer again since I left school, so I don't know what happened to him.

I hope you are well and I look forward to hearing from you again soon.

Yours sincerely
Graham Wilmer

21 June 2004
Dear Graham,

Thank you for your letter of the 18th June and sorry for

the delay in replying. I have spent the weekend looking for Martin's card but with no such luck so far. It is quite a while since I last saw it but I will keep looking. I told Stephen that I purchased a kit for an RF signal generator some time after x Mass 67, and spent time in the lab building it. I believe the first time I offended against you happened some time later (March - April?) when I brought it to your house to demonstrate it to you, using it as a short range transmitter. I think it interferred with some local police car radio traffic. I know I was using the motor bike (a Matchless 600cc G11) as I did not have use of my father's car till the summer term.

I did not know just how close you were to Martin and his family until your last letter and I fully recognise the dilemma you faced. I remember a little about the Mass, and the effect of Martin's death on the whole school. I was unable to receive communion then as I had not had the courage to go to confession until much later that year.

My memory of how you told me was different. What I seem to remember is that some time after Martin's death you asked me to come to your house one evening as you had something to tell me. When I arrived, we went for a short drive and you told me they 'knew about us'. I don't remember you telling me how they knew, in fact only by reading the internet material around December did I know you had told them and the connection to Martin. I do remember saying I would deny it and you would not believed. I just could not do it, so I went and admitted it to Fr Gaffney that night and resigned immediately. I am sure I started to tell you the following day but was interrupted by someone coming down the stairs. It never occurred to me that you still thought I had denied it. I am sure I was not playing cricket as the nets did not go up until the summer term.

The exact date of Martin's death could be quite important so are you able to contact Chertsey, I don't think I can. If not, do you know where Martin is buried as I could visit the church and look for the records! I was very surprised to learn how you were treated at the time as it seems to be against what the Salesians were all about!

I did work out my notice until July and remember one thing vividly which I told Stephen. As you came out of the Chemistry exam I asked the boys around 'how did it go?' You said 'Wasn't it easy'. My heart fell at this because it was just about the trickiest paper I had seen for a long time.

I now remeber we went up a mountain in the Brecon Beakons called Corn Du. We had almost reached the top when we got caught in a sudden downpour and got soaked to the skin.

I brought the U13 team from Battersea (and 2 other

teams) to Chertsey and towards the end you came down to the field and watched the end of the match.

I had not contacted you in accordance with my promise to Fr Gaffney, perhaps you were in Chertsey and looked in on the chance of seeing old friends that would have been in the there, but after the match we chatted, went into the pub down Station Rd. for a 'swift half' and I gave you a lift home.

I think I spoke about Battersea mostly, comparing it with Chertsey and saying how much noisier the Boys were, about an Irish tecaher at Battersea who delighted in leg-pulling and found me ideally suited!

You told me you were working in a hospital (St. Peters?) We spoke about going to Wales again but I thought later better not to break my promise.

It did not occur to me to tell you I had resigned as I probably thought and expected the Salesians would have done after my admission to Fr Gaffney.

Perhaps if I had known how they had treated you and not told you I had confessed you could have been saved the trauma you have been through recently - sorry, I think when we met neither of us wanted to talk about what happened.

I remember the trip in autumn 66. You and others were walking from Blaisdon to St Braivels Y.H. during the half term.

I was going down to my father's place to make sure it was OK and had not been vandalised. I said I would keep an eye-out for you and I remember giving you, Ralph and a couple of others a lift from the Forest of Dean to St Braivels.

That night, several boys wanted to go down to the old station at llandogs and examine it by torch light, and I think I ferried about six of you down to the station. Before doing so, I was offered a cup of tea and either Paul Meek or Tony.....(Mr Lowe's nephew) offered me some sugar. After the 4th spoon he said 'would you like some tea with your sugar!!' Another night you told me that Paul had said he was going into the local and ask for a pint, but his nerve failed him and he asked for a 'p-p-pickled egg please.'

I hope you are feeling better and continue to make progress.

Yours sincerely
Hugh.
P.S. I knew nothing about Fr Madden.
P.P.S. I will be away from 26th June for about five days to visit my cousin.

Dear Graham,

Can you help me on a totally different matter?
I have an Apple Mac computer (1973) Quadra 840AV
that packed up before Christmas. I have stripped it
down and found several badly burnt components in the
power supply. I can repair them but cannot find their
values. Do you know of any site on the net that I could
access from my library that gives circuit diagrams of old
Mac computers? I do a lot of slide scanning but cannot
manage the cost of a new Mac and software/hardware
just at this time.

23 June 2004
Dear Hugh,

Thank you for your letter of 21 June, which was very
helpful. Stephen has asked me to tell you that although
our correspondence is very difficult for me, it is helpful.
When your letters arrive, I don't open them immediately.
I wait until Stephen is available and I give them to him.
He reads them and talks me through what you have said.
I respond and he then helps me write the reply, which I
sign and send on to you.

There would seem to be some discrepancy in your
account of dates and time. However, I am very clear of
the sequence of events and the places and times that you

abused me. I definitely told you that I had told Fr Madden about what you were doing to me in the afternoon at school. I met you as I was making my way back across the playground. You were bowling to some lads in the cricket nets in the playground. It was autumn, and the nets had not yet been taken down.

The episode over the signal generator occurred at my house over a weekend. You stayed the night because my parents were on holiday in Devon. They had gone on ahead of me because school had not broken up yet. I think it was the Easter holiday. I joined them the next day, Saturday, after a long coach ride. You did not abuse me that night, although you did hug me on the stairs before we retired to bed - separately. You slept in my elder sister's bed, which was in the new extension we had had built on the side of the house. I slept in my own room. I can recall very clearly saying to you that I did not want you to sexually touch me because I didn't feel well. You agreed and went to bed on your own. You had been abusing me for some time before this event, so your recollection is not quite right here. Perhaps you may be confusing me with some other boy.

Do you remember the night I came to stay at your house in London? I recall it well as after I had gone to bed, you and your mother came and woke me up to look at a house fire that was burning not far away. We went to the window and you pressed up against me from behind, even though your mother was standing right next to me. I was only wearing a pair of underpants, as I did not have any pj's. I felt very vulnerable.

A few other things. 1) Did you offer your resignation, or did Fr Gaffney ask you to resign? 2) Can you recall the name of the pub you say you took me to in 1969? 3) Why can't you contact Chertsey to ask about the date of Martin's death?

One other thing. You say you worked out your notice until July 68. What was your relationship with me during that period? Did you simply ignore me, or did you continue to have contact with me?

You make no mention in your letter of the journey home from Wales on your bike. I wore your helmet if you recall. You just wore the goggles.

Stephen told me that you had said that Fr Foley had instructed that you were not allowed to be alone with other boys on out of school activities. How then were you able to bring the U13 team to Chertsey, plus the two other teams? Seems to me that they were not keeping such a close eye on you as they said they would.

Do you recall taking other boys camping? I have been told that you took a boy called Cleary camping with you on one, or perhaps several occasions. I was also told that you had taken some boys to your Father's cottage in Wales, the same cottage that you told Stephen that you had had full intercourse with me in.

I had never known that you had been moved to Battersea until WPC Sarah Harris told me in April 2000 after she had tracked you down, so it could not have been me that you took to the pub in 1969, where you say you talked mostly about the differences between Chertsey and Battersea. Are you sure that really happened, or was it some other boy you took to the pub?

Yours sincerely
Graham Wilmer

25 June 04
Dear Graham,

Thank you for your letter of 23rd. I am pleased it was helpful but I am sorry you find it difficult. I also find it difficult but know I must if I am to be of help to you and try to make up for what I did to you. It has depressed me very much to realise the harm I did but felt a little better after talking to Stephen.

I know there are discrepancies in our memories and have tried to reconcile them but cannot at the moment. I was always mad keen on cricket and I remember helping Fr Murphy put them up in Summer 67. I also think I remember helping him take them down at the end of term. I believe the date of Martin's death is critical, and possibly even later than I recall. I think if I contacted Chertsey they might not reply or be unhelpful.

My memory of the signal generator episode is also a bit different. It cannot have been a Friday because I remember taking you to school the following day on my m/cycle and dropping you off just before the crossing.

There was another time (later) that your Mother asked me to stay to make sure you got up in time to catch the coach to meet them. I came over with you with the intention of staying but during the evening Michael Canning came around. He said he would stay and make sure you got up in time - so I did not need to stay. Michael said he had always wanted a ride on the back of a bike, so I gave him a ride round for about ten minutes before leaving. I know it was very late! It is possible that these two events have become crossed in time.

Graham - there was no other boy!

I remember the fire. You had gone into your bedroom when my mother called us to look at the fire. I do not remember pressing up against you but I am sorry if I did. We went on the bike the following day and found it was an old church/hall that had burnt down.

To the best of my memory I think I offered my resignation without Fr Gaffney asking but cannot be sure. I did know, however, that I would have to resign before I saw him.

I cannot remember the name of the pub as it was, I think, the only time I went in, but being half way down Station Rd on the right, it was the nearest. From the time I resigned, I did not ignore you - I am not like that, but I did avoid being alone with you. I do remember the journey home from Wales on the bike. We went along the A4 which I never normally use. There were two other members of staff present, one still teaches at Battersea. They came down by train or coach, I had been home so I met them at Chertsey in my car - sorry I did not make that clear.

The first time I took boys camping was about 85-87. I trusted myself completely then but to be certain I never went alone with a boy. I cannot specifically remember Cleary, but he may have been one of a group of 5-6 boys I took then. I used the school minibus and slept in it whilst the boys slept in the school tent which I borrowed. I had permission from Fr Blackburn and the boys parents - nothing happened, or would have.

My father had been very ill in 69 - was in hospital till the following year when he had to dispose of it as he was no longer able to visit it regularly. I did not take any boys to the cottage from Battersea, I don't know where this came from but it is rubbish.

When I was interviewed by WPC Sarah Harris in 2000, the meeting in 69 and going to the pub was one of the few things I did remember at the time. Yes, I am totally sure we met and you told me you were working in a hospital (as a porter I think I remember). I also remembered that you had grown at least 3 inches since I last saw you.

I believe I became totally trustworthy after 68, or I would not have risked taking even groups of boys away. I could not face again how I felt in Fr Gaffney's office or the knowledge of the harm I could have done to a child had I repeated myself.

I very much hope this helps even if we do not totally agree on details of events almost 40 years ago. I hope you will feel better and make continuous progress.

Yours sincerely
Hugh.

29 June 2004
Dear Hugh,

Thank you for your letter of 25 June, which was very helpful. I have sent off for a copy of Martin's death certificate so that I can work out more precisely when it was that I disclosed to the Salesians what was happening. There are still a number of blanks to complete in the timeline, but I have almost pieced it all together.

I remember the day after the fire, you took me for a walk and you had some sodium in a bottle of oil. When we reached a small brook not far away from your house, you threw some small pieces of sodium into the water, where they exploded on contact. I also remember you took me to your university in South Wales. You showed me the lab you had studied in, and even made me sit on the very stool that you had sat on as a student. The irony here is that because of what you did to me, I never had the chance to go to university myself.

You may not be aware, but the Salesians are currently the subject of a huge scandal in Australia following the arrest of a Salesian priest, Fr Frank Kelp, on charges of child abuse. It seems that the Salesians covered up his offending behaviour as well, an almost identical story to how they covered up your abuse of me, the exception being that they only had to move you to Battersea rather than Samoa because you were never charged with any offence at the time.

What this has shown is that it was the policy of the Salesians to protect abusers within their organisation, regardless of the danger that placed other children in. I enclose a copy of a news article about the scandal, which appeared in on Australian news web site this morning.

There is no need to reply to this letter unless you want to add anything further that you might have thought of. I am going to try and get on with my life now so I won't be writing to you again for a while. If there is an issue you want to discuss, you can always talk to Stephen about it. Just let me know when and what time, and I will arrange for him to phone you.

Yours sincerely
Graham Wilmer

9 July 2004
Dear Hugh,

I know I said I would not write again for a while, but I have now seen a copy of Martin Allen's death certificate, which states that he died on 19 February 1968 at Atkinson Morley's hospital in Wimbledon. He was 16 years old. An inquest was held into his death on 22 February 1968, which concluded that he died from 'cerebral infarction due to internal carotid artery thrombosis following trauma during a game of rugby football.' This would mean that the requiem mass would have been a couple of days after 22 February. It also means that I made my disclosure to Fr Madden and Fr O'Shea a day or so before that.

I have thought hard about the time I told you, and

concluded that you may well be right that the cricket nets were not up, but you were definitely bowling to a couple of lads in the place where the nets used to be. I think there was a mark on the playground that represented the wicket position. You were using a tennis ball. It would not have been possible for me to have told you at my house because my confession was so close to the mass itself, maybe even the day before the mass.

What I don't know is how long did you have to give as your notice period after you resigned? If you were still there, as you say you were, when I took my GCE's, that would have meant four months from the time of your resignation. So when did you actually leave Chertsey? If you could help me with these dates I would appreciate it.

Yours sincerely
Graham Wilmer
10 July 2004

Dear Graham,

Thank you for your letters of 29th June and 9th July. The date of Martin'e death was even later than I had remembered. I do not remember Fr Taylor (Rugby teacher) saying that Martin had received an injury during the match, I think he said Martin had started to drag one of his legs when he was running and he ordered him off. Martin did not want to go off but could not continue. I believe he collapsed a little later. I know our memories on when you told me are different but I think I am correct. You asked me to meet you and when I came over, we went for a short drive and then you told me they knew about us. I believe this was some time after Martin's funeral as I never connected it with what had happened.

One thing that may be significant is that some time after Martin's death, Fr O'Shea told me he was having difficulty teaching L, VI Sc as he needed more time to attend to school affairs and wanted me to take them over. I did but he must have taken a class or two off me to make this possible. I wonder if you remember did I stop teaching you some time during 68? It may have been the physics that was taken away. There may be no significance in the above, but I think now that there was! Again, I did not make any connection between this and us at the time.

A few other things I have remembered since my last letter are:- I remember as I resigned the night you told me, I believe it was much later than February. I am sorry I cannot be more accurate than this but I hope it helps.

I read the piece on Fr Kelp, it was news to me. I understood that the Pope had made it clear that abusers should not be protected/sheltered within the church, perhaps the

Salesians had not heard!

I have wondered recently why Fr Williams told me about the post at Battersea, he had no need to as I had resigned and at the time I was effectively "History". I thought at the time he believed I would not offend again - now I am not sure. I was glad that they decided to trust me as I had nothing fixed up at the time. Before I decided on a career in teaching I had been offered a place with the G.P.O. doing research into transmitter materials. I considered either re-applying to them or going into medical research, but my heart had always been in teaching.

As I have been writing something has been going through my mind. Could you have told me twice? Once when the Salesians told you to tell me that they knew and later (perhaps in the summer term when the nets were up) you told me more? It might help explain some things.

Did the photos I sent help? If you have finished with them please send them back. I hope I have been helpful in this letter and may continue. Please keep in touch and I hope everything goes well for you

Yours sincerely
Hugh.

17 July 2004

Dear Hugh,

Thank you for your letter of 10 July, which was helpful. I think the differences in our memories of the actual date I informed you that I had told Fr Madden and Fr O'Shea what you had done to me is not really that important any more, now that I have established the date of Martin's death.

You mentioned, however, that you had seen me in Fr O'Shea's car, and you presumed I was about to be taken to Battersea. I was interviewed at Chertsey, not Battersea. I have never set foot in school at Battersea, nor do I ever want to. I will hang on to the photos of the school for a while longer if you don't object as I am still trying to trace some of the priests on them, but I will keep in touch as you suggest. I think we have much still to talk about, how and when that will occur is not a priority for me at the moment.

There are major challenges ahead for me following your disclosure, which will determine how things develop from here on. Your agreement to help me unlock the conspiracy of silence with the Salesians is proving to be an interesting challenge in its own right. Their immediate reaction to me informing them recently that I now knew that they had lied to me during the mediation process threw them into convulsions. They rushed to the protection of their fat cat lawyer who threatened to silence me with an injunction if I said another word. I told them to piss off and said that I would respond robustly in any court to argue why any such injunction would be a breach of my human rights. They backed off, of course, which is typical of them.

In the meantime, I am continuing to develop my case against them, and in due course, I will ensure that you have ample opportunity to seek legal advice before you respond to any formal request I make of you to act as a witness for me against them in my civil action in the High Court. I know that you have expressed some fear about that when you spoke to Stephen, but at the end of the day, you have chosen to clear your conscience after all this time, for which I am extremely grateful, and the court case will be the absolute proof that you really are sorry for the damage you caused me.

In the meantime, I have now published the survival guide for victims of childhood sexual abuse that I told you about, a copy of which is enclosed for you to read. I hope that when you have read it, you will think very carefully about its contents, and then think of me. I have suffered everything that is in that booklet, and that suffering is still not yet over. Hopefully, at least partly due to your decision to tell the truth at last, my recovery journey will be a little shorter than it would have other wise been. You can have no idea what it has been like living with such a terrible secret, not being able to tell any one about it because I had always believed no one would believe me. However, all that has now changed, and I can at last bring some real closure to the whole sorry saga.

Yours sincerely
Graham Wilmer

24 July 2004

Dear Graham,

Thank you for your letter of 17th and the booklet you included. I have read it twice now and it has opened my eyes even more to what you have been through then and since. I believe its contents will be a help and comfort to anyone in a similar situation. I was astonished to read that the incidence of sexual abuse is so high. It implies that 10-35% of the population are abusers. While reading this, it passed through my mind that prevention would be better than having to pick up the pieces.

I think there must be three types of abusers. (1) Those who just want a child at any cost and don't give a damn about the harm done to the child, (2) Those who do care but cannot stop themselves and (3) Those who do care and could stop themselves if they knew the short/long term effects on a child. I was ignorant of the harm that I was causing and I believe that any professional involved in childcare/education should be made to listen to a tape/video of a child actor recalling the trauma they had been through. It would not change the first two types of abuser but the third type might just be turned away from abusing children. Even if this helped only one child it would be worth it - what do you think?

The other two types could only be weeded out by psychological profiling but I don't know if it is effective - Has it ever been tried?

Please keep the photos as long as you need them and if you are able to scan those priests you want to identify send them to me. I did not know all priests on the photos, many only lived at the College and were not involved in teaching but I will do my best.

Your comments about the Salesians' reactions do not now surprise me. I think they may contact me and pressure me. If they do in writing I will send you a copy but I do feel very fearful for my future. I do not feel able to approach a lawyer as I do not trust them. I do not like the adversarial system as it will not always lead to the truth and a very smart lawyer can influence a jury more than the evidence justifies.

I am so glad that I have helped you by what I have said but now I feel terribly isolated. I feel unable to talk to anyone, even the psychiatrist I have been seeing since 98 when my mother died. I would appreciate a call from Stephen next week if possible just to talk to someone who knows.

I hope you make rapid progress.

Yours sincerely
Hugh.

ps. my cousin will be staying with me for a week or so in August but I feel unable to talk even to him.

26 July 2004

Dear Hugh,

Thank you for your letter of 24 July. I have spoken to Stephen today. He is currently on holiday, but he is back next Tuesday 3rd August. He said he would be happy to talk to you on Tuesday afternoon, or on Wednesday if that would be more convenient. Please could you let me know which day would be best, and at what time should he phone you? I am glad that you found my booklet informative, and I was interested in the questions you raised, which I will think about and reply to soon. I would not worry too much about the legal issues in relation to the Salesians. Any case against them will take at least five years to get to court - but I expect they will settle out of court before then anyway, in which case you would not have to give evidence in person. We will cross that bridge when we come to it, but I would urge you not to let it cause you undue stress.

One thing Stephen has advised is that if you do come under any pressure from the Salesians, you should not say anything to them as it could be interpreted that they were trying to intimidate a witness. Stephen says that when he talks to you next week, he will give you his personal mobile number so that you can call him if anyone does contact you, and he can then advise you accordingly.

Yours sincerely
Graham Wilmer

29 July 2004
Dear Graham,

Thank you for your letter of the 26th. It has given me a bit more confidence to face the future. I would like to talk to Stephen and will (I expect) be in on tues 3rd and wed 4th august after about 3.30 (sometimes my uncle requires me to stay and help). I am surprised that it can take up to five years to obtain justice now the facts are known. Send me any scans of people you want identified and I will do my best

Yours sincerely
Hugh.

On 5 August, 2005, Madley wrote one final letter to me, telling me that he had written to the lawyers acting for the Salesians, to state categorically that their client's continued denials that they had 'never known anything about the abuse', was a complete lie. They responded by saying simply "This adds nothing."

This is what he wrote:
Dear Sirs

SDB/Graham Wilmer and myself

I understand from discussions I have had recently with Graham Wilmer's care support counsellor, Stephen Williams, that the Salesian Order, whom you represent, is continuing to deny that they had any knowledge of the events that occurred at the Salesian College Chertsey back in 1966 and 1968, between myself and Graham. I further understand that your Client's denials have caused Graham to suffer a great deal of avoidable stress and anxiety, which has set back his recovery significantly.

In April this year, I made the decision to seek Graham's forgiveness for what I had done to him, following my discovery of the long-term harm it has caused him, which I had not fully understood until I was made aware of it in December 2003. As part of that process, I made contact with Graham through correspondence and through conversations with his care support counsellor at the survivor's group he attends. Although this was a very difficult decision for me to make, I felt that I had to do something to help him, and he has told me that it has helped him, now that I have told the truth about what happened. What still concerns me, however, and that is the reason why I am writing to you, is that your Client appears to be still trying to cover up the events of the past, at Graham's expense, in order to protect themselves.

This is a situation that I am not prepared to be party to, therefore, I am stating for the record that your Client has always know what had happened because after Graham disclosed to them in February 1968, I too disclosed to them, as they well know. The sequence of events was as follows: After Martin Allen's death on 19th February 1968, Graham disclosed to Fr Madden what I was doing to him. Fr Madden then informed Fr O'Shea, the head teacher, who arranged for Fr George Williams, the Salesian Provincial, to interview Graham.

Not long after this, Graham informed me he had told the

Salesians about us. Although I told Graham at the time that I would deny it, I did in fact go to see Fr Gaffney, the Rector, and confessed to him what I had done. He asked me to resign, which I did. He said at the time that he would see Fr O'Shea the following morning and tell him that I had resigned. Fr Gaffney asked me to promise him that I would never offend against a child again, and I made him that promise.

Some time afterwards, I can't recall exactly how long it was, Fr Gaffney died, and at his funeral, Fr Williams told me that he knew what had happened and he wanted to hear it from me. I told him the full story and he asked me why I had done it. I told him that on the first occasion, I was unable to control my feelings for Graham. He said he could accept that on the first occasion, but he asked me about the subsequent times and I had no answer for that.

Fr Williams asked me what I was doing for the future following my resignation. I told him that I had applied for a couple of posts, but had not been successful. He told me that there was a teaching post vacant at Battersea and that were I to apply for it, he would not stand in my way. He said that he would arrange an interview for me. He also asked me to repeat to him the promise I had made to Fr Gaffney, which I did.

I applied for the post and was appointed following the

interview. Fr Foley, the head teacher at Battersea, told me that I was to be supervised and that I was not to have contact with any boy on a one-to-one basis. The rest is history.

Given the seriousness of what happened, it is simply not credible that no one within the Salesian Order has any recollection of these events, and I am fully prepared to testify in court to the above if necessary.

I have copied this letter to Graham for his records.

Yours sincerely
Hugh Madley

Appendix ii

This is the document I submitted to the Surrey police on 4th May 2004, which led to the opening of a new criminal investigation and Madley's re-arrest and subsequent prosecution, twelve months later.

THE FACTS AS WE NOW KNOW THEM - HUBERT CECIL MADLEY (ABUSER) & GRAHAM PETER WILMER (VICTIM)

1. Introduction

1.1. This document sets out the full facts as now known relating to the sexual offences committed by Hubert Cecil Madley against myself, Graham Peter Wilmer (DOB 20/10/1951), between 1966 and 1968 at The Salesian College, Chertsey, Surrey, and the actions and consequences that followed.

1.2. The document relies on evidence taken from my testimony, witness statements, police statements, CPS statements, statements from the Salesians of Don Bosco (SDB) and the recent confession of Hubert Cecil Madley on 30 April 2004.

2. Background

2.1. In the spring of 1968, I, Graham Peter Wilmer, then

aged 16, and a pupil at the Salesian College Chertsey, a Catholic boys school, disclosed to my housemaster, Fr Madden, under the seal of confession, that my chemistry teacher, Hubert Cecil Madley, was sexually abusing me. Fr Madden coerced me to repeat my disclosure outside of the seal of confession so that he could inform the head teacher, Fr O'Shea, which he then did.

2.2. Fr O'Shea spoke to me about the matter and told me that I would also have to be interviewed by the then Provincial of the Salesian Order, Fr George Williams. The Provincial is the senior most member of the Salesian province in the UK.

2.3. During this interview, I was asked to explain everything that had happened. I was also asked very personal questions about my sexual knowledge and behaviour. Afterwards, I was instructed by Fr O'Shea not to tell anyone, including my parents, about the matter, and told that the school would now deal with things.

2.4. The abuse had begun in 1966 when I was 15, and by the time of my disclosure, some 18 months later, I was clearly suffering from the traumatic impact the abuse was causing me, the evidence of which was noted by my parents and other teachers at school because my behaviour and my school work had deteriorated dramatically during the period.

2.5. Despite this, I was not given any support by the school, and Madley continued to have contact with me. My father, concerned at my unexplained decline, wrote to Fr O'Shea in March 1968 and questioned my deterioration. Fr O'Shea replied saying that there was nothing wrong and that I would do well in my GCE 'O' level examinations, which I was due to sit in June of that year.

2.6. My mental health continued to deteriorate and not surprisingly, I failed all of my exams. In the September of 1968, after I had received my results, my father instructed me to asked Fr O'Shea if I could return to the school and repeat the 5th year and resit the exams the following summer. Fr O'Shea refused to allow me back into the school, bringing to an end my formal education.

2.7. In my first three years at the school, I had been in the top group of my class in performance had been awarded prizes for 'diligence in studies', by the Rector of the school, Fr Harris, in 1963 and 1964.

2.8. Having left school with no qualifications, I got a job as a hospital porter at St Peter's Hospital in Chertsey, but I was unable to settle. For the next 7 years, I had numerous manual jobs, none of which I was able to settle at. I was also unable to form relationships with other people and I took refuge in alcohol and self-injurious behaviour.

2.9. The impact of the abuse left deep mental scars, which fundamentally changed my character and seriously damaged my development into adulthood, and, although I finally did establish a long-term relationship, which began in 1976, the quality of that relationship and my life in general was plagued by the memories of my ordeal and the impact it had on me.

2.10. In 1998, aged 48, I suffered a serious mental breakdown, subsequently diagnosed as post traumatic stress disorder with an underlying chronic depressive illness. I was treated at St Catherine's Hospital in Birkenhead using a number of psychological interventions, and, five years later, I am still being treated for depression.

2.11. In November 1999, as part of my treatment, I was advised to inform the police about the abuse I had suffered, and, subsequently, WPC 963 Sarah Harris and WPC 1768 Lorraine Smith, from the North Surrey Family Support team, began an investigation into my allegations.

2.12 In April 2000, Hubert Madley was arrested and interviewed. He denied the allegations of abuse, but was able to recall extensive detail of the time he had spent with me, both in and out of school.

2.13. Fr. O'Shea was also interviewed, but he said he was

unable to recall any of the events of the time, and there was no record of my disclosure, or Madley's subsequent move to Salesian College Battersea. Fr George Williams, the Provincial at the time, was not interviewed and Fr Madden had died in 1998.

2.14. An advice file was submitted to the CPS who decided that there was insufficient evidence to support a prosecution. The Chief Crown Prosecutor at Guildford, Sandie Hebblethwaite, gave me a full explanation for the decision.

2.15. The CPS decision rested on three points: 1) The case rested solely on my word against Madley's word, 2) There was a lack of any corroborating evidence that could be tested in court, and 3) Madley's right to be able to mount an effective defence; the period of 30 years between the offences and my allegations being deemed to be too long to be relied on.

2.16. Consequently, the police investigation ended with no charges being laid, but the case details were added to the surrey police computer system, where they would remain in case any further evidence came to light. My allegations were not, however, filed on the National Police Computer.

2.17. Following the collapse of the criminal investigation, I began civil proceedings against the Salesian Order for their failure to carry out their duty of care. Madley was not included in this action. The process proved extremely difficult for a range of reasons, not least of which were the huge costs involved and the strengthened position the collapse of the criminal case had given the Salesian Order, who continued to maintain that they knew nothing about the events of 1968.

2.18. Eventually, I took over the case myself as Litigant in Person, reducing the cost significantly. The consequence of this was that the Salesian Order decided to offer to mediate with me rather than face an action in the High Court.

2.19. The mediation concluded in February 2001 with an offer from the Salesians of £20,000, who still denied any knowledge of the abuse, and an agreement that I would not pursue them, the LEA or Madley (although they was not party to the mediation), in any court in the future.

2.20. My need to secure some form of settlement from the Salesians was not about money; it was to enable me to regain my self-respect by proving that I had faced them once more, but this time as a man and not as a child.

2.21. The Salesians decision to give me the money, despite them still not accepting any liability, was enough for me to move on with my recovery process, or so I had thought at the time. Had I known the true extent of the knowledge SDB actually had about the abuse, and the further damaging impact their deception, once discovered, would have on me, I would not have settled the matter in any other place than in a court.

3. The Catholic Clergy abuse explosion and the Soham murders.

3.1. In 2003, when the full scale of child abuse by catholic priests began emerged here and in the USA, it became clear that the Catholic Church (of which the Salesian Order was part - being the third largest catholic order in the world) had covered up abuse for years, under papal instructions.

3.2. The realisation that this was why the Salesians at Chertsey had sworn me to silence became a growing problem for me in my recovery process, and I began to suffer further psychological problems. I was advised that I would have to revisit the problem if I was ever going to reach the point of closure. However, having signed the mediation agreement in 2001, which prohibited me from even talking about what had happened, I was unsure how to proceed.

3.3. The breakthrough came following the tragic murders of Holly Wells and Jessica Chapman, which brought into focus the issue of allegations of sexual offences not being recorded on the police national computer (PNC), unless a conviction had been secured, and the potential, therefore, for un-convicted pedophiles to go unnoticed in future CRO checks made prior to employment.

3.4. Consequently, in November 2003, I began to correspond again with Surrey Police and with the lawyers acting for the Salesians, to press the argument that times and events had changed, and that it was not safe to keep the issues I had raised locked away under legal restraint any longer as there was the real possibility that in doing so, Madley would be able to continue to abuse other children.

3.5. The course of action I proposed was that I be allowed to instruct the police to begin a private criminal prosecution against Madley, which, even if unsuccessful, would at least enable the allegations to be registered on the PNC.

4. Salesians step back from the agreement

4.1. The Salesians at first strongly resisted my argument, but after continued pressure from myself, they finally gave ground and agreed that they would not enforce the breach of the agreement that would occur were I to launch a private criminal prosecution against Madley. The reason they gave was that they would not wish to be seen as 'having protected any one who had abused children'. They continued to maintain that they had no knowledge of the abuse, saying: 'You will understand, in the context, that [this reason] is a general statement of principle, and is not to be taken as a specific reference to Mr Madley as to whose activities the Order has no information other than that which you have supplied.' They continued to insist though that were I to try and re-open my case against them in any way, they would seek an immediate injunction to stop me.

4.2. Consequently, I advised Surrey police of my intentions and sought their help. On April 1, 2004, I also wrote to Hubert Madley to inform him that I had asked Surrey police to begin a private criminal prosecution against him.

5. Madley responds

5.1. Given the vehemence of Madley's original denial to the police after his arrest in April 2000, it was a major surprise when, only days after I had written to him, he replied, not with furious outrage, but with a request to meet with me. He included his ex-directory phone number and asked me to phone him to make arrangements.

5.2. I responded by saying that I did not want to meet him any where other than in front of a judge. Madley replied again saying that he now realised he had done something wrong back in 1966/68.

5.3. He wrote to me again on 17 April 2004, saying that he wanted to help me in 'the only was I can at this late stage'. He also said that he hoped I understood exactly what he was saying as he was 'too nervous to put it in writing'. He also asked again if he could talk to me, or meet with my counsellor if I was not willing to talk to him in person.

5.4. This was a significant development as it was the first real evidence that Madley was acknowledging he had done something wrong and he wanted to put it right. I contacted the police who took the view that this may be sufficient to persuade the CPS to allow it to be tested in court, thus allowing the original CPS case to proceed. They told me to seal the letters in a bag and they would arrange to collect them from me.

5.5. In the meantime, I wrote back to Madley, saying that I would arrange for my counsellor to telephone him to discover what it was that he wanted to say to me.

5.6. 1 He replied by return post, giving the dates and times when he would be in, and on Friday April 30th, my counsellor, David Williams, a trustee of The Lantern Project, a charity that provides support for victims of sexual abuse, phoned Madley at a pre-arranged time and recorded the conversation.

6. A full confession

6.1. The conversation was a total revelation as, without any prompting, Madly made a full admission of the sexual offences he had committed against me, plus a detailed explanation of who knew about it in the Salesian Order, who had been involved in transferring him from Salesian College Chertsey to Salesian College Battersea following his resignation over the affair, and the restrictions he was placed under at Battersea, where he remained until he retired in 1998, all of which was organised to protect him and the school from prosecution. He repeatedly asked for forgiveness during the conversation and said that he realised that the police could prosecute him at any time.

6.2. David Williams had a second telephone conversation with Hugh Madley on May 5th, during which Hugh Madley repeated his admission and added more detail as to the involvement of the Salesians in covering up the offences and in moving him to another school (Battersea) run by the Salesian Order.

7. Madley's account of what had really happened

7.1. On the day I had disclosed to Fr Madden in confession that I was being abused; I also told Madley that afternoon that I had told Fr Madden about us. Madley had responded by saying that he would simply deny it and they would not believe me. As no action seemed to follow my disclosure, other than my interview with the Provincial, I had always thought that that is what had happened - they had not believed me, which was why Fr O'Shea had refused to allow me to re-take my exams.

7.2. What had actually happened, according to Madley's confession, was that, later that same day, he had realised that he could not bring himself to deny what I had told them, and although he realised there could be serious consequences, he decided he would have to go to see Fr O'Shea and admit the offences.

7.3. Fr O'Shea was not there when he went to see him, so he asked if he could see Fr Gaffney, the newly appointed Rector. Fr Gaffney told him that he already knew what he wanted to discuss, but he asked Madley to tell him everything that had happened in his own words, which Madley says he did.

7.4. At the end of the discussion, Fr Gaffney told Madley that he would have to resign. Fr Gaffney told Madley that he would see Fr O'Shea the next morning to sort out the details of the resignation. He then asked Madley to promise him that he would never 'offend' against a child again, to which Madley says he agreed.

7.5. Fr Gaffney also instructed Madley that he was not be alone again with me at any time. The following morning, despite this instruction, Madley met me alone in the stairwell that led from the playground up to the chemistry laboratory. He claims it was his intention to tell me that he had admitted what he had done to Fr Gaffney and had resigned. However, before he could tell me this, someone came up the stairs, so he had moved away without telling me what had actually happened.

7.6. Not long afterwards, while Madley was working out his notice period (he should, of course, have been suspended on the day of my disclosure and removed from working with children) Fr Gaffney died, and at his funeral, Madley said he was approached by Fr George Williams, the Provincial at the time (the head of the Salesian Order in the UK), who asked to see him.

7.7. They went into a private room and Fr Williams said that he knew everything that had happened, but he wanted Madley to tell him in his own words. Madley said that he repeated the story he had told Fr Gaffney. Fr Williams then asked him to explain why he had abused me. Madley said that he had had 'feelings' for me, and he had not been able to control them the first time it had happened. Fr Williams told him that he could accept this explanation for the first offence, but what about all the other times? Madley said he told Fr Williams that he had no answer for that.

7.8. Fr Williams then asked Madley what he was going

to do for the future. Madley said he told him that he had applied for two posts, but had been unsuccessful in both applications.

7.9. Fr Williams then told him that there was a vacancy teaching chemistry at the Salesian College in Battersea that had arisen following Fr Perla's move to become parish priest at Battersea.

7.10. Fr Williams then asked him to repeat to him the promise he had made to Fr Gaffney not to offend against children again. Madley gave him that promise and Fr Williams then told him that he would not stand in his way if he applied for the post at Battersea.

7.11. Madley did apply and was accepted for the job. When he arrived at Battersea, he was interviewed by the then headmaster, Fr Foley, who told him that he knew about what had happened at Chertsey.

7.12. Fr Foley told Madley that he was not allowed to have any contact with boys on a one-to-one basis, and that he would be watched closely at all times. He told him that he would be monitored by the deputy head, Fr Blackburn, who taught in the laboratory next to where Madley would teach.

7.13. Madley also revealed that he had also told Fr Golding, the head of science at Chertsey everything that had happened.

7.14. In the period between Madley resigning and him taking up the new post at Battersea, he was allowed to work his notice period at Chertsey. During this time, the school did not give me any support, and Madley was allowed to continue to teach me. Now that we know that the Salesians knew everything about what he had done, it is totally unacceptable that they placed me back in danger knowing full well what Madley had done to me.

8. Further Evidence

8.1. Following the telephone conversations, Madley wrote to me a number of letters confirming all that he had said in the telephone conversations and asking me to forgive him. These letters have been handed to Surrey Police who are currently investigating the case.

Declaration:

I believe this summary to be a true statement of fact.

Graham Peter Wilmer - 4 May 2004